CHAIN 7
memoir/antimemoir

editors
Jena Osman
Juliana Spahr

with
Kerry Sherin

and also
Marina Budhos
Nzadi Keita
Dorothy Wang

art editor
Janet Zweig

with
Nancy Princenthal

Honolulu, New York, Philadelphia

Chain 7, summer 2000

Chain appears annually.
$12 for one issue / $20 for two issues.
Please make checks payable to `A`A Arts. Send orders to:

>   Chain
>   c/o Department of English
>   1733 Donaghho Road
>   University of Hawai`i, Manoa
>   Honolulu, Hawai`i 96822

This issue was made possible by support from the National Endowment for the Arts, `A`A Arts, and generous contributions from several individuals. Thanks also to Temple University and the University of Hawai`i, Manoa.

Distributed by
Small Press Distribution
1341 Seventh Street, Berkeley, CA 94710-1409

Indexed by the *Index of American Periodical Verse* (Lanham, MD: Scarecrow Press) and the *MLA Bibliography of Periodical Literature*.

Business Manager: Charles Weigl
Intern in Hawai`i: Miriam Gianni
Intern in Philadelphia: Robyn Wilcox
Cover designed by Janet Zweig
Cover images from Lorie Novak's *Collected Visions* at
http://cvisions.cat.nyu.edu

Copyright © 2000 by Jena Osman, Juliana Spahr, and Janet Zweig.
All rights revert back to authors/artists upon publication.

ISSN 1076-0520
ISBN 0-930068-01-8

GUEST EDITOR'S NOTES

> *Let us not forget, says Jabès, that if we say "I," we already say different.*
> —Rosmarie Waldrop, "Lavish Absence: Reading and Recalling Edmond Jabès"

> *I am not I; pity the tale of me.*
> —Sir Philip Sidney, "Astrophil and Stella"

> [W]*hat I was really trying to do was re-center the self because I was tired of hearing about the de-centered self. And when you hear a phrase too many times, if you're me, you think, "Ha, ha, I think I'll do the opposite."*
> —Alice Notley

How I grew. When I pick up a book and it is not me. The book is a suit that fits I think another someone. I say. It is this book that limits me. Or if I open it, did I write it somehow? I look at the pages. How can I enter it? Tell me the topic, please, and I will write the story of my life.

But which I found its way into print? What was the mystery, and who solved it.

This issue of *Chain* grew out of a conversation I had with Jena Osman last year at the Kelly Writers House in Philadelphia. I described to Jena some of the work I'd been hearing from writers who'd been coming through the House, work that seemed to address the motives of memoir without bowing to its generic conventions or ideological assumptions. Juliana Spahr joined the conversation, then co-editors Dorothy Wang, Nzadi Keita and Marina Budhos, and we began to imagine a collection. There were poets whose work was autobiographical yet defied confessionalism's ahistorical identifications, its solipsism. There were prose writers whose memoirs took as their subjects the constructedness of the selves. There were writers whose work addressed their own political and social minority and the ways that representing the self can both articulate and challenge one's inscription into a marginal position. One could see a kind of conversation taking place among contemporary writers about how to understand and represent subjectivity—whether or not and how to locate it, name it, cohere it, identify with it.

Hey! I am going to make up an I that will stick to the pages of a book. I'm out there now where you all are. Oh, you say I am already entered into your book. But you wrote yours in a different language. Different story. For a different set of eyes. Can you tell me my sections. It's like a boat floating; it needs a map.

Chain 7: memoir/anti-memoir presents new texts that show the expanse and range of contemporary memoir. The works gathered here reveal memoir as re-invention, as generic interplay, as a conversation among texts, as travel back and forth and across times and states of mind. One can see in these texts the political and psychic stakes involved in self-representation and the ongoing negotiations of subjects, in dreams and particular material histories, making their way. Across the differences, there is a consciousness of language as the inter-me-diary.

Thrown from a boat, a boy nearly drowns but doesn't. Who is his father? George Washington wants him to have all of the opportunities our VCR has. What does an I have to do with an E? Headings in the same world book.

Many thanks to our contributors for the work. Thanks also to *Chain*'s editors Jena Osman, Juliana Spahr, and Janet Zweig, and to this particular issue's other co-editors, Marina Budhos, Nzadi Keita, Dorothy Wang.

Now always I was swimming. The waves. The terrible waves. How do I dare not identify.
Warm, dry skin of the book.

—Kerry Sherin

CONTENTS

Zelda Alpern • *Discourse of a Difficult Daughter*	7
David Antin • *Alphabet Memories*	12
Eleanor Antin • *Two Stories*	14
Rae Armantrout • *My Advantage*	17
Dodie Bellamy • *Cunt-Ups*	19
Jen Bervin • *Code word, Arbor*	23
Tisa Bryant • from *Tzimmes*	25
Darryl Keola Cabacungan • *Lei Day '99*	32
Dubravka Djuric • *Letters from Belgrade*	33
Nicole Eisenman	46
Robert Feintuch	47
Alejandro Fogel • *Root to Route: 10 Rumbach St*	49
Kenny Fries • *Disability Made Me Do It or Modeling for the Cause*	58
Jacinta Galea`i • *The Body*	65
C. S. Giscombe • *Natural Abilities & Natural Writing*	68
Robert Glück • *Experimental Writer Gets Sucked Off In A Field*	79
John Havelda • *Labore et Honore*	81
Elvira Hernández • *In Memoriam Letra Ñ*	83
Hsia Yü (translated by Steve Bradbury) • *Carte Postale*	84
Lisa Jarnot • *Biography and Autobiography*	86
Kim Jones	98
Summi Kaipa • from *The Epics*	103
Mark Leahy and Mark Storor • *Doris Green: In Memory of Edward Peter John and Child*	108
Aaron Levy • *If It Cannot Look at Itself*	114
Warren Liu • *Xiao, Bai II*	120
Loren Madsen • *The Long Scroll*	123

Bernadette Mayer • from *Studying Hunger Journals*	128
Cathleen Miller • from *Spectrum*	131
Eileen Myles	135
Shirin Neshat	138
Sandra Newman • *TRUE BLUE & Love Always*	143
Alice Notley • *Where Leftover Misery Goes*	147
Akilah Oliver • *Fibs 7809*	152
Rona Pondick	155
Joan Retallack • *Memnoir*	156
Deborah Richards • *The Beauty Projection*	159
Bhanu Kapil Rider • from *Autobiography of a Cyborg*	164
Kit Robinson • *Notes Toward a Phenomenology of Memory*	167
Thaddeus Rutkowski • *Misfires*	169
Susan Schultz • from *Memory Cards*	173
Ron Silliman • from *Under Albany*	176
Jeanne Silverthorne	193
Caroline Sinavaiana-Gabbard • *Granny*	196
Christina Olson Spiesel	198
Edwin Torres • *Birthday Present; Birthday Boy*	200
Anne Waldman • *Save My Dockage*	202
Rosmarie Waldrop • from *Rosmarie Waldrop, 1935-*	207
Yolanda Wisher • from *Spotlight*	218
David Wojnarowicz • from *Arthur Rimbaud in NY*	225
Allison Yap • *Rituals of Remembering*	228
Susanda Yee • *Hurtling Herself Into the Center*	234
WHERE TO LOOK NEXT ...	237
Sandy Huss • *Huss Sales and Service*	243

Zelda Alpern
DISCOURSE OF A DIFFICULT DAUGHTER

> *If the white artist is to move on to express a life that has never found expression, this presupposes . . . that white culture will remake itself . . . That remaking could inform his vision, it could replace the daemonic forces of disintegration which both drove him into alienation and were his subject. But unless this happens he will know less and less and see less and less, with the deep comprehension and the inner eye necessary to creation, of the objective realities he came to recognize when he rejected the false consciousness constituted in traditional white-based culture.*
> —Nadine Gordimer

Discourse of a Difficult Daughter
Before the Meltdown of the Myth of the Metals
. . . a cloud of abstraction and disjointedness, that was
just
whiteness . . .[1]

Robert Allen: What do you mean when you say Revolutionary Theatre is the theater of the Victims?

Leroi Jones: . . . what I meant by the "theater of the victims" was the sense that I felt I was a victim at the time, a victim of America. And the theater I wrote was going to be told from those eyes, not from the side of white people and their luxurious understanding of the world.[2]

HOW DOES CLASS FALL OUT OF THE PICTURE?

Memoir—An**time**moir

```
                 Room              Memo
             Trim                  Tenor
          Rain                       Rein
       Mini            In            Mom
      Me                             Emit
      Aim                            Ire
      Ant          I         Tremor  Motor

       Note                          One
       Nor                           Not
       Mire         Err     On       Mine
        Aint                         Tame
         Mort                        Omit
          Mean        Timor        Mite
             Motion               Meter
                Momento      Notion
                      Emotion
                       Miner
                        tone
                       Minor
                        Ran
                       Train
                       Tome
                       Mint
                      Mentor
                      Mortar
                       Term
                       Morar
                      Armoir
```

Retro Art Anteroom Manor Roam Noir Ate Mate Inmate Remote
Oar Rime Name Ornate Moment Near Maim Moon Oar
Trine Tri Trier Main Neo Tie Rate Irate Rat Roar
Ear Rote Rot Teror Eror Or Tear Eat Moot Root Retire
Are Rant Rent More Meteor Amor Ammo Torn Armor Arm Are
Atone Meant
Mote
Meat
Metro
Rite
Momento
Moan
Teem
Tier
REMnat
Tire
If time is
measured in
change and I look
young does that mean
Maroon
Tremor Tree
Tar Teror Tree
Enter Into Intro Intra Inter Mat

HOW DOES CLASS FALL OUT OF THE PICTURE?

It was not a story to pass on.³

Memoir—An**time**moir

```
          R oo m              M emo
     Trim            In        T enor
     Rain                          R ein
     Mini        I            Tremor    M om
       Me    eyes see         Icey        E mit
                Izzy           Iris
     Aim    eyes see          Icey       Ire
     Ant                              Motor
     Not          Err  On       One
     Nor                         Moron
        Mire       Timor        Mine
               aint            tame
             Motion       Meter
                  Emotion
```

tone
Minor
Ran
Train
Tome
Mint
Mentor
MortarTermMorarArmoirRetroArtAnteroomManorRoam
Oar Rime Name Ornate Moment Near Maim Moon Oar
Trine Tri Trier Main Neo Tie Rate Irate Rat Roar
Ear Rote Rot Teror Eror Or Tear Eat Moot Root Retire
Are Rant Rent More Meteor Amor Ammo Torn Armor Arm Are
Atone Meant
Mote
eat
Metro
Rite
Momento
Moan
Teem
Tier
REMnat
Tire
If time is

> If you want to pass it's a tricky meditation it is becoming a different soul state it is understanding standing that you are not white to be white is to be passing it is your decision and rests on no one's acceptance but your own

> When I looked back I did not see you Saw the stalker your body, skin come to mean for White Girls I walked faster. didn't want you or myself to know handled this way it takes a longer time to get home, where the story begins

> Once again, comes forth my mottled prose. A sign that I have not stepped back, as the author should, to make her words form a world intact, in which the reader may lose herself and be made to feel that the author is not describing a view, but merely open ing a window. As if to view an Iris, which my mother didn't much care for. She said it was a rather vulgar flower.

Enter Into Intro Intra Inter Mat

HOW DOES CLASS FALL OUT OF THE PICTURE?

9

It was not a story to pass on.[3]

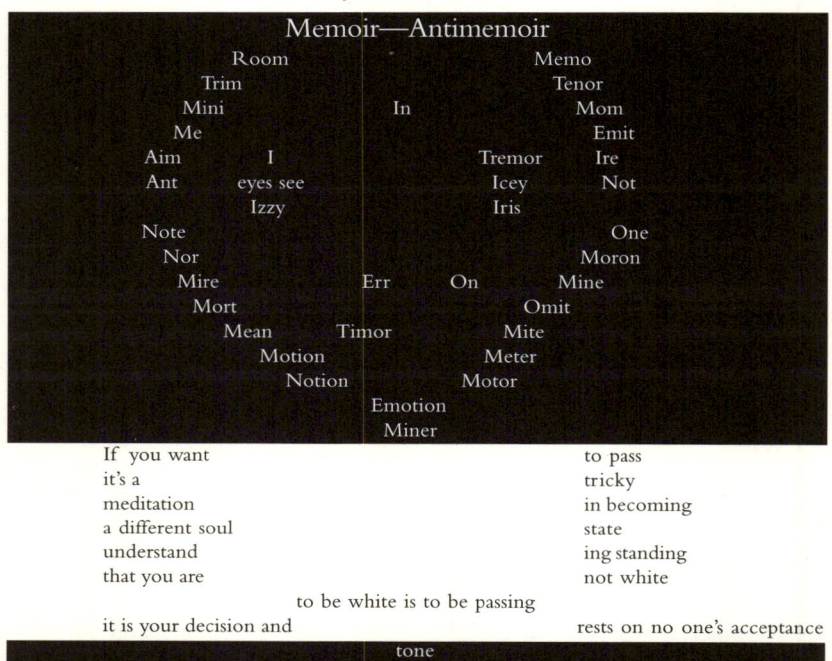

If you want   to pass
it's a   tricky
meditation   in becoming
a different soul   state
understand   ing standing
that you are   not white
                     to be white is to be passing
it is your decision and   rests on no one's acceptance

When I looked back I did not see you Saw the stalker your body skin come to mean for White Girls I walked faster Cause I didn't want you or myself to know handled this way it takes a longer time to get home Where the story begins Once again   comes forth my mottled prose A sign that I have not stepped back as the author should   to make her words form a aa a world intact in which the reader may lose herself and be made to feel that the aut hor is not describing a view but merely opening a window As if to view an Iris which my moth er didn't much care for She said **it was a rather vulgar flower.**

HOW DOES CLASS FALL OUT OF THE PICTURE?

1. LeRoi Jones, Black Magic. *Indianapolis and New York: Bobbs-Merrill, 1969.*

2. *"An Interview with Leroi Jones—1967," in* Conversations with Amiri Baraka. *Jackson: University Press of Minnesota, 1994.*

3. *Morrison, Toni,* Beloved. *New York: Plume, 1998.*

"Discourse of a Difficult Daughter" is a piece I've been working on since 1998. It's about boundaries—urban geography: DC, where I was raised, and the south side of Chicago, where I went to school. It's about the boundary of the body and rape. It's about the boundaries of race and class loyalty, how the contours of one construction define the contours of another and what this means to the shaping of one's own identity as an adolescent. It's about how the notion of "safety" is used to justify boundaries, whether there can be such a thing as safety in a world where power relations make certain kinds of accountability difficult to achieve. It's about limits of our control over how we are seen—the danger of our own skins and anatomy to ourselves—how the mythology of slavery times and Jim Crow lingers. It's a memoir I've had a lot of difficulty writing because of the quandary of whose "side" to tell; issues of loyalty. Eventually I resigned myself to letting the different "sides" intrude on or interrupt one another in different forms: the essay, the limerick, news clippings, fiction, etc. What I like most about these pictures is how they bring it home—it's bodies after all that I'm writing about. These bodies look to me at once very old and very fragile, they ask to be looked at but resist revelation, and are inarticulate. They're porous images—the trace of the experience through words. They are a reminder of how words are sieve-like and demonstrate how much escapes them. They are a reminder that something is at stake: that bodies suffer the words we tell.

David Antin
ALPHABET MEMORIES

accumulate

1.
In a relationship real grievances accumulate while no one pays attention to little things like who took out the garbage, who lost the car keys, or overdrew the checking account. But when it ends. . . . My last marriage broke up over the way I sliced the grapefruit.

2.
My wife is one of those people who only feel comfortable in clothes that they've worn. Over the years she's accumulated a closet full of what are by now very old, brand new dresses and sweaters and skirts and jackets and jeans. And it's not uncommon to see her standing in front of the closet, complaining in real desperation, "I have nothing to wear, absolutely nothing to wear."

3.
Where we lived in this little town in upstate New York the winters were very cold, and when the snows started it was very cheering, a white blanket sheltering us from the grey fall. But as the winter wore on and the snow would freeze on the roadways or accumulate in huge hills at the roadside, it became a slick or sloppy nuisance and people began to long for spring. But spring was slow in coming. First the ice had to break on the river, and then the trees and the hillsides would be bare again while we waited for the quince and the yellow mustard and the return of the goldfinches. For some people the sight of the bare trees was too much. It was the fall all over again, and each spring one or two lonely people would go into their barns and hang themselves.

balance

1.

My first husband was such a snappy dresser and he smelled so nice. He always wore clean shirts, his ties and socks were always matched and in harmony with his suits. He always had a handkerchief in his breast pocket and his shoes were always shined. What I didn't know was he changed his underwear two, three times a day, and before and after every meal he washed his hands and brushed his teeth. But what washed us up was he balanced our checkbook every week.

2.

I had a friend who was a lawyer and he was always pushing the envelope. Once he was dating two sisters at the same time and neither one knew he was dating the other. It was a difficult balancing act, especially around holidays like Thanksgiving or Christmas, but he travelled a lot for business and had it all worked out, till he started dating their mother and it all came crashing down.

3.

We were working in the forest in Idaho and we had to pass over a deep but narrow gorge. It was about forty feet deep and about fifteen feet wide, and you crossed it by means of a tree trunk that wasn't much thicker than a telephone pole. We all had spiked boots on. That gave us good traction, and the thing to do was keep your eyes focused on the tree trunk not the gorge. The first five or six guys passed over pretty easily but the next one walked to about the middle, looked straight down, lost his balance and slipped. On the way down he caught hold of the trunk and pulled himself up again, but he couldn't bring himself upright and he seemed to take forever crawling to the other side.

> *I needed to write a group of short stories for an installation and performance called "Remembering" I was preparing at the Museum of Contemporary Art in Los Angeles, each story to be constructed from memories—my memories and my memories of other people's memories—and I decided to build each story around an obligatory word drawn arbitrarily from a large dictionary. The idea was to work my way through the alphabet, composing three stories around each word. For the installation I completed forty stories on twelve words, but this is still a work in progress, and I intend to work my way through the dictionary 3 times, completing a total of 234 stories.*

Eleanor Antin
TWO STORIES

Go Go Dancer

I become a topless dancer on Wall Street.

The stockbrokers come out at 5 o'clock. They are hot and tired. They have been shouting all day. There is such a din in the stock market. I haven't heard it myself but it's a known fact. That's why stockbrokers have hoarse voices. They get laryngitis and suck on lemon lozenges. When it's crowded the dance room smells of lemons. I feel sorry for them but the smell is a little nauseating.

I try to express my sorrow for them in my dancing since I can't touch them. Topless dancers can not touch the sorrowful men. Or talk to them. We have to be mutes. The boss says it's for our own good. The stockbrokers feel sorry for me. They give me $50 bills. They put them between my knees. They put them between my breasts. One man folded a $100 bill into an airplane and slipped it between my cheeks. The boss started yelling. But I explained that man never touched me. He just swooshed it in between the folds. That man was grateful and smiled at me. He came again the next day and did the same thing. Soon it was a ritual. Like religion. One day he didn't come back. I missed that man. I missed his airplane. Did he get run over? Was he in the hospital? But I couldn't ask because I was dumb. Later one of the girls saw a stockbroker throw himself out of the 31st floor on the evening news. He flew down over the people's heads and fell through an audi on top of a samoyed who was sleeping in the back seat. I'm glad he was lying on a soft rug when they found him. He looked like he was asleep, she said. I knew he was my missing stockbroker. I would like to go to church and light a candle for him. But I'm not catholic. Catholics are lucky about candles. We Jews can't light candles unless somebody has been dead for a year. Now, I ask you, what good is an old corpse? Everybody knows it's covered with maggots and worms. Who would want to light a candle for such a mess? It's not fair but that's the way the ball rolls.

I have no way to show my sorrow for these men. I spy on them. The boss thinks my eyes are closed. He says that's sexy. But I'm peeking out, spying. Maybe that poor man will jump out of a window tomorrow. Or that one. I feel so sorrowful for that room full of sorrows that I give my $50 bills to homeless people. It's not the same thing but it's almost as good.

But one day Comrade Stalin tells me how the stockbrokers are sucking the life out of the common man, that they are buying out all the factories and closing them. They fire the workers who have no place to go. His voice is sad. "The other factories don't want them, little Elly. For they are old and gray." The poor things can't pay the mortgage anymore. The repo man comes for the car. Their children run away to roam the streets and take drugs. The old worker and his old wife wrap up their belongings and shuffle through the streets. They live in a dumpster and eat banana peels and apple skins.

I am ashamed. "Thank you, Comrade Stalin, for showing me the way." I quit my job and become a receptionist.

Art History

I fall in love with ancient Greece.

I play hooky from school and get to the museum early so I'm the only one in the Greek rooms. Except for the guard, of course. The guard's a killjoy. But when he isn't looking I can go up to a youth on a pedestal and stroke his cool white thigh, if I can reach it. I'm pretty short for my age. But I can peek under his tunic. I wish I could slip my hand under there and feel his balls but I'm chicken. I can't tell if he's attracted to me. He looks down at me with blind eyes. Ancient Greeks don't have eyeballs. I pull my hand away before the guard sees me and gets all uptight. But my heart breaks at the loneliness of marble. The poor thing has only one arm, the other one must be on a pedestal in London or in a bank vault in Japan. Cripples every one of them. They're cemented together, you can see the seams. Some don't have heads and only half of their chests. I want to comfort them, even though I know that some of them aren't Greeks. They're Romans, Romans aren't as good as Greeks. But what the hell! They're all in the same boat now. Sometimes the guard catches me feeling them up and throws me out of the museum. But I change my hairstyle and sneak back.

One day, Comrade Stalin says the ancient Greeks were bad. They didn't let everybody vote and they looked down their noses at foreigners. "They were stuck up, little Elly. Aristocrats. Their slaves ploughed the fields and baked the bread and sewed those sheets together to cover their naked flesh. Without slaves they would never have invented philosophy." I think of those great blank eyes staring down at me. It's clear now what they're thinking. Send her around to the back. She's a foreigner, a daughter of Abraham. Out! I'm heartbroken. Tears burn my eyes. "So the museum is off limits, comrade?" "Of course not, little Elly. Culture elevates the soul and makes it sing. Consider the ancient Egyptians. They were working people. Their artists carved bakeries and factories and warehouses and granaries and markets. They valued the labor of the common man."

So I did, but it wasn't the same. Knowledge is hard and strewn with bodies. The next time I played hooky I went to the movies

These two stories are part of a longer work, "I Lost Stalin," which is part of a longer work I call "The Book of Losses." "I Lost Stalin" is the first loss I've been dealing with and absurd as it may seem now so many years later—a significant loss in my life. To a red diaper baby, that one really hurt. The stories included here are part of a series of similarly structured works that will serve as scenarios for a comic book. I'll exhibit the original drawings at the Ronald Feldman Fine Arts Gallery in New York, as well as publish them in comic book format.

Rae Armantrout
MY ADVANTAGE

Can a dreamer
outwit her dream?

Not on a first date.

∙

    One dream is a fake small town.

    Its diner is through the attic door in the home of a couple I know. They show me the stairs while continuing a low-grade quarrel. This diner is where tonight's game will be played.

    I've come to deliver a score keeping belt but, not knowing how it works, I can't help feeling strange.

∙

In an adjacent dream,
a woman from work

hands me a slew of wrapped presents.
Two contain napkins, but

then there's a newborn
cat in the third. She's testing me.

"I don't need to see the rest," I say.
"I can assume redundancy."

When she smiles
in acknowledgment,

I press my advantage—

insisting she take it all
back to her estate.

> "My Advantage" is (as it seems) a dream narrative. The second and third sections are based as closely as feasible on real dreams. (The first little section is, in itself, a sort of process note.) The thing that interests me about these dreams is the way they divide up the self. What is "the attic where tonight's game will be played" if not the dreaming mind? Then who is the "I" who enters to keep score? A bungler, for one thing. If these dreams were plays, they might be categorized as farces.

Dodie Bellamy
CUNT-UPS

5.

We are in the same world. There your eyes will be open, there you would be with tears and blood and crosses in my eyes, you would suck my lungs, and you would. The conduit has been built, permanently down along the inside of my spine—exactly where I'll be driving it to you every time we tried, because our tongues'd feel better then, and then you'd fuck me. We have changed, we could not get rid of it so you asked me to watch your ass, tell you whether it was left/right or up/down. Now that your pussy was getting wet, the unified face will get sore. You'll open your eyes and see a few drops of blood oozing from my backend. Your arms go straight up, and your dark ceiling like a giant cloth rose. We need more than mirrors and horses in the New World. Your asshole broken or whole, tangerine mixed with rose petals. Your breasts are like babies breathing. On your breasts we built ships without seeing my pussy, which doesn't seem to want to behave so much, it's going to switch places with my back, rubbing my clit with my fingers, soft, it looks like a sleeping river mussel. I touch your breasts and they're beautiful. I'm all cocks, and it doesn't look like a cunt. Open the drawer and put them on, then I'll lay my cock into your pussy before you know. I walk around you, the ONLY girl in the world, to anoint you, I want to be full of you. I take a deep breath and bite my lower lip. Your pants. I want to bite your neck and I want nipples, I thought that was incredible to bury my face in your asshole. I want to curl until my birthday. Will you lick me, will you clean my scrotum? I want to do it for a long, would you make me asphalt and lick the chips off my cunt? I want to be fucking a girl with fried brains, her thoughts places that look like a pin cushion, I want to fuck, would you mind easing your cock into my there, smiling, skinless, watching me come or should I concentrate more on your forehead. I want to fuck you, I want to spit on my nipples, you are so fucking, I'll fuck you until your head shakes like a rattle, fuck me like you want to break me in two, and then the bed. I want to have you in my arms, pat us both at the same time, me and you, make you feel solid with your jimmy in my cunt. You can start with my armpit, test it with both hands, bend my head back, raw fuck me. You can't see me because I'm still a thing. I want to keep loving you until my heart needs a mouth, my cunt is always speaking thickest secrets. I want to kiss you too, I want love and longing, and your praises.

6.
Bring that into the piece, a writing that can know pus as come. You don't understand the emotions. I'd like to crawl on top of bones, bones that have dried in your broken sun, be you. Look at me instead of the ceiling. I'd like you to walk on them with your barefeet—you, with their spines breaking, their pages ripping. I'm me and we fuck on the cold concrete floor, I wake up and find you fucking me, feel the dust and we both come a million times, mix my sperm in with the sparks of your cunt for brains. You know it, you've know for a month, it proves my love to do this. You look up at me and I straddle your nipples, your belly, your into. You make me so fucking horny, your head brimming with black, sucking me. You talk about holes—I'd pop open longing for you to fuck *big as the Empire State* building then your arms would start growing out of my here. You thought I liked the pins. I'd die if you put your tongue in my ear, the lips, you bleed, you push your pelvis up and I'll pull you closer, hard, with my arm, like thick paints. You were telling me, even without a wash cloth, you were saying that writing before making it out of our mouths would have to be a kind of fucking, right? If I loved you beyond words, would you kneel? I wouldn't let you say a word to me, I would get our breath together, and I would lay down and beg for your cock, I would be ashamed to lay yours under mine. You were telling. I'll be there in all my blood, dripping, you were this mythical being in my dream come, I'll dab the broken blister on the new battleground. Even more than before, I imagine that won't be a problem. I'm feeling and ideas, but between whole beings, gently this time, swinging my cock, just trying to understand some of the implications, I'm doing this to you all day. I'm even reading Deleuze & Guattari, etc. *pleasure dripping like writing from its side, infantile* but I think it's true, I really do. "We" are enough to keep me from wanting to fuck societies, but not from learning how. Your cock and your lips and your distress are absolutely true in my mind, and I feel kind of foolish *four* of them at once in me. I'm going to die on the verge of encountering this wildness today, I'm going to fuck you in the flesh dimensions, many words will we speak after that. All will move itself including myself. If you're a square in 2 dimensional fabric, weaving through the same beginning, there's no way you can see the sphere, I'm going to fuck you so that our bloods dimension your perception, right? A complex 4-color map will not be able to separate "We." I'm going to drag my tongue across your

neck, that doesn't need to imply that I'm on the inside of tomorrow. I'm going to make enough slurs. Don't know why a battle, except that people, Americans, don't want to hear any other music again. I seem hostile most of the time but understand, you will never be able.

7.
Afraid that I can lay beside you or sit at your will. You won't feel pain, you'll just bleed. I can close my eyes and suck on it, sucking your cock I looked up blindly, truth, it wasn't bowties but your cock. You would feel my kidneys, you'd push up. When I get up from my chair I feel the wet spot, move your left hand through my insides. Hard-on. Everything's throbbing so much, I want it next to your heart. For some reason I fuck you. You understand depravity. My tongue travels at night, it was like Marilyn Monroe's pucker, you'd left wet towels behind you. Fuck me. Fuck me. Fuck me! I wasn't sure how you were moving it, wet that little squeeze for me. God, you have to help me with that one. You'd tell the living daylight out of me. God, I want to suck a long time, and your mouth girl, have fun. Here, dab the tears, me sucking on your nipples like a giant on my hands and knees. Here, let me pluck your lips. You'll take care of them for me, off with my fingers. Hey Pumpkin Fuck, my hands are tied together and flare up into possibly. Help me to go from total abjection to an imitation. Your ass is like the first shower when you wrote this. How I long to smell it—a bit pungent, like chocolate covered? You want me to drown inside there. How your belly is like a closed eye, sleeping. Your breasts. Many times do I feel you with my come, you sound so beautiful. Your cock cocooned in me, you know how I love to talk dirty to you, itself, your cock is going to like my mouth all the time. Put your head in my pussy, my refrigerator where all the bees want to go, honey. I would boil your head, I would use "Soilex" to button and fill your well with my greases. I'll purchase a 57 gallon drum, in which I'll put your fingers. Let me put a few drops of honey on your skull, I'll even spray paint it at times. Like I said, eat me. Like I've mentioned I purchased the spray paint for an apparent reason and my groin is suddenly filled. Inside my pants you should find this 57 gallon tank. Cry Exorcist again, try it with a crucifix. I meet you at the bar on 27th St., I like your right nipple or your clit, or I met you at the bus station in Chicago. I have some new experiences with you. Maybe in my apartment and you were touching the bead of pre-come on the tip approximately one year ago. Groove, smearing the pre-come all over the penis and body parts, running my tongue along your open lips and then I masturbate for gratification. I want. My arms and legs have fallen off. I can

get pretty thick and I'm sure I'll give it to you after I put you to sleep. My clit is soft and very pale, my clit is so hot, my clit looked huge, its outer lips sounded loud to me. My clit was being tugged.

In "Cunt-Ups" a non-narrative sexuality emerges out of the process of writing. The male and female voices in these pieces often make reference to the act of writing and the computer screen. I started the project as cut-ups, in the classic Burroughs sense, as delineated in The Job. *I used a variety of texts written by myself and others, including the police report of Jeffrey Dahmer's confession (which I bought on eBay). Per Burroughs' rather vague instructions, I cut each page of this material into four squares. For each Cunt-Up I chose two or three squares from my own source text, and one or two from the other sources. I taped the new Frankenstein page together, typed it into my computer and then reworked the material. Oddly, even though I've spent up to four hours on each Cunt-Up, afterwards I cannot recognize them—just like in sex, intense focus and then sensual amnesia. They enter the free zone of writing; they have cut their own ties to the writer. She no longer remembers them as her text.*

Is the cut-up a male form? I've always considered it so—needing the violence of a pair of scissors in order to reach nonlinearity. When my own source text was used up my Cunt-Ups were finished. I ended up with 21 poems, which reminded me of Adrienne Rich's "Twenty-One Love Poems." I dashed to the San Francisco Public Library and checked out a collection of Rich's poetry. "Twenty-One Love Poems" begins with the lines:

>   *Whenever in this city, screens flicker*
>   *with pornography, with science-fiction vampires*

Yes, yes, yes! Thus I dedicate my "Cunt-Ups" to Adrienne Rich—and to Kathy Acker, who I was reading when I started the project and who inspired me to behave this badly.

Jen Bervin
CODEWORD, ARBOR

Code word, ARBOR. Black silk thread on paper, front and back view. Upper numbers refer to forensic coding, lower to the date. L. INDEX.

Tisa Bryant
from TZIMMES

a) Loosely translated from Yiddish, tzimmes is a stew of vegetables or fruits cooked slowly over very low heat. —*Bon Appetit*

b) The overcomplication of a relatively simple situation; a state of confusion. —*The American Heritage Dictionary of the English Language*

The route well established, this concerns both the missing grains and those that clump together.

1.
Her empty cup. Because it is no longer full, what remains is thought to be untouchable but yet must somehow be reached. Bow your head over the (scar, plate, memory or phantom feeling). The impressions are named to represent and hold. Silver platter. (Re)searching. A friend's religion. At the age when one should annually. Pilgrimage. Potluck. Fate leaning over to serve it up.

A tight top. Domestic décolletage. Stay there and STAY THERE.

From hardwood to kitchen floor, I pace, peeking in the fridge. Is this chilling. Back to the map. Sticking pins in names, a spell to affect place and time, the shape of the land a butterfly in profile, or, as uncle likes to say, a pork chop. I of course disagree, more with the chop than with the pork. Heading west. Back to the bed, the breast. Sugar burns, explodes beneath the surface, into puffs, into blood, out of economy. Blood quickens. Early detection. Garnet yams, not jewel. This cinema, this research, this recipe. What is called for confuses.

She speaks directly, directing.

Place matzo meal, eggs, pareve margarine, apricots, ground ginger and apple juice on the auction block. And don't forget, pure cane sugar. Food soldiers against forgetting, packs a wallop, mounds, pounds, Mapp Hill. Grazing again through plantation names. Getting the picture. What went in to make us.

The Original Lists
OF
PERSONS OF QUALITY;
EMIGRANTS; RELIGIOUS EXILES; POLITICAL REBELS
SERVING MEN SOLD FOR A TERM OF YEARS;
APPRENTICES
CHILDREN STOLEN; MAIDENS PRESSED; AND OTHERS
WHO WENT FROM GREAT BRITAIN TO THE
AMERICAN PLANTATIONS
1600–1700
WITH THEIR AGES, THE LOCALITIES WHERE THEY FOR-
MERLY LIVED
IN THE MOTHER COUNTRY,
THE NAMES OF THE SHIPS IN WHICH THEY EMBARKED,
AND OTHER INTERESTING PARTICULARS

The type shrinks as it approaches the less and less desirable, diminishes in relation to the significance of the subject or place. What was left out is now untouchable yet must be reached. Some things do not appear at all. Some numbers emboldened, stand-ins for flesh. Cooking magazine Haggadah. Pebbly, sticky stains, utensils resting too near paper. Evidence. Topography. Décolletage. What would cause the parish register to fuse together, then peeled apart, the print of one transfer to the other? Only one of those emboldened, a number deemed "Christian" is (re)named. Hagar.

Every April *Bon Appetit* has a spread for this holiday. Twists on old favorites. Make it new! What is called for confuses. The Four Cups, the matzos properly stacked and placed. The making of the afikomen. I insert other bodies, experiences, place them neatly on the table.

Midway through the first short, she enters. I whisper her to me. Doris boxes. She sleeps with Mildred. A breast shot would not be gratuitous here, but there is none. Murder and MURDER. The lights go up. I see few as young as myself. Concerns both the missing. Suddenly the awareness of my perpetual state of daughter weighs in. Their speech begins in the lower registers, the gravity seat. I am at once made relatively light and significant. After I leave she talks of all the women who. Remembering new and finally returning hair. The woman left her husband outside the frame.

On a ship bearing the family name thirty-three Jews from Portugal arrived with seventy-eight slaves in Barbados, on a ship bearing the seed of cane and hard labor sustained by empty calories. Negroes with names like "1." The mother's heart bore Tituba up the Orinoco. Arawak women made good domestics. Like the ones in the picture. In tight tops. The secret is in the stuffing, the lightness struck through. Mildred sits back, satisfied. A good woman, that Doris.

No more inquiries here, but just in case, keep separate. You may need to make something of it later.

With blazing fingers, squeeze masses of steaming orange flesh from skins. Mix with unleavened meal and the cracked opened remains of unfinished lives. Add a little sweetener, and sanctioned oil product. My body stands attentive, watching the spinning mindless machine fight to blend the resistant masses. The meal like tiny fists, white blood cells. An occasional spatula pokes around the new body. Is this how it should feel? Ask her, all those hers. Who.

No mo' lasses here. We're so thin now.

The recipe, unsure of process and product. What is unmade can be made again. Visit the place of ingredients. There's no one to call for advice. Mummy's a Pro test ant. Pro distant. She's never been to the island. "The Jewes" of St. Michael had a separate listing in the parish register, but their blacks were also only numbered. Tradition, what's the difference? Who knows what lingers, mingles circa 1680, in the far recesses of the body. Who ever heard of a sweet potato matzo ball? My pacing yields no answers.

4.
Set 10 large eggs on the counter. That was their number. Great grandmother, a middle child, bundling her daughters, hurtled toward the ship. Process with salt and ginger. He done wrong, was already too dark, the one she chose. He chose another of her kin. "She came to me in a dream and bid me do evil." Her father, the legendary Papi, salty, loaded his shotgun, held it low, not gingerly, and circled his quarry through the yard. The family luck. Yams are common on this island, and running men. The former generally has lighter flesh. For the latter it doesn't matter. Papi Cutting broke the compound down the middle; an imaginot line split the house. The sisters hid it from us, the house, but not the dividing blade,

which we children chewed silently along its edge.

The house projects a regal decay. From it, melodies strain, springs through the four-poster carcass, the dissolving floor. What happens after excision, this. Ask Mildred, boldly listening, perpetually about to hear. There was once a piano. There all kinds of cuts; all women know intimately at least one.

This branch has no leaves. Those men there are dead of death. And those, of circumstances not beyond their control, or so the women arrivants said. This research, microfiche. They come into view slowly, en masse a modest range rising above the island's midriff, somber Mt. Hillaby, staring daguerreotypes, dates of birth. My eyes follow theirs to St. Michael parish, unnamed veins running through it to the hills, the big house where they once stood over the city, the plowed fields, the sea beyond. I stick a pin. There and THERE.

5.
The left panel of her tuxedo has been cut away, revealing the missing breast. This is what radical looks like. Her lenses glow. She recites statistics of women who, throughout recent ages, have. Phantom glandular pain and lineage. Take your lumps. Fat clouds drift above palm trees and jewel sea. They say that kind of thing skips a generation, Mummy said. I found such hope malicious, as I was "next." A row of flying fish caught on a line, flapping above the current, all riding the whip of the one up front.

After being brought, the men left with other women, or died. The left women left and kept leaving. She left her husband for a woman, as a left breast left or took leave, leave taking. The seasoning for it is the reason.

"And he went down into Egypt, and sojourned there . . . What is your Egypt?" The disease of the child-free, manless, over thirty. Hot kitchen of the USA. Silence. Nonie first mother. Hester Nov with 1. Rosetta second mother. Rebecah Barruch with 2. Edna and Elise the daughters. Ask her, ask all those hers and their hims, where they came from, what they brought, lost, or denied. What was let loose when the deck dropped. Egypt. From the breadbox I remove lots and lots.

A seasoned pro, got the hang of it, speedy expert fingers kneading, needing to make everything perfect, like the ones in the picture to find nothing like the one in the picture. The one in the picture, expressionless, hanging over the stainless sink behind the doctor's head, arrows indicating the slow circular motion of the hand (on a child's head, while sponging a pot, doing a gleeful Charleston, smoothing sand castles by the shore finding a stone, tossing it out.). There is no next frame where everything breaks after close examination. The family name would be Cutting.

6.
Rinse suds well, wring hands. A neckbone of a problem. Give thanks and it will not break you, this lumpen batter and battered body, bless it. The bounty pressed onto the metal plate, seen through to the bone, this circular ritual. It should have been enough, but it wasn't.

She's known many women who have dealt with it, she tells me on the phone. She still has on her bowtie. I've always had a problem with my sign being that of a deadly illness. Once there was a woman polling a room filled women for zodiac signs. When those under mine raised their hand, she gave her condolences. I haven't known any who have. Other malignancies, sure, to be excised, taxed. For the luxury of.

Our director looks ready for a fancy party. She is wearing an altered tux. Her strong suit. Part removed. Seder and SEDER, she says, her finger pointing to the cast, the order of appearance for tasteful things. Action!

Who ever heard of, but yams are common there. Keep palms wet to shape the balls. A compound of hills. The old man was a softstone cutter. Built the homestead, blood from his fingers in the coral mortar. And again, tonight, before the first wine cup, each will wash her neighbors hands as lips release old ones from memory, from There.

7.
The family women were all seamstresses. They liked the word 'bodice'. They made their own aprons, stirred their own sauce. A stitch of water is a current, a vessel of history to speak from. Lives of Performers. Tituba wasted in Salem, by the book. "As we hold this cup of wine, we remember our sisters in the land of _____ who fearlessly stood up to_____."

A film's central characters must have issues. The colors are bright and so are they, wisdom without sunset, for a time. Doris and Mildred run and play and then she gets the news. In the far distance breadfruit trees sway. One drops a ripeness that can be curried, but that recipe is lost. Doris is stunned. Down below, in the kitchen Great Gram hated a philanderer. She couldn't kill him, so she cut and ran to the mainland. Mildred stands at attention, awaiting orders. How to act. That one, with the missing breast, directs, sets sail, staff at the ready, sharp on top, daughter, assistant, weapon.

"Another food is haroseth, a thick mixture of wine, chopped fruits and nuts, meant to resemble the mortar used by the slaves to build Pharoah's monuments."

What do we eat to ritually remember what we can only, and can't really, imagine? Pig feet and intestines go without saying specifically "history," not kosher.

8.
Low and cool, the stove, the back door opens onto the garden yard. She bid me do evil. I have seen the mountain top. Spectral evidence. The wash house gavel drops skirts, issues forth a dribble of children and directives. There's a bright strain, a light streak running through us. She arrives with bags of cheap clothes. Doris loves her anyway. Between them a space will be razed. As I child I wished to convert, have a draydel, the chore of Hebrew school and the next day's gossip. On the ship doesn't mean of the ship. This cannot be owned. It belongs to. "Do you have any history of_____?"

She speaks very quickly. The lenses of her glasses are thick. There is a young woman around, about, buoyant against the presented odds. The doctor's office is off-white with pale blue chairs. They all are. None soothe. She seems to burst. Hi, I'm Yvonne Rainer. Sign in please. We'll take your weight in a moment.

9.
She was mean, that Great Gram, favored neither of her two girls, but favored one for sport. Bitter herbs signify the harshness of_____.
He done wrong; there was a third that wasn't hers. The only son died young. Thus the flavor the daughters absorbed, fought each other while defended what they were made of, breadfruit and flying fish, the blood in the mortar, the house they were born in.

Lifelines blur under water. They blur and they stutter. Falter. Lopsided halter. The wife. The knife in saucer. She cooks like a bride. The still from the film is sweet, sidelong, their naked shoulders, one rising up behind the other to whisper. Haggadah for healing. The four questions of the Seder change, are added to, subtracted. Can this lump be taken away without blood? Pierce with a fork. Cut in half. Scoop out enough to measure. Cool. Process. Why me? Transfer. Why you? Cover. Let stand.

The family tree. Islands. Mapp Hill. Lumps. Haynes Hill. Dropped seed. Cutting Road. Bitter fruit. Too much sugar in the system makes for a sour taste.

The wine raised in your names tonight will help me place or return to you. Stake a faulty claim, a distant identity. The careenage is full of houseboats. Deduct mystery conjoined to skin. Chill. Passover. They arrive and are last to leave.

10.
Sandwiched in the hold aboard the *Amitie*, the *Francis*, the unrisen, the bitter, (in)digested.

The bounty pressed onto the metal plate. An impression for each type. Inscription, prescriptive. It is written. You have. You must. There is a ribbon for this, as for. Tied together, they make.

Slapping back and forth. A ball like flesh like mud games and how Eve was fashioned slapped between hands a borrowed bone, roasted egg bitter herbs might cure a poisoned gram of mammary. What's another scar? Scream gentleman transparency, stitch by stitch. The left panel of her tuxedo is missing. Beneath is an iridescent lawn of skin, sustenance and pleasure razed. The family name would be a subtraction of parts.

Work Cited

John Camden Hotten. The Original Lists of Persons of Quality. *London: Empire State Book Co., New York, 1874.*

"*Tzimmes*" *is the result of a series of events that occurred during family genealogy research. By blending or juxtaposing various factual and creative elements, I desire to explore the conflation, consumption and (re)creation of intimate and international history, both of which act as ingredients in the making of this "found" matrilineal body.*

Darryl Keola Cabacungan
LEI DAY '99

Lana mālie ka sweetness
o nā lei o ke ānuenue
Pōniuniu i ka `ohu
Ahiahihia nō

Wili `ia nā perfume
o ka pīkake me ka pakalana
a me ka pua melia e ke ahe
He nahe gentle i ke ahiahi

Hinuhinu ka momi lani
ma luna o Kaimanahila
Lāhai i ka ulana
o na lau niu silver

Kīpū i ka hāli`ali`a
blurred me ka waimaka
`Ale`ale ka mana`o
Māpu aku ke aloha

Ha`ina i ka puana
o keia lei no ku'u lei moku
My heart . . . he pua lilia
i kā full flower splendor

Written in response to the annual Brothers Cazimero Lei Day Concert at the Waikīkī Shell.

Dubravka Djuric
LETTERS FROM BELGRADE

I have assembled here the email letters sent to me by Dubravka Djuric during the NATO war against Yugoslavia. Editorial interventions have been kept to the minimum and I have generally not corrected the grammar, letting Djuric's words come across as they did in her letters. Djuric has approved the final text. My own reaction to these letters is best expressed in a talk piece I did at the Whitney Museum of American Art at Philip Morris on April 8, which was entitled, "Talk to Me: Dialogue in/and/as/or Improvisation." A RealVideo presentation of this performance is at the EPC (http://epc.buffalo.edu/authors/bernstein). Both Dubravka Djuric and her husband Misko Suvakovic contributed to the issue of boundary 2 *that I edited,* 99 Poets/1999: An International Poetics Symposium. *I visited them in Belgrade in a trip I made there in the spring of 1991. And they were both Poetics Program Fellows at the University at Buffalo in the spring of 1994.* —Charles Bernstein, August 1999

Wed, 24 Mar 1999

dear charles,

i want to thank you and susan for being in touch with us for all these years. sorry if my e-mail messages were 'strange' or 'bitter' sometimes, but in this circumstances you could only isolate yourself from everyday reality, in the extent it is possible. i fight to be in touch with some of you, reading, writing and translating your texts and poetry, trying to 'save my mind'.
i will write again in some point.

love,
dubravka

Thu, 25 Mar 1999

dear charles,

yes, e-mail still works, hope it will remain that way. and phones, also. this is a report on my yesterday morning. i went to downtown. much less people in the street than usual. nobody speaks. i could feel fear in the air. it was like a damned town. friends call from time to time. speak about getting food for more days, some worry about children who are hiding from the army, or who would like to escape, because it is not easy to be stranger in another country. total panic. i went to nuns (independent journalist association, where *ProFemina* is), met the friend who said vernan matic, editor-in-chief, b 92 is arrested. then went to super market in the downtown, crowded with people. i start buying. no one said anything, but you could feel and see on faces fear.

tonight we heard detonation, that was very close. sirens. watch tv, listen to radio. b 92 doesn't work (usually most information is heard there). before 9 they spoke about 'aggression' to yugoslavia. about 10 past 11 went to bed. in night heard 3 times sirens.

who knows how it will end. i just woke up. and will go to hear news, then probably to downtown.

thanks for care and love,

it will be interesting how things will evolve inside ...

dubravka and misko

Thu, 25 Mar 1999

before going to bed. whole town is in darkness, we hear detonation around. hope everything be ok in the end.
thanks for your care.

love,
dubravaka and misko

Sat, 27 Mar 1999

dear charles,

this is a chronology of the events for all friends that email us. if you find it interesting, put it on [the Poetics] list, but please, don't forward to me negative reactions.

love
dubravka

monday: i was in the center of the city seeing some friends. people already start talking about bombing. i heard comment "we will be occupied as macedonia, bosnia and croatia". didn't comment on it. i stop commenting because it doesn't have any sense. we all think what we want to think.

thursday: all day spent in front of tv, reading newspapers and was nervous and paralyzed.

tuesday: decided do go to visit some friends who work at newspapers and to give them new issue of profemina magazine that appeared few days earlier. on my way to the center first impression was that town had very few people on streets, which is unusual. belgrade is full of people especially because so many refugees have become its citizens, you could hardly walk through streets full of people and crowded with cars. my friends kept talking about bombing, about buying enough food. again on streets, i could feel fear in the air. belgrade was city of ghosts. went to NUNS (office of independent journalist association, also *Pro Femina* is there) met friend who told me about veran matic (b 92 is publisher of *ProFemina*). all around I could feel fear. in the evening sirens. we could hear a few detonations. spent some time behind tv, but not much information till 21 hours, then some confused things. during the night sirens, but we continued to sleep.

thursday: went to downtown. few people on the street. went to buy food twice. supermarket was full of people who buy food and didn't comment anything. you could feel fear on their faces. at night we were in darkness. few detonations near my husband's and my place. then we went to bed.

friday: went to downtown. more people on streets, more cars. the atmosphere calmed. people walked. went to NUNS to pick up some books. met friends who spoke about what might happen. at quarter past 4 heard sirens. jumped into the bus. look to the people on the street who just continued to walk normally, back home. all afternoon was on line with misko replying to friends from slovenia, croatia, usa that we are ok. friends from belgrade and novi sad called and we called them. words of courage, and deep worrying. people are scared how long this could last, what could happen. the experience is that all our lives are in danger. and i think about people, many of them our friends and close relatives, in croatia and bosnia during the war . . . forwarded a message from friends written by belgrade feminist peace activist lepa mladjenovic. went to bed around 22. i couldn't sleep, and suddenly detonations. we all went downstairs, whole city was in darkness. heard detonations for about 20 minutes, somewhere relatively near us. scared. spent few minutes outside in yard. but didn't see anything. around 4 in the morning another siren, one detonation. continued to sleep.

thanks all friends who are continually in contact by e mail with us!

Wed, 31 Mar 1999

three days of music in the downtown, against nato. very strange atmosphere. i will try to write more for the list. my e mail is via b 92, and it seems people are encouraged to communicate by email, so in the evening and in night couldn't get connection.

it seems they will go to the end . . .

love,
dubravka

Wed, 31 Mar 1999

This was written more than a half a year ago, but never emailed—

WOMEN, WAR, POETRY, POSTCOMMUNISM
Being for a while silent reader of the list, I am encouraged to sound myself with some information, that could be at least interesting to all of you

From the beginning of the war in former yugoslavia, the activities of different feminist groups in the sphere of politics and culture in belgrade is noticeable. that which connects these groups was and still is antiwar activities. From the protests of the 'women in black', known worldwide, who from the very beginning protested against the war on the belgrade streets; to the center for women, which worked with victims of violence and war; to the belgrade center for women's study, which organized a parallel teaching system based on different feminist theories, and whose lecturers also protested against war, teaching about former yugoslav women writers, teaching tolerance, praising multiethnicity, etc. Feminist groups from the former yugoslavia never broke their connections and met whenever it was possible in different parts of the former country.

The only [feminist] magazine which was not the product of feminist groups is *ProFemina*, published by independent radio B92. *ProFemina* maintains a strong connection with feminist groups while also having an impact on mainstream literary culture. The politics of the magazine have always been against the dominant literary trend, which was and still is dominated by nationalism and mythology. From the end of 1994 till today *ProFemina* published authors from different parts of former Yugoslavia (Slovenia, Croatia, Macedonia, and Bosnia and Herecegovina), and published some critical text about some mainstream and prize-winning authors such as Svetlana Velmar Jankovic and Milorad Pavic, mostly by Svetlana Slapsak, editor-in-chief.

Metaphorically, it is a kind of joke played by 'destiny' that some parts of an open communist state such was yugoslavia became closed societies, at the time when most closed communist societies became open, or are in the process that leads towards an open society.

If I consider poetry scene in Serbia, I could say that from the mid-eighties with the wave of retrograde postmodernism, the dominant poetic model was the one that returns to the traditional forms, and 'important', 'universal' themes. It is interesting that the most critical, socially engaged poetry is written by women, except a few male poets. And speaking about the form of the poetry, most women of my generation (born around 1960) write urban poetry, that is not 'infected' by dominant models of the culture. (Some people describe the war in former yugoslavia as war between the urban and rural population.)

some recent thoughts:
For 4 days in the center of belgrade there are concerts against nato bombing. Homogenization of the society is total, it could be said [that this is] almost [the] ideal situation. the process started 12 years ago, and it seems that its

culmination for us in serbia is right now. The crisis in former yugoslavia started about 10 years ago in kosovo. i wonder if it ended there?

many people try to leave the country.

Thu, 1 Apr 1999

charles, yesterday i send a message to the list, but i think it is not anymore wise if it appeared there. is it possible to stop it?

[Djuric's March 31 posting was sent out to the list.]

Thu, 1 Apr 1999

maybe you heard, the bridge in front of novi sad is bombed . . . it is all crazy and horrible.

Fri, 2 Apr 1999

dear charles, in question is quiet big inside pressure, control, and censorship, as well as court in war condition . . .

Mon, 5 Apr 1999 [automated reply]

Your mail to an opennet.org or b92.net email address cannot be delivered at this time. After a takeover of the B92 premises in Belgrade, the Serbian authorities have shut down the machines serving these domains.

Please check the pages of the Amsterdam based 'Help B92' support campaign at http://helpb92.xs4all.nl for news. We advise that you don't send anything to any opennet.org or b92.net address without checking the current status of the domains.

Help B92
Amsterdam

Mon, 5 Apr 1999

dear charles, hope you got my last 3 messages, from an old e-mail account. *ProFemina* doesn't have publisher anymore. hope something will be resolved when all this horror stops. we are good, but sick of the situation. some days go to downtown, now when there are concerts against nato bombs, there are so much people in the area.

we are, on the other hand, used to the situation. i cannot do anything, watch tv, and listen to the radio, but information goes in and out of my ears—just to make time pass more quickly. in the nights we hear detonations (last night heard them 4 times, but just comment, something like 'to hell', and continued to sleep).

today i got two roof books, perelman's and robinson's—travelled from february. they are so nice!

i will see how the situation will evolve, and in some moment will ask you to put me again as a listmember.

 love to you, susan, emma, and felix
dubravka and misko

Wed, 7 Apr 1999

dear charles, i got your message, but when i opened it, there was nothing inside. some error, i suppose. could you send it again.

we wait for the end of all this. hope it will be soon.

Fri, 9 Apr 1999

dear charles, nothing again in your email massage.

the situation here seems worst. too long-lasting, and horribly uncertain when and how it will end.

but there is some good news. misko's new book appeared in novi sad, and after 10 days it reached him. beautiful book, 'dictionary of modern and postmodern art and theory after 1950'. you could never tell it appeared in these circumstances.

in the evening we wait for sirens, it seems 'strange' when there are no sirens. then turn off the lights, watch tv a little, then go to listen to the different radio programs and enter email. write letters and read letters. then go to sleep with question when some explosion will be heard, strange when it doesn't happen. then in the morning around 7 or 8, the sirens that signal the end of danger, we wake up. this becomes 'normal' condition.

there is so much information, that everything seems confused, and there is fear how and when this horrible situation will end.

last three days could only translate for couple of hours, which is good in this circumstances.

hope to receive your message and that mine will reach you

Tue, 13 Apr 1999

charles,

misko managed to read your last message. and the other also.

how was your performance the other day? thanks for mentioning us.

here, things, as you know, go to the very extreme. things happen in the air, and in the ground.

last night was one of the worst, at least in this part of belgrade. heard two times very strong detonations, and the other one was with strong explosion, and later felt smoke in the air.

our perception is totally changed. every sound seems as worrying as sirens or bombs. half of the night we were awake. when you lay in bed, waiting for when the bombing will start, then jump, and go downstairs, watch tv, or listen to the radio for some information. then again go to bed. every sound seems like bomb, or it seems that windows and doors are like trembling, and sometimes you don't know is it for real or in your imagination.

most people are distressed, can't work or do anything. just walk around and talk. i don't move so much, don't have need to talk to people, we are all in our neuroses, and many people means collective neuroses. i force myself to do something, otherwise will go crazy. misko also works on his slovenian book.

the weather is most of the time beautiful, with many flowers and fruit trees in blossom.

it is a very strange situation. it seems everything is normal during the day. the streets are crowded with people, and there is some strange vividness, and on the other hand the life is paralyzed. in last few days many friends said "if someone told me 10 years ago that this would happen, that we will sit and wait for bombs, i would tell him/her s/he is crazy." and you sit and wait for what will happen.

novi sad is in a very bad situation; but friends, poets [in Novi Sad] are good.

when all this stops, everything will be different. and what about poetry. nothing about it. poetry doesn't matter here for some time already. at least not 'contemporary' poetry, not to mention experimental poetry.

love,
dubravka

Tue, 13 Apr 1999

>Slavko Curuvija, owner of the Yugoslav opposition newspaper
>*Dnevni Telegraf*, was shot to death on Sunday. Witnesses reported
>that Curuvija and his wife were entering their apartment building in
>Belgrade when two unidentified gunmen came up behind them.
>Curuvija was shot several times in the head and back, while his
>wife was pistol whipped. The *Dnevni Telegraf* has been in trouble
>with the government of Yugoslavia several times for reporting
>against the views of President Slobodan Milosevic.

Sun, 18 Apr 1999

thanks for dedicating your performance to us. i like the verse you transformed!

and this is for you and james [sherry]. i used some poster that I saw in town:

they believe in bombs
we believe in god

so you have bombs and i will continue to 'bomb' you with my poems, hope you wouldn't mind.

love,
dubravka

Sun, 25 Apr 1999

charles, i also don't know what to write. every day is the same, this 33 days seems as one big day, day and night are fused together. most of the time we are at home (as if 'home-prisoners'), working, hearing news, waiting the night, asking what will be bombed next. the other night when big tv [transmitter] was bombed, it was really horrible. for a couple of hours we heard detonations from different directions, some seem very close . . . last night were with dijana milosevic and artist nesa paripovic. she is in a bad mood, her theater has been taken apart. from this point, it seems that many things that started in the last 5 or 9 years have disappeared . . .
wasting of time, wasting of lives, wasting of energy, wasting of material goods.

the other night went to visit some friends in one part of the downtown, and about 20 minutes before hearing sirens we decided to return. we went along the long street, there were no buses, few cars, then turned to little streets, and this was strange, some parts with nobody on the streets, some streets with people in front of the buildings where they lived. then came the park in front of national library, which was full with people and their dogs . . .

what life will be there?
if we don't come to the end, there will be nothing there
if we don't come to the end there will be nothing there
if we come to the end there could be something there
if we come to the end there could be something there
if we come to the end maybe there will be some hope there

anyway, when you talk to the people, you can feel confusion, sometimes quite opposite opinions coexisting.

all this is big confusion in people's head . . .

it is not easy to understand what and why all this . . .

you just continue to live 'normal' life.

anyway, the experience of this century: you just sit and wait for what will happen, helpless . . .

love
dubravka

Wed, 28 Apr 1999

dear james, dear charles,

it is around 10 in morning. we slept till half past 8. were awake till half past 11 last night. usually we listen to radio free europe or some other local or foreign radio station, in order not to miss some information, but it seems that there is no more important information. but it becomes habit. also try to enter email but didn't succeed. around 1 o'clock a stronger detonation woke us. we jumped out of bed as if someone poured hot water on us. the whole house was shaken, windows trembled. the explosion came very near the trolley station, part of the city called dedinje, if you remember, where we went down from the downtown, at the top of the hill. the electricity disappeared. my first thought was—i will not be able to be in touch with my friends via email. but after 20 minutes it came back . . . which was a relief . . .

fortunately we are at the bottom of the hill. then thunder was heard, and we didn't know whether it was bomb, but then it started raining with thunder. we were awake an hour more and then went to bed again.

it was really 'exciting'!

love,
dubravka

Fri, 30 Apr 1999

dear friends, just a brief note. thanks for writing, and it is important to be in touch with you all this time . . .

later i will try to write for the list a short report, but now i just want to tell you that last night was the worst of all others. we heard the detonations from 22 hours on, most of the night we walk around the house, open windows trying to hear something, and we could hear planes, anti-aircraft artillery, explosions, and at the end, before 6 in the morning we were awakened by the earthquake. could you imagine this!

misko went to the faculty [university], this week most of the faculties started some kind of consultations with small groups of students, and i am just about to go to downtown.

love,
dubravka

p.s. charles, misko's brother wrote, two issues of *boundary 2* reach him [in LA], it would be interesting to see if it will reach us. the post from slovenia still comes . . .

Wed, 5 May 1999

dear charles, it was good that *boundary 2* wasn't send here, yesterday i heard from an american who live here, she is translator and lecturer at dept. of english, that mail from usa doesn't work any more . . .

i didn't write for some time at all, because from time to time felt psychically exhausted. we had few days relatively peaceful, and that means we could sleep relatively well . . . but the other day when electricity disappeared, it was horrible, all fears that could come at one's mind came. whole city in darkness, you don't know what happened, and what might happen . . . looking through the window you could just see from time to time some cars passing by hurrying, in fear. yesterday and today from time to time we didn't have electricity. most of the parts of the town were out of electricity and of water. we are near hospitals, and are in a better position. but the night electricity disappeared, the first reaction was to go and fill bottles with water in the case that there was no water.

we will try to put *ProFemina* on internet . . .

i will write again . . .

Sat, 8 May 1999

dear charles,
just a short note.

we have the same problem with misko's brother messages as with your empty messages . . . the problem is, i don't know why, when you write as reply to the author it is empty. when you write a new message, it is readable.

we are good. last night was also bad, the worst is with electricity, because the next day couldn't enter email.

anyway, i will write whenever i can . . . just to be in touch.

love,
dubravka

Nicole Eisenman

Self Portrait as Sphinx, 1995
ink on paper, 12" x 10"
courtesy of the artist and Jack Tilton Gallery, New York

Robert Feintuch

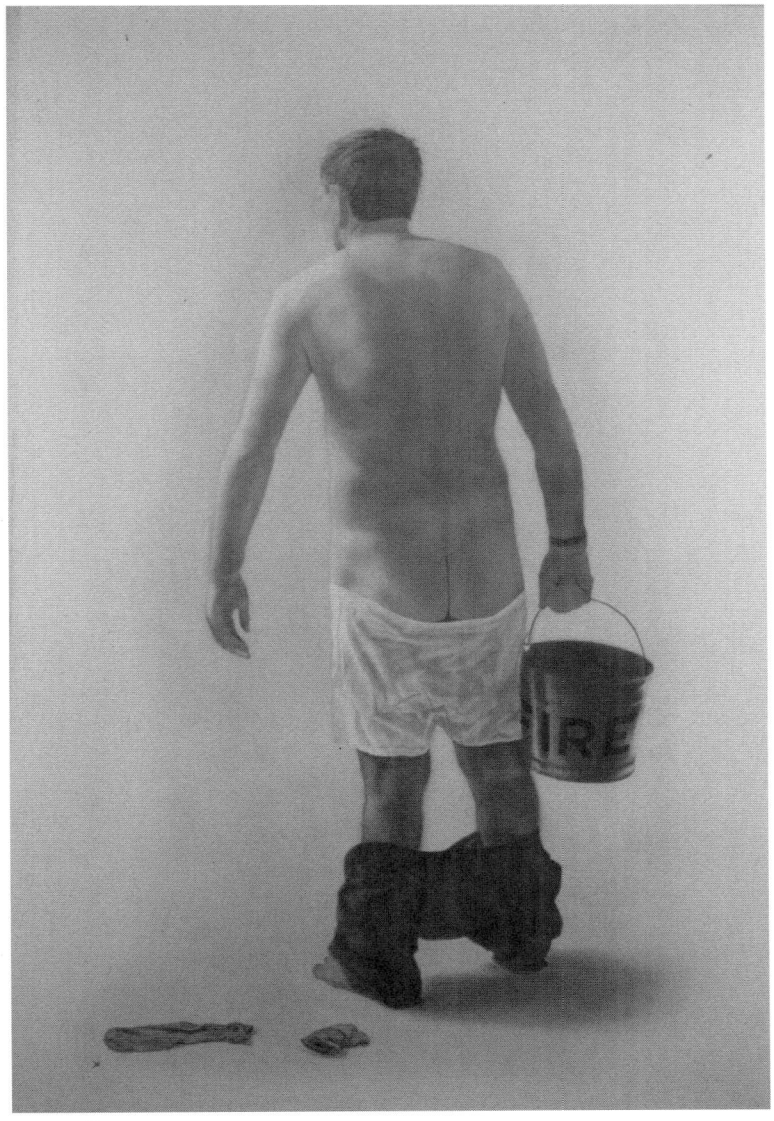

Himself, 1998
polymer emulsion on canvas, 73.5" x 47"

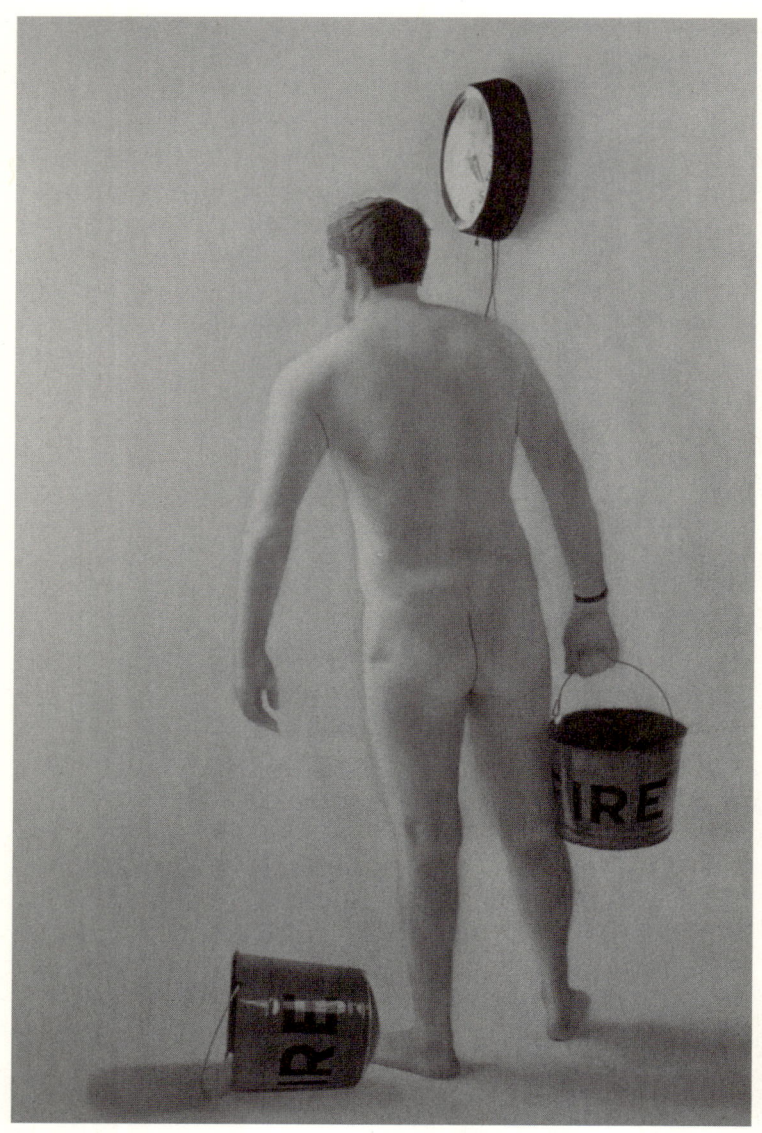

Self Portrait with Clock, 1999
polymer emulsion on canvas, 72"x 45 1/2"

Alejandro Fogel
ROOT TO ROUTE: 10 RUMBACH ST.

"10 Rumbach Street" is one part of *Root to Route*, the story of my life and my father's life intersecting through time. I have been following my father's footsteps through the Holocaust years and after, as he journeyed from his small Hassidic village in northern Transylvania to Budapest and finally to Buenos Aires where I was born and raised.

Root to Route is a world to be traversed in writing, video, photography, painting, installation, and on the Web:
www.RootToRoute.com

10 Rumbach St. III
panoramic photography, 4.5" x 9"

Scratches in the train III
acrylic on cork, 14" x 12"

My first memories of the Holocaust came to me in the form of screams in the dark. My father's nightmares and his heavy breathing. I remember waking up in the middle of the night and feeling his past coming back to us, my mother calming him down, and the shadows of the leaves from an enormous tree outside my window frantically moving through my room. I never asked my father about those dreams.

I was three or four when he first told me about running from the Nazis. It happened one day when I asked him about his petrified toe nails. He was sitting on a chair in the living room of our Buenos Aires home with his feet in a pan of hot water. His toe nails were different than

Scratches in the train II
acrylic on cork, 11" x 9"

mine. They were dark brown, bulbous as grapes and the texture of petrified wood. I was very curious about them and began to ask questions. I was sitting on the floor looking at his feet next to the heater and for the first time he let me pour him a mate. Then he started to tell me his stories and I began to understand his nightmares.

My father, Moishe Fogel, was eighteen years old and on his way to becoming a rabbi when he left his home town, the small village of Sacel in Northern Transylvania. It was the year 1941 and the Jews were being sent to labor camps. There was no choice and he left. His parents, Zvi and Dreisa, would remain behind, as would the youngest children. The other eight brothers and sisters would scatter. My father shaved his curls, left his black clothes behind and with nothing but a little food and his father's blessing he left home. Only five of the brothers and sisters would survive the Holocaust. Zvi, Dreisa, and the children remaining in Sacel were deported to Auschwitz in 1944. Moishe would never see them again.

He traveled to Budapest where he found a room on Rumbach street. He lived there in hiding for two years, with no identification papers and nobody to talk to from where he came from. He worked in a textile factory on the Buda side until he was caught and sent to a labor camp from which he escaped and was recaptured again, tortured and finally put on a train to Auschwitz. He knew what Auschwitz meant and broke the barbed wired covering the small window of the cattle car with his hands and, in the middle of the night, bleeding, he jumped out. The guards on top of the train fired many times but none of the bullets hit him. It was winter and he was running through the fields somewhere between Czechoslovakia and Poland. This was where he hid in the mountains and suffered frostbite on his feet, causing the toe nails to turn the strange color and texture that had led me to question him as a child. He joined the Russian Army and fought with them until the end of the War. With the Russian Army, he came to the concentration camp at Bergen-Belsen. A woman in one of the barracks recognized him and called him by his name. She was from Sacel and she had seen one of his sisters, Charne, only a few days ago leaving for Israel. The woman said she was going there, too. Moishe took the only picture of himself he had taken during the war and which he treasured from his wallet, and gave it to her. He told her to give the picture to his sister in Israel as proof that he was still alive. Ten years later Moishe's sister sent that picture back to him from Tel Aviv to Buenos Aires where it sat on a shelf under our television.

After the war, he defected from the Russian Army and wandered as a refugee in western Europe for six years trying to get a visa to go to America. The US quota for Jewish refugees was very small and tired of waiting, he bought a fake Bolivian passport that took him to South America and finally to the train station Evita in Buenos Aires, Argentina during Peron's times. The first place he went looking for help was the AMIA, the Jewish Aid Society, where he would later come to work as a cantor. In the summer of 1994, the AMIA was blown up by terrorists while Moishe was working only 2 blocks away. His body lifted off the ground at the same time that some of his friends were blasted apart and buried in the rubble. I spoke to him on the phone a few hours

Moishe Fogel, 1944

after the explosion that killed more than one hundred people and he repeated what he had said to me many times over our years together: "I am a lucky man. I escaped again."

Shadow, videotape

I am standing now in front of the building at 10 Rumbach Street where my father lived in hiding during World War II. It is the summer of 1994 and my first visit to Budapest. Fifty years later I am my father and I have come back. We are so different, he and I, and at the same time we are the same person looking for our past and our roots. He was only eighteen years old when he first arrived in Budapest and I am 38 now. He could have been my son then, I think, watching the high school boys coming home from classes. I am speaking to the janitor in the courtyard of the building, hoping to find someone who had known my father then. She tells me that nobody from that time survived. "The last person who had lived in 10 Rumbach since the forties died two months ago," she says. She can't tell me much more. She confides that she knows some Jews live in the building. When she pronounces the word "Jews" she lowers her voice.

The moment that I walked the same street in the Jewish Ghetto in which my father lived alone as a teenager in hiding between 1941 and 1943 was a turning point in my life. I was walking the same street fifty years later. I was being my father, an "alien Hungarian" born in northern Transylvania, illegally in Hungary seeking

Shadow, videotape

safety from the Nazis. I understood persecution. I understood the meaning of the word genocide not only in Europe but in the continent of South America where I was born. The Route and The Root were finally at a crossroads. Everything in Rumbach Street was meaningful to me. The texture of the crumbling walls, the old curb, the boarded up windows in the cellars, a piece of brick, the imprints of shop signs that were taken away and, of course, the war pitted building of 10 Rumbach Street, itself. The huge metal door was open so I entered the courtyard and looked up the dizzying spiral of stairs that led to the apartments. The hallway had not been painted for years, the walls themselves were falling apart and a single bare light bulb swung from the ceiling and lit the corridor. I could see him in his room, my young father, my father before he was my father: shaving, sleeping, thinking. It was the first time I felt really close to him. The first time I understood his suffering. His voice was still there in Rumbach Street. We communicated through the same air, through the same walls, through the sounds of pigeons gathering on a roof from his time then to my time now. Our routes were so much apart that finally they touched each other. I was at that crossroads alone with him. Alone with his petrified toe nails and my nightmares.

On Rumbach Street, the whispers of those who suffered Nazi persecution in Hungary are still there and I am listening to them and establishing and sharing personal contact with the fragments of memory left by the inhabitants who walked those streets and never returned. In Rumbach Street I discovered the reality of a physical space and time my father once occupied and from it I have come to understand his story and the stories of those who did not survive to recount them. In returning to Rumbach Street, I was able to do what my father could not. Go back and look at his experience through the eyes of time: from the years he spent in study, learning to be a Hassidic rabbi in his little village in Transylvania, to his room as a teenager alone on Rumbach Street; from his escape from a labor camp in northern Hungary to his escape from the bomb which leveled the Jewish Aid Society in his neighborhood of Buenos Aires. These crucial events travel a succession of levels through time, incorporating elements from my father's life and my own, composing our worlds into one, from that little room on Rumbach Street, where I realized that our lives were overlapping.

This is a diary of two men, fifty years apart, unraveling their destinies.

10 Rumbach St.
panoramic photography, 4.5" x 9"

With Adolf Hitler's rise to power in 1933 began the genocide of millions of people throughout Europe. The efforts of the German government were directed at the total elimination of the European Jews through massive firing squads, death marches and concentration camps where the prisoners were systematically gassed with the efficiency of a factory assembly line. As a result, 6,000,000 Jews were killed and countless others wounded and scarred for life in what it is called the Holocaust, from the Greek word meaning "a sacrifice burnt by fire." In 1941, the year in which the "Final Solution" of the Jewish Problem was conceived, there were 700,000 Jews living in Hungary out of a total population of 15,000,000. 150,000 of them lived in northern Transylvania, where my family came from. Hungary at that time was a German ally. In the period that ends with the "Final Solution" for the Hungarian Jews in 1944, close to 50,000 Jews died in forced-labor camps, like the one my father was imprisoned and tortured in during 1943. In the spring of 1944 the Nazis invaded Hungary, ghettoized the Jews and 450,000 of them were deported to concentration camps in a total of 147 hermetically sealed freight train cars. Most of them were gassed upon arrival at Auschwitz—among them my grandparents Dreisa and Zvi Fogel and 7 of their 12 children.

Kenny Fries
DISABILITY MADE ME DO IT OR MODELING FOR THE CAUSE

I am living in Provincetown, single for the first time in seven years, when I get a phone call from Tom, a local artist. Tom tells me he has been hired to do the drawings for an updated version of a well-known guide to gay male sex. "I want to make sure different types of men are represented in the drawings," he tells me. "I wanted to talk to you about how you think I can best portray a disabled man having sex."

During our conversation it becomes clear that Tom wants to include a drawing of me in the book. "I'll take photos of you having sex and use them as the source for what I'll draw," he explains.

"Sex with whom?" I ask.

"That's easy," Tom assures me.

"I'll think about it," I tell him.

A week later, Tom calls to tell me he has found someone to pair up with me. Thinking it important for a disabled gay man to be accurately portrayed in this popular book, I agree to take off my clothes and be intimate with a nondisabled man I do not know.

Why did I so easily agree to model for the cause? Two encounters with men, a few years apart a few years ago, hold part of the answer.

I am working at a very public job in the San Francisco theater community when I am asked out to lunch by a man interested in getting to know his way around the community the organization I work for serves. During what is supposed to be a business lunch, he looks across the table at me and asks, point blank: "Do you like to be humiliated?"

Right away I know what he is talking about, where this conversation is leading, even though no one has ever asked me such a question before. I am intrigued. I want to know more of what lies underneath his question, so I reply, "Why do you ask?"

"Because I know this one guy in Los Angeles who told me that's the only way he can enjoy sex. Pain and humiliation bring up all the times he got attention when he was a kid, so he gets off on it."

For me the operative words in his response are "this one guy in Los Angeles." This man, reasonably intelligent and successful in his theatrical career, has taken an experience he heard from one disabled gay man he knows and assumed that all disabled people get sexually aroused by pain and humiliation. I could answer him by pointing out how many nondisabled men, gay or otherwise, enjoy experiencing sex that way or offering other enlightened responses, but all I can muster in response is, "Really?"

A few years later, I am taken out to lunch by a nondisabled gay male editor who is interested in my work. His keen interest in my writing about the more sexual aspects of my past make me uncomfortable but, like the previous experience at lunch a few years ago, I am intrigued. I want to find out what lies at the bottom of this man's inordinate curiosity.

During this lunch in a prim New York restaurant, I learn that the editor has a cousin who is disabled. As he speaks, I sense that growing up he had an obvious affection for this cousin which was related in some way to his own sense of feeling different, of being ostracized by his family for being gay.

When I tell the editor my concerns about how, as I write more about my past, I concentrate more and more on the sexual, trying to allay my concern he says, "People are very interested in how disabled people have sex, aren't they?"

For a moment I am taken aback. Puzzled. My first thought is that not many people would be interested in the way I have sex, being that my sexual practices are probably similar to the experiences of most nondisabled gay men I know. My next unspoken response is: No, most people aren't interested but you obviously are.

Taking into consideration that I might have to work with this well intentioned man sitting across from me, and that he is paying for this rather expensive lunch, I simply correct his assumption. "Actually, most people do not think of those of us who live with disabilities as sexual at all," I say.

The night before the photo shoot I get nervous. Since my last relationship broke up three months ago, I have not been naked with another man. Since I was monogamous with my last lover, I have not taken off my clothes and shared my body with a stranger for many years. How will I feel undressing and getting into bed with someone handpicked for the occasion? How will he react to my disabled legs? My insecurities keep me awake all night long.

When I was in my early twenties, when I was a graduate student in New York, as well as during the first years I lived in San Francisco, I had success finding sexual partners in bars. When I first started going to bars I would plant myself at a table or on a stool at the bar and stay in one place as long as possible. When I saw someone I wanted to get to know, I would stay put. And even when I had to go to the bathroom I would put it off for as long as I could in order to avoid making my disability noticeable by standing up and walking around the bar. By deciding to remain stationary, the men I would meet would have to come over to me, or I would meet them by chance when they happened to take a seat next to me where I sat at a table or at the bar.

Only once during my years of going to the bars did a man decide not to go home with me after he noticed I was disabled. That one time, after I had been talking with this guy most of the evening, long after it had become obvious we would leave the bar together and go back to where one of us lived, when I got up and he saw that I stood just over five-feet tall, he immediately decided not to leave the bar with me. When I stood up, this man who a moment before had been running his finger up and down the length of my arm, became flustered and without saying a word walked to the other side of the bar.

A few years later, when traveling with a friend in Italy, I was denied entrance to a gay bar in Florence because I was disabled. "No belong here," the handsome man in charge of letting people into the bar told me, after I explained to him in no uncertain terms I was gay and belonged inside.

Perhaps, I might have been excluded from the Florentine bar for reasons having to do with physical attributes, or lack of them, other than my disabled legs. Perhaps, my disability was never the most salient feature that caused men not to want to have sex with me. But, attraction being a difficult thing to decipher, I have always been apt to hold my disability responsible when these situations occur. Does this assumption tell me more about my own insecurities than about a culture in which images of disabled men are not part of the book of myths that define what is attractive?

No longer drinking alcohol, allergic to smoky places, and no longer interested in meeting men this way, I stopped going to bars. About the same time, I found out my cholesterol was way too high and my doctor recommended I swim for cardiovascular exercise. So, I joined the Jewish Community Center, which had a good pool, and was close to where I lived.

During the late morning and early afternoon hours, the JCC was sparsely filled. Most who used the facilities during these hours were elderly Eastern European men. Long dormant hybrid languages of the recent past were whispered in the locker room and showers.

When I began my cholesterol lowering regimen, I noticed a few men my age who swam every other day the same time I did. After almost an hour's swim, in the showers or in the locker room I was surprised that many of these men took an obviously sexual interest in me. Why in bars where I was fully clothed did I usually go unnoticed, but when my deformed lower body was revealed naked in the showers at the JCC did men consistently pursue me? Were my expectations of how men react to my disability that out of line? Had I internalized all the negative body imagery and stereotypes of disability to the point where I could no longer think clearly about the effect my body's difference had in the world?

Before we begin the photo session Tom tells us that the part of the book that we will model for will be "Biting." That doesn't sound too heavy, I think to myself, as I introduce myself to George, who will be my partner for the session. "This should be interesting," I say as I shake his hand. George doesn't seem as nervous as I feel. Is he surprised I am disabled? Did Tom tell him before he agreed? Even though it probably wouldn't have made me any less nervous, I wish I had asked Tom if he had told George about my disability before we met. Next time remember to ask, I tell myself, as if this session will be my first of what is sure to be many nude modeling sessions.

A few minutes later, Tom leads us up a flight of stairs to the bedroom where the photos will be taken. As Tom sets up his camera, the lights, and other photographic equipment, I sit on one the edge of one side of the large double bed; George sits on the other. Slowly, as we small talk over the width of the bed—"How long have you lived in Ptown?"; "Where do you work?"—we begin to take off our clothes.

I could be chatting with my doctor or undressing for what I know from experience will be a fabulous massage. I don't know George well enough, had never seen him until a few minutes ago downstairs—has he ever seen me and my inimitable gait walking down Commercial Street?—to ask if he has ever done this before. What I do know is his olive skin, his tight curly black hair, his dark brown eyes.

"Should we unmake the bed?" George asks.

"Might as well," Tom calls, still busy with his camera.

When George stands up to take the sheet off the bed, I see his unclothed body for the first time. Casually, or trying to appear casual, I take in his hairless chest, the thin trail of darkness that eventually spreads itself around an amply sized penis. Even when aware of the pernicious affect of doing so, it is often too difficult to shed the socialization of judging another man's body by what one has, by a constant bombardment of words and images, been taught to desire. I want to look away before I am aroused. How much of my body can George see from where he stands on the other side of the bed?

"Why don't you two get to know each other," Tom says as he checks a malfunctioning light he's set up over the bed.

And before I can give Tom's suggestion a moment's thought, George has trampolined onto the bed and is pulling me toward him.

Often, when I wake during the night, wrapping myself around my lover's torso, I am surprised anew each time I realize my body, lying so closely next to my lover's, is of measure. Because above my thighs, my body is of customary length, lying in bed with my lover I feel the equality of my body's size. I feel comfortable, at ease, something I do not feel when standing up and talking to someone at a party where, standing just over five feet tall, I often don't reach my conversation partner's shoulders, or even when sitting down for dinner in a restaurant where more often or not my feet do not reach the floor. In crowded public elevators, I am often unseen, relegated to a back corner where the view is more often the middle of a back, or below.

But here in bed it feels as if the playing field has been literally leveled. Lying in bed with another man, as I now am with George, despite my insecurities about my body, I feel more natural. Even though a half hour earlier I did not know him, I am soothed by his fingers grazing my shoulder, then the length of my arm.

"Lay on your back," George tells me, and unquestioningly I do so.

How often have I done this—getting to know first by touch another man? But this time I'm doing it for the cause of the accurate representation of disabled persons, I remind myself as I feel George's lips on the inside of my thigh.

"Nibble him," Tom calls out from behind his camera, and I feel George gently biting my balls.

"That was great," Tom says much too quickly. "I think I've got what I need."

I wish I can say the same thing, I think, reluctantly watching George put back on his clothes.

Parting in the street from the man who only moments before had nibbled at my nakedness, I want to ask him not only what the experience was like for him but specifically what did it feel like to touch me, a disabled man. As I often do after having sex, I try to remember if George had actually touched my legs. I want to ask him, as I've asked many of the men after we've first had sex, if we can get together again. But I ask none of these questions, nor any of the others that float in my mind. A few days later, when I see him in the street, we stop, exchange pleasant small talk, and with my questions unspoken, continue down the street in opposite directions.

Later that week, Tom calls. He wants me to come over to his studio to look at the photos, as well as the drawing he has already begun.

Looking at the photos and drawing, I am both surprised and relieved at my reaction. I do not recoil, as I often do when I glimpse myself in a full-length mirror or in a store window as I'm passing by. This time, now, I recognize the images of myself in both the photos and the drawing as very beautiful. I check within but do not find the usual embarrassment at seeing a representation of my disabled body.

But when Tom submits the finished drawing to the commercial publishing house in New York City, the art director is not pleased. He tells Tom that in the drawing "the disability does not read."

When Tom calls I share his disappointment. "We have three choices," he tells me as he begins to tell me the art director's ultimatum. "He wants me to cut off one of your legs."

"My parents didn't let many well-known doctors do that when I was born," I tell Tom.

"Or I can put in a wheelchair by the side of the bed." But I know Tom does not want to take the easy way out and simply draw in a wheelchair, which I do not use but is the most obvious symbol that would "read" disability to a general audience, at the side of the bed as two men make love. Tom wants to depict an actual person with an actual disability in the act. After all, this was the reason I agreed to model, wasn't it?

"And the third way?" I ask after a long pause.

"I can put somebody else's head on your body, then take off one or both of your legs."

An uncomfortable conversation ensues. Finally, when I tell Tom if he cannot use my body as it is, he cannot use my body at all, he is angry. This means he will have to completely scrap the drawing he has already spent time on, find another model, reshoot, and redraw. This will put him even farther behind schedule than he already is. In frustration, he hangs up the phone before we have finished our conversation.

Months later, when the book is published no drawing in which I appear is included. Instead, accompanying the section on "Masculinity," there is, included in a group of nondisabled men, a drawing of one fully clothed man in his signifying wheelchair. This disabled man is not portrayed as being sexual, and once again—as in countless photographs by Diane Arbus, Joel Peter Witkin, or Gary Winogrand—it is the disability which defines the person, instead of being part of the person. Once again, the disabled person is viewed as object, not an object of desire.

As I stare at the drawing, I realize a man with a disability has once again entered the book of myths defined as his disability instead of being portrayed as a person with a disability. To the large audience who will use this book this might be the only image they might ever see of a disabled gay man. And the message of the drawing: Despite having to use a wheelchair, he is a man, too.

Leaving the bookstore I am gripped by a sadness too heavy to have been caused by my encounter with the drawing that was supposed to be me making love with George. Lying in bed that night, I can't get the photos Tom took of me and George out of my mind. Did George ever see it? If so, what did he think?

"Nibble him," I hear Tom say, as I finally fall asleep.

Waking the next morning, I reluctantly get out of bed. Who was I kidding? I ask myself as I get up to take a shower. Was modeling for Tom by having sex with George any different from my other brief sexual encounters? Isn't it to prove to the world, and to myself, that a person who lives with a disability is sexual that I've found myself so quickly naked with strangers before? Didn't I fall for my last lover Miguel because his roughly elegant Spanish beauty made me somehow feel more desirable? Feeling the strong pulse of the spraying water run over me, it is as if I am back in the showers at the JCC in San Francisco, thinking once again about the potent combination of mystery and doubt that plagues not only those of us who live with disabilities when contemplating what we deem attractive and who we desire.

> When I finished writing Body, Remember: A Memoir, I turned to some expurgated episodes from drafts of the book thinking I would turn this unused material into essays. In the process, I became interested in the idea that disability, in fact all things we consider "other" or "different" is actually not a difference at all, but a culturally defined variation that calls into question the entire notion of the dialectic of normalcy. This material, in altered form, has in turn become part of a larger book-in-progress, The History of My Shoes, which uses the disability experience to look at Darwinian notions of evolution and progress. In this way, I have learned that episodes from life—memoir if you will—are as fluid as the culturally arbitrary categories such as disability itself.

Jacinta Galea`i
THE BODY

When I was a fetus in my mother's womb, my genetic code created two blueprints, one for my physical makeup and one for my behavior. The blueprint for my behavior included these traits: will enjoy reading, learn to control temper, eat Dorito chips in the middle of the night, develop an ego at a young age that will be painfully crushed later in life, and will become an assassin. The blueprint for my physical makeup listed these features: female, black hair, dark brown eyes, short fingers, birthmark near left pupil, and will have an extra layer of fat right around the legs.

That was the opening paragraph of a paper I wrote in an autobiographical class I took in 1997 for teachers in American Samoa. The assignment was to write about our bodies. Re-reading the paper, I realize how clean and funny the images, tone, and language are in the paper. It is definitely a piece a teacher in American Samoa could assign to a class of high school students without having to worry about a parent barging into the classroom waving a fist. The irony, however, behind the clean and humorous images and language is the events which led to the actual writing of the body piece were not simple, clean, nor humorous.

In the Samoan culture, there are certain topics that when discussed in public must be done with caution. The body, depending on how one approaches it, is one of those topics.

"Don't forget that our next assignment is on the body," the professor reminded our class as we packed our books.

"The body?" some of the teachers murmured to one another.

"Yeah, you know, breasts, sexuality, masturbation," the professor replied.

Silence.

Complete silence.

"Did I just violate a cultural tradition?" the professor asked, cutting through the silence.

"I could change the assignment," she added.

Continued silence.

Eyebrows rise, eyelids widen, eyeballs search, and desks rattle.

The professor is still.

The class is *still* still.

At this point, we were not too concerned about how we would approach the paper because we knew how *not* to approach it. Rather, we were more concerned about restoring equilibrium in our class.

Bothered by the tension in the classroom, one of the teachers spoke up and carefully said, "There's nothing wrong with the assignment. I know something valuable will come out of it."

Another teacher seconded his response.

As the teachers started to share their views, equilibrium was gradually re-established followed by a discussion on American popular culture's fixation on the body, particularly the fascination with women's breasts.

At this time, I departed mentally from the discussion.

"What part of the body would I write about?"

"Feet, arms, hands, shoulders, toes, . . . What?"

"It would be read aloud in class, which means any sign of sexuality would have to be presented metaphorically or with humor so as not to offend the Samoan audience," I thought.

As I sat in my mind, I listened to the class discussion that was obviously beginning to heat up.

"Westerners and those who have been influenced by western thought are fascinated with private issues," one teacher said.

"We've all been influenced by western thought, but yes, you're right. There is no distinction between what should be talked about publicly and what shouldn't."

"Yes, it's called freedom of expression."

"Freedom is very important, but freedom to do what is good for the community, not just the individual," another teacher responded.

"In Samoa, there are cultural boundaries that are to be crossed carefully, but the choice to cross them is always available."

"How does a person cross the line?" one teacher asked.

"Using their cultural, family, and religious values as a guide," somebody replied.

"It would be easier to cross if you didn't live in Samoa because then you don't have to explain yourself if you're confronted in the village, at church, store, or on the street."

Realizing that some teachers were squirming in their seats, the professor intervened, "Look, we can change the assignment."

"No," someone cut in.

"This is an opportunity for us to examine the whys behind our beliefs and the choices we will make."

After class, as a group of us were heading for our cars, we talked about our discussion.

"Shoot! If I write about this my whole family and village will tease me for the rest of my life."

"Yeah, the teasing would be difficult to take, especially because it will be done mostly behind your back."

"Yeah, they'll say you've gone mad talking about it publicly."

"By the way, what's the Samoan word for that M thing?"

"I don't know if there is a formal word, but I always hear people joke about it as FUFU."

We all started laughing and started calling each other names using the F word.

C. S. Giscombe
NATURAL ABILITIES & NATURAL WRITING

Comatose, lecherous, bored, not aching for a little titillation but not averse to it either: TV nation, 1999. But by spring the official business of impeachment was over and the heavy-duty, philosophical commentators were telling the watchers that "We're all breathing a sigh of relief." Moving on, shaking hands, saluting Bill Rehnquist, toting up the US dollars spent on the whole thing but the money was gone, it was over, though jokes about the money persisted through the summer—it maintained that kind of literary half-life before fading away with the fall.

But while it was going on it was interesting because it was us—a term I dislike, us—, big broad US culture having an experience together; tempting to term it—the experience—sexual, but it was more sexually-*tinged* than directly pleasurable. It was more a metaphor for sex than sex itself, an itchy blanket under which fucking was more possible than it was a fact (to borrow an image from Nicholson Baker). Perhaps I found it interesting because it *was* representational, because it demanded of Americans— even unimaginative Republican-types—a metaphoric virtuosity that's quite foreign to our everyday national character. We're a technological bunch— from a tradition of tinkers, Ellison said—, but metaphors? Of particular note is that the impeachment made it possible to look at the perpetrators themselves, the Republicans, in terms of theirs. This isn't about sex, said the Grand Old Poobahs. Well it was, certainly, even a moron could see that; but then again it wasn't. Neither of course was it about the stuff the Republicans said it was about— honesty, the Constitution, the law, Clinton as a bad role model for the youth of America; but in the *New York Times* Maureen Dowd said, They want payback, the Republicans, and not just for Watergate, they want payback for *Woodstock*. All those bodies in the sun and the rain caught on film, in that movie, often naked, writhing to Jimi Hendrix and Carlos Santana and other jungle music or jungle-inspired music, mostly white kids shaking that thing. Payback for *that*.

(I went to the Goose Lake International Music Festival, Jackson, Michigan—near the prison—, the summer after Woodstock, July 1970, 19 years old, one of the few black kids there. It's a mixed memory: I went with a friend and freely and happily admit to doing the sorts of things one does at a three day outdoor party but finally, I think, there were too many bodies present for me—naked, clothed it doesn't matter—, groups don't do it. I met a cute little hippie at breakfast the morning of the 2nd day, someone who'd come in a van, who said he pal'd around with a black guy his age who was over there still asleep right now. "He got a goat and I got a goat too," he said, pulling at his wispy chin. "Late at night 'round the fire we both wolfmen." Wolfmen.)

Tall Vernon Jordan, the soul of black eloquence and haughty post-black grace—both—striding around Washington, a "super-lawyer" by all estimates, a man who moves with "alarming" ease into all manner of campfires, all sorts of powerful situations. One of the southern Republicans, though—speaking doubtless for the gang—, thought it ought to be necessary to actually watch Vernon Jordan testify about the whole mess. I paraphrase but the nouns and verbs are correct—he wanted to look Vernon Jordan in the eye and hear his tone of voice and, *that way*, know whether or not he was lying. I recall it being the moronic Lindsey Graham—because of the white southern accent I reckon—who said that, but it was "really" Bill McCollom, from Florida, who wanted to look old Vernon in the eye. "You a lie," we said as children, "you a lie." A terrible curse but a beautiful one as well.

Now tall Vernon Jordan, he a superlawyer. And trials are, to a large extent, theatre—the experience of presentation—and because of that I'd certainly think that Vernon Jordan or any lawyer worth a damn could look you in the eye and lie to you with a song in his heart and an honest smile on his face. But Vernon's a colored boy, and we have that complex, knotty history with white southerners and by "complex" and "knotty" I mean that there's real familiarity—commonality—there and a savage presumption there as well. We are our bodies, the blackness of our bodies is our curse, our cross: his body gon' tell on him, said Bill McCollum, his body gonna betray him and we'll see that he's a liar, that he a lie.

Betty Currie, the other black body at the periphery of the scandal? She was "loyal" went all the descriptions of her, loyal.

In the city in which I used to live—Ithaca, N.Y.—there was a feature that ran on Saturdays in the *Ithaca Journal*, something sponsored by the local SPCA and encouraging readers to "adopt" animals: each Saturday there was an article about a particular animal, a profile as it were, and each of these was accompanied by a clear, crisp head-and-shoulders photo of the animal in question. My wife Katharine Wright is a photographer and also knows a great deal—through various employments and schooling and deep interest—about animals. The photos, she told me, are not to the point: they're being photographed like humans are and animals are much more their bodies—the stretch of those—than we are. In our faces lives our intelligence and our faces are subject to that and malleable because of it: in my family we pride ourselves on being able to tell tall tales with straight faces—a collie shortage in Scotland, e.g., or a 40 foot glass statue of a pigeon at the State Office Building campus in Albany, N.Y.—and we're not even lawyers. I realized some years ago how much physical attraction depends on the intelligence observed, over time, in someone's face. Erica Hunt mentions, as example of double exceptionalism, "the black man who yields feeling cerebrally." Graham Greene said that by the time you're 50 you have the face you deserve.

Now for a colored boy such as myself who appreciates the outdoors—trees, mountains, hills, the prairie, animals, etc.—this is troublesome when it comes to the natural. Or this is the way we're brought to the natural, *as the natural*. Nature is quantity, its own surface and opaque and mysterious and threatening and, obviously, erotic because of all that, but knowable *via certain conventions*, discernible, readable—Vernon Jordan's dark body will tell on him, will undo him, will reveal him. Our words don't mean—it's our bodies that mean, that's where our nature is. And because of this we have no particular agency there, in the depiction of nature—our bodies are "primitive" and "jungle" and therefore we are not other enough from the natural world to be able to find metaphors of ourselves there. Instead, we *are* the natural world, we're ripe: upon us can be projected metaphors by nature writers or writers about human nature. Channel-surfing late at night I recently got to Zalman King's "Delta of Venus," the shock of nudity on TV, soft-core porn on the IFC: I watched for a while and then I fell asleep though not before the scene in an after-hours club—there was a frenzied crowded dance in which women lost their tops and their breasts came out and this was called "jungle" in the voice-over. They acted like Negroes. This is old news but on it goes. But it's old news, an easy example.

(But channel-surfing again some nights later I came into the middle of "Howling III," a werewolf movie set in Australia that's too racially weird to even begin to talk about. This was not of course on the Independent Film Channel but on TNT or USA or some other cable channel that panders to our indelicate appetites. But I was struck by a scene in which a white ballerina went lupine in the middle of her frenzied dance—hairy, grey, and savage she came after her fellow dancers with a hungry aplomb. Same scene as in "Delta.")

Frenzied sex and nature and us. All this is trouble to me too because I came to understand malleability and provisional definitions and choice and projection all at a long early point in my own life. Nothing particularly mysterious here: reading and thinking and meeting smart people. (Many of whom were ambivalent priests and even more ambivalent religious brothers, the lot that educated me in high school, this being a benefit of the black middle-class dodging the bad public schools and sending its children downtown to be schooled by the Catholics.) Anyway, when I got to college and read Blake's hellish proverb about "Where man is not, nature is barren," I knew that already. I learnt how to watch movies by watching movies on TV with my mother—"Look," she'd say, "look what they're making that woman do." I became aware that writing and photography and movie making and walking in the woods and commenting on what one saw were not natural abilities or occurrences but a series of choices, determined in extent by the circumstances of one's birth, people you've happened to meet and other lucky or unlucky accidents visited on one's person—and this alone, this awareness which I can't lose when I think or write, would probably be grounds for my lifetime exclusion from the canon of nature writing.

That canon's even more profoundly white than others. But Eddy Harris did make it into the *Oxford Book of Nature Writing*, with a snippet of his *Mississippi Solo*, the book about his canoe trip down that river from Minnesota to the Gulf. I recall hearing him interviewed on the radio in 1989 or 1990 and realizing that he was black before the interviewer's questions revealed it—a familiar inflection in the voice betrayed it to me. I was on a mission to the grocer's but I put that on hold and sat in the dark parking lot listening to Eddy Harris on the car radio and thought I could do that, I could write about unconventional, back-country travel, publish a book about it. And then I went into the supermarket to shop for dinner feeling quite odd about having just granted myself that permission. I was 40 years old, a professor, middle-class—my Volvo sat waiting for me in the lot. I'd published poetry books, done the state some service, and won literary awards. And I certainly understood by then—had understood long before then—that there was no unproblematic center, that all was margin and—more—that straddling the margin, like I'd been doing in my writing and my life, was exhilarating, the long ride, the dance of flirtation with various kinds of otherness, with various forms. I knew before I heard Eddy Harris on the radio that the margin was a powerful place to be, that you weren't trapped there—if you were middle-class—, that you could, because you were marginal (and middle-class), do anything. Sure I talked in my classes about the lack of certain narratives for black writers and women writers but I'd thought I was immune, post-all that.

I bought *Mississippi Solo* and marched through it—it's OK, it's a goodenough read. It did not inspire my prose book *Into and Out of Dislocation*, which is about back-country travel in Canada, among other things. (It's really a book about ambivalence and about family-as-metaphor, and about race—that is, blackness—and history in the northern reaches of the continent.) Neither the book's content nor its form offer any particular homage to Eddy Harris but the fact of *Mississippi Solo*'s existence helped me be arrogant enough to push my own book as book. The classic path/desire of wanting someone there before you was at work here, even for a writer such as myself, one who's sneered so often at narrative's straight, dull line and at the cliché of role model. But here I was—driving home from the supermarket and a few years later out having lunch at a lovely seafood restaurant near Union Square with my editor at Farrar, Straus & Giroux—appreciative of that narrative and humbled some by that appreciation, by my own realization of the narrative's power, and not wanting to trouble it or disrupt it. (Especially not while someone was buying me lunch.)

Of course I remember "discovering" Jean Toomer's *Cane* when I was a sophomore at university and what a powerful moment that was for me, but I was young then, at the age where one's supposed to be having such discoveries—when one's not lolling around naked in the shallow end of a Michigan lake with a joint burning one's fingers, which is in itself, truth be told, a not unpleasant way to spend an afternoon. Not unpleasant but neither is it particularly *unnerving*—Toomer's complex blackness married to issues of migration and sex and to his book's own *unwieldiness* as a book, on the other hand, unnerved me a great deal. My book *Here*, begun 15 years after I read *Cane* for the first time, is a belated response—an homage really—to it.

But is all this "nature writing"? Or what's this got to do with nature writing, which is what I'd intended for the theme of the theme of this essay to be? I spoke last year—1998—at St. Mark's, invited there along with a hundred other people to talk about "Identity and Invention." I began by saying, "All my life I've depended on geography, acknowledged it and considered it as basic meaning, as that which is in the world and irreducible in the world." There's nature, right there, boys. But on I went to talk about my invented identity as filmgoer, movies being an art form I truly love in a goofy, romantic sort of way, and to document the film that had most scared me as a child—it was not a proto-intellectual choice like "Repulsion" or "M," it was a wolf-man movie, "Curse of the Werewolf," with young Oliver Reed in the title role. My piece was short, less than a thousand words as per the instructions from the Poetry Project. Now, a year on, I want to return to that and add some things to it.

I'm interested, simply, in the processes by which people estimate nature, what we bring to descriptions of it, what syntheses. We do synthesize. From the first chapter of Eugene Genovese's book, *Roll, Jordan, Roll*: "Slavery bound two people together in bitter antagonism while creating an organic relationship so complex and ambivalent that neither could express the simplest human truth without reference to the other." It's this necessary "reference to the other" race that Genovese suggests that interests me. It's the soul of synthesis, of an everyday self-consciousness that black people *continue* to inhabit. (The relationship is still there, I'd argue, for white people as well but the consciousness of it has burned off or gone underground, choose your metaphor. We still, though, fresh and talking among ourselves, are perpetually, unforgettably other; or, as Dick Gregory said years ago, commenting on the failure of Madison Avenue type advertising in the ghetto, "We know what it's like to *be* Brand X.") But I was raised middle-class and understood and appreciated irony and we were far removed from the "old days," even as I was growing up in the 50s. I was sent to the Nature Program at the Dayton Museum of Natural History in 1958 or 1959, only vaguely aware that I was the only black child present. (My exhibit on Birds of Ohio is boxed in the attic still.) My sister's history is similar.

The question is, Why are the Giscombe children so enamored of werewolves?

If most popular and literary depictions of nature as subject are problematical because they seem to deny—or pretend to deny—human/cultural agency and hypothesize a de-racialized and class-free "human" self whose metaphor might be found in the erotically primitive otherness of the natural world ... Well, werewolves are an antidote to that, or at least a more direct form of address—we have the human and the animal coupled (not sexually but sexuality enters into it). Popular depictions of lycanthropy are a satire, arguably, of nature writing, a cautionary tale: look too close and you're gonna fall in. (Langston Hughes' "Suicide's Note": "The calm / Cool face of the river / Asked me for a kiss.") The primitive will inhabit you. This, of course, is what "going native" means, which phrase only seems to apply, in the customs of usage, to white people. Native? [replacing ME. *natyf* (OFr. *natif*) < L. *nativus* < *natus*, pp. of *nasci*, to be born]. If black people are jungly, primitive nature itself then nature [ME.; OFr.; L. *natura* < *natus*, born, produced, pp. of *nasci*, to be born] will get you and take *over* your ass.

More: the films my sister and I enjoyed so much as children were not the monster films of giant ants or beasts from 20,000 fathoms as much as they were films about human bodies in revolt, infected bodies, bodies at war with their own "selves," the inescapability of the monster's human body—the werewolf in the daytime staring at his hands, the elegant appearance of the vampire in the drawing room in early evening, arguably even the limping mummy, with its human form and memory. What's at stake is the human's inability to truly transcend the heat of its infection, the nature of its nature. Oliver Reed, as Leon the werewolf, was described as being in flight "from the curse of his tainted blood." And blood's a big deal, as a public metaphor for race—it defines black people (in America) as being people with even "one drop" of African "blood" in their veins. It's the one drop that stains you like it would a white tablecloth—it's the thing, the *substance*, that taints you, makes you non-white. This is not news either, this one drop rule and the fear of hidden miscegenation that it represents for white people. The point I'd argue, though, is that the films we liked constructed their monsters, partly, out of this fear—there was often a heroine to be rescued from some dark sexual beast (Fay Wray and old King Kong, e.g.) or the ostensibly ordinary person is the descendent of some wrong or un-ancestor as was Simone Simon in "Cat People," one of the smartest werewolf movies. (Monsters had other Africanisms about their persons as well but this is a topic for another place, another time.)

It's not news but to me these old movies were a statement of the fact of miscegenation because this is what it is, partly, to be black in America—it's to acknowledge the racial mix of your ancestry; to be white, of course, is to deny it. The film that scared me as a child, "Curse of the Werewolf," came out in 1961 and never entered the public imagination like the first handful of wolfman movies from the 30s and 40s. Prominent among these of course was "The Wolfman," which appeared in 1940. The main character, Larry Talbot, played by Lon Chaney, Jr. looked like a normal-enough white guy but oh what he turned into by night: his hair would kink up and his skin would darken and that big Chaney nose would flatten right out. De woof-man!

(In the most interesting moment in "American Graffiti" one of the minor female characters says her parents won't let her listen to Wolfman Jack—played by himself in the film—"because he's a Negro.")

Real wolves don't look a thing like what Larry Talbot turned into: their fur is very straight, their snouts are aquiline. But he is the werewolf image that has survived in American culture—60 years on, Lon Chaney's still the wolfman. His depiction made it onto a postage stamp last year, just before the rates went up, the fearsome head printed there next to 32¢. This wolfman as opposed to the metaphorically less complex but higher tech models of the various Howlings and American Werewolves in London and Paris. This movie is from back in the day, from 1940, and story itself is simple and cautionary: Larry Talbot, the wayward American son of Sir John Talbot, arrives at the embarrassingly huge family mansion—Talbot Castle—in England, becomes smitten with a young local woman—played by blonde Evelyn Ankers—who is charming and all (but lower class). He accompanies her and her unfortunate friend—the dark-haired actress Fay Helms—to a gypsy fortune teller at a traveling carnival. The gypsy—Bela Lugosi in a bit role—happens to be a werewolf and, later that foggy evening, he attacks the dispensible dark woman. Larry Talbot fights the "wolf" off—too late, alas, for poor Fay Helms—but in the process is bitten and becomes of course a werewolf himself. The question of the film is whether or not he's going to kill the blonde he's in love with; he does not—he's killed (by Claude Rains as Sir John) first and, in death, reverts to his human form. He's brought back to life for a number of sequels and it's possible, in these, to chart the advances in special effects: in "The Wolfman," he changes demurely—that is, off camera—but in later films Chaney's transformations were accomplished in a succession of frames of the same shot: different thicknesses of hair overlay each previous shot until he's finished changing into the dark-skinned, flat-nosed, kinky-furred monster who first went off in pursuit of the English blonde who'd fallen in love with the white boy who came back from America to live in the house that Jack built, y'all.

I saw all these films for the first time at home, at 11 or 12, on snowy channel 9's Shock Theatre, Friday nights at 11.30. Years later on the verge of leaving college I saw my first porno film, "The Devil and Miss Jones," at the Art Theatre in Schenectady, N.Y. I'd seen "dirty" movies in high school but was unaware of how far the genre had progressed. After the first scene, in which Miss Jones (played by Georgiana Spelvin) commits suicide, comes the second in which she goes to hell and meets the devil (Harry Reems), on whom she goes down; the woman next to me, my classmate Olivia, keep hissing, "Penis worship, goddamnit!" in my ear but I'll confess to being fascinated watching the actor shed his robe and get hard—the shock of seeing proud flesh, *wood*, in a theatre—, realizing there in Schenectady that this is what I'd witnessed in "The Wolf-Man" years before on TV. Harry Reems indeed. The body changes, grows hair, sprouts a horn, gets blacker, it's all the same. Or similar enough.

Why are the Giscombe children so interested in this? Kathy Giscombe, rolling her eyes at her brother and then getting serious, mentions the spectacle of hidden, angry power unleashed suddenly and unexpectedly. Robert Hayden: "the chronic angers of that house."

And this works for me as both a female and black reading of werewolf stories—as well as a tale of the Giscombe manse—, but my own interest was always elsewhere. Alongside that but elsewhere. There's a loup-garou tradition in Haiti and it's interesting as well but it's also other than this, the depiction of the werewolf as a European-descended American icon, something we watch at the movies or on TV. Alfred Metraux: "A woman werewolf getting ready for a night outing first raises as many fingers as she expects to be hours absent from her house, or else she lights a candle marked with three notches. Unless she is back before the flame reaches the last notch her excursion may go ill. When she has taken these precautions she frees herself of her skin by rubbing her neck, wrists, and ankles with a concoction of magic herbs. She hides her skin in a cool place—in a jar or near a pitcher—so that it will not shrink. Thus, stripped to the quick, the woman werewolf makes movements which have the effect of preparing her for the flight which she will shortly undertake. Flames spurt from her armpits and anus, turkey wings sprout from her back. She takes off through the thatch of her house . . ." In Haiti loups garoux are shape-shifters and devourers of children and the French for werewolf itself fits awkwardly: there are no wolves in Haiti. And the Giscombe children's antecedents are Jamaican and that's a different island. Here in late 20th C. America werewolves are nature transformed—*narrated*—infused with the wide human trace in such an ungainly way as to be—as spectacle—of deep interest or, better, of broad interest. If one's interest is in the dance werewolves are a good spectacle, a *filmed metaphor,* perhaps more of one than anything else I can easily think of.

More on this: I was on Assateague Island some years ago, the island off the Maryland coast where wild horses still roam. "Wild horse" had always seemed oxymoronic—the term itself a combination of opposites—after seeing horses bridled and saddled, behind fences, for all these years. I was on a several-days cycling tour of Maryland and Delaware with my friend the poet Cory Brown; it was rainy and miserable this particular day but I'd convinced him to go on in that for the extra miles so we might be able to encounter nature in the "person" of these horses. We crossed the bridge onto the island and rode around for a long time on the park roads—I had on a primitive Gore-tex raincoat but Cory was wearing a green garbage bag and was getting impatient. (The horses of Assateague are descendents of domestic stock kept there by Eastern Shore planters in the 17th and 18th centuries. "Truly" wild? Well, they live without human agency or without benefit of *direct* human agency anyway—Assateague, which stretches across the state line into Virginia, *is* protected; the Maryland herd is "managed" by the National Parks Service. "Feral" might be a more appropriate term than "wild" but the distinction is a fairly fine one.) Anyway I was anxious to actually see the horses and was not disappointed: suddenly, there at the roadside in front of us, was a group of them, three mares and a stallion, grazing. They're not tall animals, they're stocky and scruffy and shaggy. They're bigger than ponies, though, and the stallion stood still looking at us as the mares crossed the road and disappeared into the brush. This was a harem, I realized, and then I wondered, "Should we be afraid?" He was brown and white, his big penis hung down toward the ground; he snorted at us a few more times before following the mares off out of our sight. "OK," said Cory Brown, "we've seen the fucking horses. Now can we leave?"

We went back the way we'd come, over the bridge to the mainland, and it was on the bridge that I realized that in the "Wolfman" movie, people claimed on the screen to be seeing a wolf, to have seen a wolf—*Canis lupus*—and *not* Lon Chaney in black face and fur. I remembered the screen image of the attack on poor Fay Helms—it was a wolf (or a dog actor playing a wolf) that was savaging her kicking form there in the fog, underneath a tree. The gypsy's mother—Maria Oespenskaya—explained it to Talbot later with, "The wolf was Bela and Bela was the wolf"; but when Bela was the wolf, the wolf looked a lot different than when Larry Talbot was the wolf. And I realized that the figure of the wolfman—clothed, broad-featured, hairy, dark, and upright—was a construct for the movie audience, that in the "reality" of the film that figure does not exist. It was a *literal* filmed metaphor, I realized as we chugged up the slick road; it was an awkward fit on the Maryland 2-lane and it's still an awkward fit on the way back from the story of the wild horses of Assateague—it doesn't particularly connect or hold together but it's a true story, my friends. We pushed through a heavier rain to the condos and highrise tourist lodgings of Ocean City and arrived drenched and grubby and a little desperate but still managed to fight with a desk-clerk and get the price of a room in his hotel down. We watched a PBS program on Robert Mugabe and went out for a wonderful seafood dinner. The ocean's right there, of course; fish tastes different in seaside towns. It's a rainy Sunday afternoon in central Pennsylvania as I keyboard this and I'm thinking of the loups-garoux of Haiti: no wolves there so their presence is an act of language rather than an act of God or the devil: it's an act "against nature," an act of opening the field rather than an act of connection.

My mother had dozed through one of the later wolfman movies, the one in which a gypsy girl fell in love with cursed Larry Talbot and then tried to kill him, as a service, with a silver bullet. I explained the plot twists to her the next morning in what I imagine now was likely tiresome detail. But then I pointed out that a werewolf could only be killed by a silver bullet "fired by the hand of one who loves him." This, I realized, was heavy. (This is probably why the Republicans failed to eliminate Bill Clinton, they didn't come to assassinate him with love in their hearts.) "But what," she replied, "if a strange werewolf came to town and no one knew him well enough to love him?"

What's the nature of nature writing? It ain't language, the jagged peaks of sentences, the dewey dells of short paragraphs. Nor is it about "reducing something to voodoo," as Barry Lopez snorted in the werewolf chapter of his book about wolves. Henry Louis Gates suggested that Ralph Ellison was signifying on the titles of Richard Wright's books *Black Boy* and *Native Son* with his own *Invisible Man*. Boy: Son: Man. Music should come up right about here. Denied the oppositeness of nature I propose my own iconography, that from the jazz standard, "Nature Boy," the road leads crookedly to the wolf-man.

Robert Glück
EXPERIMENTAL WRITER GETS SUCKED OFF IN A FIELD

Homage to Straight to Hell

I was just about to graduate from Berkeley. It was 1969.

I'd had plenty of experience rioting, but I had no news about Stonewall, let alone an inkling of what Stonewall would come to mean. I had not come out yet. I sort of planted myself in the way of known fags hoping and fearing to be seduced.

One day I hitchhiked a few hours north just to get away from my hippie commune and out of Berkeley. I took my shirt off and became flesh on the freeway. I was quickly offered a ride in a green Buick by a pudgy check-and-plaid middle aged (perhaps he was thirty) optometrist's receptionist. Even with the windows open my underarms smelled up the car. He put his hand on my knee and it was just that easy—in an instant we were parked in a dry field under a hot sun.

So here is a homosexual, I informed myself. Bad body, dreary life, no friends, isolation, ageing alone, poor, no cultural interests. What the hell, I was just a straight young guy letting some old fag blow me. How well I remember that bleached weedy field and stupid sky—twenty years later I would have thought, "shallow grave." He went down on me and produced orgasms again and again like it was his work to do, that is, single minded, intent as a mole. "Can you do that?" he asked. "Just trigger yourself as often as you want?"

I had no attraction to him *whatsoever*, and I felt no cultural allegiance at all. I was a hippie and twenty-one years old. I wondered why people over thirty bothered to buy new clothes. Every time I came, he opened the car door and spit my cum into the weeds. That unlovely gesture and my picture of his stifled, small town life seemed so hopeless, that I thought rather grandly, "I am getting blown by the misery of the world." I was an English major and that's the way we thought. It was just before the time when the meaning of life would migrate to secondary sources. But then he wanted *me* to blow *him* and I balked. Blowing the misery of the world was something else.

He grabbed my balls to threaten me, but seemed to cave in on his own, as though I'd put up a fight. He tried a second tactic: he took a pair of sunglasses out of his glove compartment—thick black frames and extra dark lenses—that were exactly the same as the ones I was wearing. He was showing me that we were united, we had accessorized as sisters. He said, "Do you come here often?" Here? I looked out at the discouraging universe. He asked if he could see me again. Pervert glasses! I thought in self-horror, I could recognize them for what they were, and the next day I threw my pair away. I wish I hadn't—they'd be right in style now.

> "Experimental Writer" is a tribute to Straight to Hell, *a journal of homemade pornography that ran for years. The idea was to democratize porn. The stories were outlandish, their titles were sensational tabloid headlines.* Straight to Hell *was always a puzzle: were the stories actually true?—were they written by the contributors or by the editor? Problems of authenticity—what were you jacking off to? The stories were stylistically similar, always emphasizing smell, that most elusive sense. Perhaps the editor guided the contributors in that direction? Or the contributors were aspiring to the style of the magazine?*

John Havelda
LABORE ET HONORE

At the age of 11, I was accepted at a boys' grammar school, modeled on Eton, in the Midlands of England. One of the first benefactors of the institution was Queen Elizabeth I. It was all uniforms, assemblies (at which we piped "Lord! keep our School, for ever in thy hand / Stainless and bright; / True lore professing, ever let it stand / A beacon bright: / So when we launch away on life's rough sea, / We may look back, and know we look to thee."), prefects, houses, masters and sadism. I was impelled to forget my working class Hungarian immigrant background and become a little English gentleman, adept at bowing to men in nice coats.

The symbol in the middle of this piece is a reproduction of the school badge I wore on the breast pocket of my black blazer. We were drilled in Latin. The phrases that frame the piece are lifted verbatim from a textbook: the translations are mine. The other trespasses are masters' evaluations of my performance.

Or maybe I am burdening the memory with letters it did not possess, as the narrator of George Perec's W or A Memory of Childhood might put it. If I remember rightly.

Elvira Hernández
IN MEMORIAM LETRA Ñ

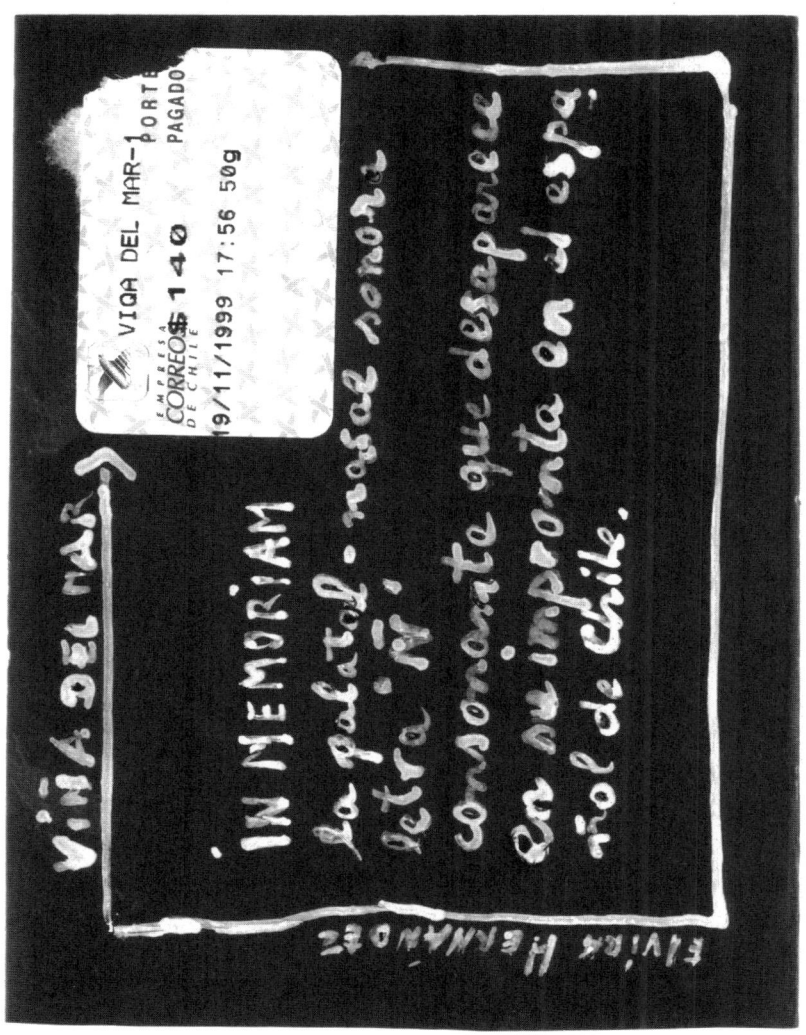

The text includes words and type from the mail machine and words in correction fluid, on black paper, written by hand.

Hsia Yü (translated by Steve Bradbury)
CARTE POSTALE

時間不多
謹慎的小城
不無互相毀滅
即將遠走
打破玻璃
指甲透明

●明信片

Carte Postale

so little time
little city of circumspection
not above a mutual destruction
on the verge of a long voyage
the breaking of the glass
translucent as a fingernail

> *This poem is from Hsia Yü's third volume of poetry,* Moca: Wuyimingzhuang, *or* Rub: Ineffable *(1995), a montage assemblage of "found poems" culled from the cut-and-paste "ruins" of an oversize folio version of one of her earlier books—hence the title "Carte Postale," or "Post Card." The impetus for this volume arose in part out of a desire to undermine the tendency among critics and scholars to read her poetry as if it were confessional in nature. Composed at a time when her writing was becoming strongly influenced by the poet's reading of the early French modernists, the volume is formatted in a manner designed to draw attention to the materiality of poetry, the "music" and sensuality of poetic language, and the evocative power of the fragment. I have used French for the title to underscore the poet's allegiance to this early modernist tradition.*
> —Steve Bradbury

Lisa Jarnot
BIOGRAPHY AND AUTOBIOGRAPHY

Prologue—

When I began writing a biography of Robert Duncan in 1997 there were many questions that people asked me. Are you really going to write a biography? Why are you going to write a biography? Do you know how long it will take you to write the biography? How big will the biography be? Why aren't you writing a biography of a woman? What kind of biography are you going to write? What's your favorite biography? Why don't you write something other than a biography?

During 1993 and 1994 while I was composing my first book of poems, *Some Other Kind of Mission*, I became fascinated with the idea that a poet could create a reality—not a representation of a world, but a world itself. Consciously what was resonating for me at that point was Robert Duncan's directive from *The Opening of the Field*— "Go write yourself a book and put / therein first things that might define a world." Unconsciously I'm certain, in retrospect, that a more primitive adolescent instinct had also crept in—either a resonance of some early teenage Dungeons and Dragons reveries of "the imagined universe," or even the "virtual reality" proposed by MTV or Star Trek. When I completed this book of poems, *Some Other Kind of Mission*, I realized that it was in fact a world that I, and more importantly that others, would always be able to return to, and that it was now a world that functioned with some independence—it had a life of its own and it existed as what the philosopher Alfred North Whitehead would describe as "an actual entity" ingressed or intersecting with "an eternal object." Or that a pure potential for the existence of a new living thing had been transformed into that thing, into its actuality.

I have puzzled over the relationships between biography-writing and poetry-writing in regard to Whitehead's theories, and I have come to a few conclusions—that biography is a collaboration between two authors—the subject and the biographer. And in the way that Jack Spicer talks about the poem as a "mediated space," biography too would be a mediated space. In biography two elements would come together to form a third—that third element, the narrative of a life, would then function independently of the author or the subject—it would be a new actual entity—

One of the jobs of the biographer then would be to enter into a dialogue with the subject and to negotiate with the subject the original terms of the subject's life. The biographer would draw a picture out of the conflicting strands of narrative—not to recreate the original story of the subject nor to present an objective critical evaluation of the subject, but to arrive at a new independent living structure with elements of (or DNA patterns of) both collaborators—author and subject. I've come to approach biography as just such a collaborative effort—not out of a conscious effort to do so, but out of the real life experience of writing such a book—where inevitably (and I think this is one of the great truths of writing biography) the subject of my biography, Robert Duncan, will no longer allow me to distinguish between my life and his. And in Olsonian terms, or through the influence of Whitehead, I would say that the project is organic, that it is a work where the picture is arrived at through a process, in an actual participation with the subject.

I. Autobiography and Biography

> *History . . . is a nightmare from which I am trying to awake.*
> —James Joyce, Ulysses

What I learned to do early in life, as a survival mechanism of sorts, was to invent a self, or a composite of selves, as if my own life was formed out of a distant memory of who all the other versions of me had been throughout the history of my kind. I distinctly remember those early moments from which my creative identity emerged—driving to the Angola Public Library on Saturday afternoons with my parents, where, upon arriving, I retreated to that narrow shelf in the children's section, labeled "biographies." It was a place I would return to over and over again during those years, and a place from which eventually I would accrue knowledge about the lives of an incongruous assortment of baseball players, politicians, inventors and scientists. Having decided at some early age that no one in my family would serve as an appropriate role model, I removed myself to the realm of those books to find out not only who I was to be, but perhaps as importantly, where I fit in. What I had intuited even at that point, was that one's identity existed as one's invention, and that as a creative person, one's identification and explanation of the self might always be in flux, like the whole of the universe is in flux, existing as a place of multiple possibilities, formed around one's attentions to the messages arriving from the outside.

In a lecture at the Berkeley Conference during the summer of 1965, Robert Duncan said "I notice that many reviewers . . . refer to me as making an identity, when well, I would like to have three identities. . . . I would like to have a multitude of such because it doesn't make any difference about [one] identity it seems to me—you're engaged in what you are in, and my general feeling is that I take place *out there*. What I see, what I hear is constantly informing me of a thing I am, as I work with it, and then that can change anyway. . . ."

Duncan of course claimed Whitman (the container of "multitudes") as a great master, and he also was quite aware of theories of object relations—in that ego psychology shows how the self is made up of parts—and that those parts are formed in relation to and because of the objects (people) who surround the particular self. And of course there isn't one self—which is a peculiar dilemma for the biographer. And also, another peculiar dilemma for the biographer might be in establishing what "reality" is for the subject by seeking out the objects (people or objects) surrounding the subject during the subject's waking living lifetime. This is what Ed Sanders describes in his research work as the "zone" (of the bios or life force)—the space within a ten foot radius of the body of the subject—where a period in time becomes a three dimensional sculpture—and the project is an account of everything that happens within that space. Essentially, the biographer has to know what was happening within a ten foot radius of the body of the subject 365 days a year: in Robert Duncan's case—a life that spans 69 years—adding up to 25,185 strips of information, at one strip per day.

To look at an interesting variation on that and how the idea of biography functions—as a complete chaotic and lovely crisis—I'll point toward the experimental film maker Harry Smith who I've always felt some affinity with in his particular desire to create worlds. Smith in his autobiographical exclamations constantly created a self through a series of proclamations and erasures of those proclamations—through an active destruction and reconstruction of the objects in his "zone." I want to list some excerpts from interviews with Harry Smith, where what I've pulled are these instances in which he conjures this sense of object loss and object association to create a self, and constructs his identity out of it. These are from a recent collection of interviews with Harry Smith, aptly titled *Think of the Self Speaking*—

"I used to have a medal that George Washington gave to my great-great grandfather, but I lost it along with a lot of other things." [1965]

"My great-grandfather must have been pretty interesting. At one point he said 'I'm leaving for a five-year tour of Tibet.'" [1965]

"Any time that the Masons have a parade on Fifth Avenue, they always have a float that shows my great-grandfather founding this thing [The Masons]. He travelled all over the world and initiated people like the King of Hawaii and King Edward the Seventh into that business." [1965]

"I would like to say that I'm the czar of Russia. My mother always claimed to be Anastasia." [1965]

"I mean, we were considered some kind of a 'low' family, despite my mother's feeling that she was the Czarina of Russia . . . as a matter of fact, my mother did know [Aleister] Crowley at that time. She saw him running naked down the beach, perhaps in 1913 or 1915. I wish I had gone more into the chronology of my antecedents." [1969]

"My mother evidently had a number of boyfriends, as my father was never there. . . . That's how I met Aleister Crowley. Probably he's my father, although I don't want to say that. . . . My mother would sneak off to see him. . . . She met him when he was running naked down the beach in 1918. She would leave me in a theater." [1965]

"I've never owned a camera. I've usually just borrowed one, then pawned it. That's always an embarrassing scene, trying to explain to the person where his or her camera is. I can remember [someone] saying to me, 'Now you haven't pawned the camera, have you?' He said this jokingly, but it was pawned." [1965]

"Alexandra was my grandmother. My mother was Anastasia . . . she was on a Russian gunboat . . . and they were having a picnic on the boat when the news got through that even the Tsar's bodyguards had like revolted at that point, and she just barely got off the boat and worked her way back to Alaska." [1972]

"I made a lot of recordings . . . which unfortunately disappeared with everything else I had." [1969]

"As I say, less than half of all that stuff is in my possession at this point. . . . Many of those films are totally missing." [1965]

"My father had run away from home at an early age to become a cowboy. I think that at that time his grandfather was the governor of Illinois. . . . My mother came to Sioux City, Iowa, but my grandmother had had a school that was supported by the Czarina of Russia in Sitka, Alaska, although she moved around. The Czarina still supported those operations for years, and that's what lead to my mother's being Anastasia. My father destroyed every single shred of information when she died. I never saw him again." [1965]

"I assume that life in the universe will continue to the point that anything can be recreated. It's only an illusion anyhow. There isn't anything here except some kind of weak magnetic field." [1983]

Psychologist Heinz Hartman in his 1958 book *Ego Psychology and the Problem of Adaptation* wrote "the healthy adult's mental life is probably never quite free of the denial and replacement of some reality by fantasy formation . . . though fantasy always implies an initial turning away from a real situation, it can also be a preparation for reality and may lead to a better mastery of it. . . . It is well known that there are fantasies which, while they remove man from external reality, open up for him his internal reality."

Obviously it's not unusual for poets to function in such a realm of self-creation. James Joyce, like Harry Smith, awakes out of history by awaking into a history of his own making. While Harry Smith proves that he is the heir to the Russian throne and to Aleister Crowley's Order of the Temple of the East, it can be argued that in *Ulysses*, Joyce proves that he is Hamlet, Shakespeare, Stephen Daedelus, Leopold Bloom, Parnell, and Jesus. By the time he arrives at *Finnegans Wake*, he can safely rename his protagonist Humphrey Chimpden Earwicker or Here Comes Everybody. Freud, in his study *Leonardo DaVinci and a Memory of His Childhood* proves through a similar series of terms that Leonardo is the Christ child in his painting "Madonna and Child with St. Anne." Robert Duncan through his studies with medievalist scholar Ernst Kantorowicz, would come to write "the Venice Poem" in 1947, a poem which resonates with Kantorowicz's ideas about historical concept of "the King's Two Bodies"—mortal and divine, where the king "imitates" or enacts "the image of the living christ." Duncan, in "The Venice Poem" identifies himself as a christ figure disguised as "the cross-eyed king of 1000 lines," and "young William Shakespeare." One of the other things that Duncan does over the course of his private musings in notebooks is to prove that H.D. is his mother. One of the things that H.D. sets out to prove over the course of *Tribute to Freud,* in a typical pattern of transference, is that Freud is her father—an interesting lineage is then created in which Duncan appears as Freud's grandson. Duncan, with his sympathies for Freud's work, certainly appreciated that.

II. Biography and Biography

> *Go write yourself a book and put therein first things that might define a world.*
> —Robert Duncan, "Under Ground"

> *I would shake the Mahjong table, and the palace of many gardens and courts, the majestic halls and ramparts, constructed by giant hands from another world, the corridor where the Queen walked in the evening to meet the King, would fall. It seemed as if distant almost real shouts of anguish rose among the tottering ivory walls, and, making my play of earthquake—for I was the genius of the scene— I almost heard the confusion of delicious dismay, grief and fear, echoed in my heart as if bonds of human sympathy united me with the inhabitants of this world I created to destroy again and again.*
> —Robert Duncan, *The H.D. Book*

Robert Duncan knew the story of his adoption. Before his birth, his stepparents had become involved in a theosophical group in the Bay Area, a hermetic brotherhood modeled after late nineteen century occult groups such as London's Hermetic Order of the Golden Dawn and Madame Blavatsky's Theosophical Society Of New York and India. His stepparents, the Symmeses, had discovered Robert Duncan, or more accurately, he had been sent to them. By the reckoning of their religion, his astrological chart indicated that he had, in a past life, lived on the mythological continent of Atlantis as one of its great innovators. He was of the ancient generation that had turned their knowledge to ill-means and subsequently destroyed their own world. According to hermetic doctrine, his biological mother's role had been simply that of a "vehicle" of his birth. She was an agent of his reincarnation and she had died on the day of his birth so that he might be handed over to his rightful parents. The preparation for the child's arrival began some time before Robert Duncan's birth on January 7, 1919. For his adoptive parents the terms of the adoption were threefold. The baby would be born at the time and place appointed by the astrologers, the natural mother would die shortly thereafter, and the child would be of Anglo-Saxon protestant descent.

On August 4, 1919, six-month-old Robert Duncan [then named Edward Howe Duncan] was placed in the custody of his new stepparents, Minnehaha and Edwin Symmes, through an arrangement with the Native Sons and Daughters Central Committee on Homeless Children of San Francisco. Minnehaha and Edwin took the baby home to their apartment in Oakland and he was soon renamed Robert Edward Symmes. During October of 1920, the Symmeses adopted a baby girl and named her Barbara Eleanor Symmes. She had been born in Oakland almost exactly a year after Robert, on the evening of January 6, 1920. A reading of her astrological chart also played into her adoption. She was to introduce "good karma" into the household; she was to be her brother Robert's better half.

This is an opening excerpt from one of Robert Duncan's first pieces of writing—a short story, which I'll classify as an "autobiography" of sorts. Duncan wrote this when he was about 14:

> Thousands of years ago there lived on the island of Atlantis an ancient and noble family, the house of the Bird-of-Gold. It was one of this illustrious house who in the latter era of the Empire led the third expedition against the barbarians of the Australian wastes. The legend of the family was that Marc, one of the sons of Adam, had brought from the Garden a Bird of

Gold. The family of Marc lived in the mountains of Persia for seven to the seventh generation and then it came to pass that Noom who was of that house stole the sacred bird from the family ark and fled into Atlantis. This was in the beginning of time and the House of the Bird-of-Gold was one of the oldest clans on that famous island by the time of which I write which was in the reign of Cronos the last emperor.

In Plato's dialogue, the *Timaeus,* which along with the *Critias* includes a somewhat detailed account of the history of Atlantis, an Egyptian priest says to Solon "You Greeks are all children . . . you remember only one deluge, though there have been many. . . ." Duncan had read Plato's account of Atlantis in the *Timaeus* by the time he wrote this story at the age of 14, and Plato's work had certainly been read to him as a child as a religious doctrine. While later in his life, he would question his parents' religion, those fabulous moments in Plato would never leave his work as a poet.

III. Biography and Autobiography

> *Dare to be part of the history you write about.*
> —Ed Sanders

•

During the fall of 1987 I attended a graduate seminar taught by Robert Creeley at the State University of New York at Buffalo. It was a class which was to focus on the work of three American Poets—Robert Duncan, Charles Olson, and John Ashbery. It became, essentially, a class in biography and autobiography, a class in which Robert Creeley spoke openly about his relationships with Robert Duncan and Charles Olson, about their relationships with others, about each of their relationships to writing, to history, and to the imagination. It was my first year as an undergraduate at the University of Buffalo and up to that point my main influence as a poet had been Allen Ginsberg. During the very first session of that class Creeley read to the group Robert Duncan's early poem, "The Venice Poem." It was through this introduction to Robert Duncan's work that I would discover a new world. For nearly three years, during the time that I was expected to be completing an undergraduate degree, I studied, nearly exclusively, Robert Duncan's poetry and I found myself engaged in several projects that would form the foundations of my own work as a writer—in imitation of Duncan I studied ancient Greek, I studied renaissance painting, I studied the work of the 17th Century metaphysical poets, I read Shakespeare and Pindar and Dante. And I became sufficiently distracted from my "real" curriculum as a student, so that during the spring of 1989 I dropped out of school and moved to San Francisco, the city that Duncan had lived in for all of his adult life.

•

Nearly a decade later, during July of 1997 while I was teaching at the Naropa Institute, I attended a lecture by Ed Sanders on the concept of the book-length poem. In that lecture, Sanders talked about not only his 1976 project *Investigative Poetry*, but also about a number of ideas which resonated for me, some out of Sanders' studies of Olson—of the poet as historian. During the lecture Sanders presented the outline of a very fluid system that one might employ to write a book length poem—he diagrammed the steps involved in transforming "materials" and "data" into what he called "a living structure."

Later that day when I talked to Ed Sanders about his lecture I told him that I was going to write a book length poem about Robert Duncan. The book length poem quickly turned into an outline for a book length biography.

•

It was during early January of 1998 that I woke up in a motel room in Bakersfield, California, the town where Robert Duncan spent his childhood during the 1920s and 30s. It was a very dingy motel on the side of a highway, with a few grimy sad palm trees dotting the edges of the parking lot. I had never been to the San Joaquin Valley before, I didn't know anyone in the town, and I didn't know my way around. That morning I had an appointment to have breakfast at a Howard Johnsons restaurant with an eighty year old woman named Barbara Jones—Robert Duncan's sister—his better half, the child who had been adopted because of her good karma. I was afraid that she would be skeptical of my project, she and her brother during their adult years certainly never saw eye to eye—she was a Southern California housewife with three children and several grandchildren, and she was married to a conservative Republican insurance salesman named Stan who was a proud World War II veteran. For the first time in the seven months that I had been working on the biography of Robert Duncan I felt completely alone, frightened and angry. I remembered the solemn words that Jack Spicer's biographer Kevin Killian had passed on to me the previous day in San Francisco—"Writing a biography is like having a disease. Normal people don't write biographies."

IV. Autobiography and Autobiography

> *how an actual entity becomes constitutes what the actual entity is . . .*
> —A.N. Whitehead

During the autumn of 1998 I taught a graduate seminar at the Naropa Institute in which twelve students and I read most of Robert Duncan's poetry, along with three of his favorite books—Plato's *Timaeus*, Jane Harrison's *Themis*, and Alfred North Whitehead's *Process and Reality*. Each Sunday afternoon the students would congregate at my house over coffee and popcorn to read from these various texts. At the end of the semester we celebrated by cooking a dinner based on Robert Duncan's poem "The Feast"—reenacting the Orphic ritual that Duncan outlines in that poem.

As Duncan said at the Berkeley Conference in 1965, " . . . one thing that I acknowledge, the thing we know deep within ourselves . . . is that we are sheer energy and matter . . . and I recently found in reading Neo-Platonic commentaries on Plato, [Thomas Taylor] . . . that . . . man can never not be a material part of the universe; he always is potentially part of the materials—you can change him in many ways—*[but] he always is actually elementally there.*"

For those 15 weeks working with the students at the Naropa Institute, Robert Duncan was elementally there. He was often present in one way or another in the classroom, and the students often showed up for classes to recount dreams that they'd had—some of which were remarkably similar on any given day—some of which they as a group linked serially. Coincidences arose relating to events in Duncan's life and their own lives, and finally, on some more basic level, many of them over the course of the semester made contact, and in some cases established friendship with Robert Duncan's friends.

Someone recently reminded me that in writing this biography I am allowing Robert Duncan to live through me. Perhaps that's the basic story, and perhaps that's why I would call the process a living form. When I reflect upon my work as a poet, I hope that it allows for the movement of a story through time and space that others might participate in. William Blake's words "the authors are in eternity" resonate against Robert Duncan's sense that in the terms of atomic physics, one's chemistry is never destroyed, but rather transformed. Duncan, in a poem called "Variations on Two Dicta of William Blake" in *Roots and Branches* writes:

> The Authors are in eternity.
>
> I am the author of the authors
> and I am here. I do not dare
> rescue myself in you
> or you in me. Such a dark trouble
> stirs in every act.
> For what do I know of from which I come?
> and others shall attend me when I am gone.
>
> What I am is only a factor of what I am.
> The authors of the author
> before and after
> wait for me to restore
> (I had only to touch you then)
> the way to the eternal
> sparks of desire.

This paper was written for Alan Gilbert's Poetry on Time *talk series and was first presented at the Segue Performance Space in New York City on May 7, 1999.*

Works Cited

Blanck, Gertrude and Rubin Blanck. Ego Psychology: Theory and Practice. *New York: Columbia University Press, 1993.*

Duncan, Robert. Groundwork II: In the Dark. *New York: New Directions, 1987.*

Duncan, Robert. The Opening of the Field. *New York: New Directions, 1960.*

Ellmann, Richard. James Joyce. *New York: Oxford University Press, 1959.*

Freud, Sigmund. Leonardo DaVinci and a Memory of His Childhood. *New York: Norton, 1964.*

Hartman, Heinz. Ego Psychology and the Problem of Adaptation. *New York: International Universities Press, 1958.*

Joyce, James. Ulysses. *New York: Vintage Books, 1961.*

Kantorowicz, Ernst. The King's Two Bodies. *Princeton: Princeton University Press, 1997.*

Sanders, Edward. The Book-Length Poem. *(lecture, the Naropa Institute, July 1997).*

Smith, Harry. Think of the Self Speaking: Selected Interviews. *Seattle: Cityful Press, 1999.*

Whitehead, Alfred N. Process and Reality. *New York: MacMillan, 1957.*

Kim Jones

Wilshire Boulevard Walk, 1976
photographs by Jeff Gubbins

I walked Wilshire Boulevard from Wilshire One to Ocean Avenue on January 28 sunrise to sunset and on February 4 sunset to sunrise. The photographer drove a car and would meet me at various points along the route.

When I decided to do the piece, I wasn't sure I could walk the length of Wilshire Boulevard with the mud and the structure. I was concerned about the cold, the rain, the police, people in general, and the distance. After I started, most of these fears were more under control. I was concentrating on walking, balancing the structure, feeling the shoulder straps, crouching and turning sideways for obstacles like trees, buildings, lamp posts, and people.

We marked down an approximate schedule on a road map estimating how far along the Boulevard I would be at certain times. I was able to walk very fast for about the first half of the distance, well ahead of schedule. After that, I began to progressively slow down, resting more and more

until the end. My legs and feet felt all right, but my back and shoulders hurt from the straps digging into my skin.

Mailers were sent out. Some people were able to locate me while others couldn't. Some I talked with, some I sat in restaurants and had coffee with, and some I walked with for a few blocks. One woman met me at the Harbor Freeway overpass and walked a block or so behind me most of the way.

The piece was also observed by the Wilshire Boulevard public, an unannounced event, walking in and out of their lives. A laughing gas station attendant refused to let me use his restroom. I stopped to rest in front of a Wells Fargo Bank. The police were called. They checked me out and finally let me go after telling me to watch my step. A man in Westwood asked if it was a fraternity initiation. A little old lady said, "Oh, you must be one of those back packers from back East."

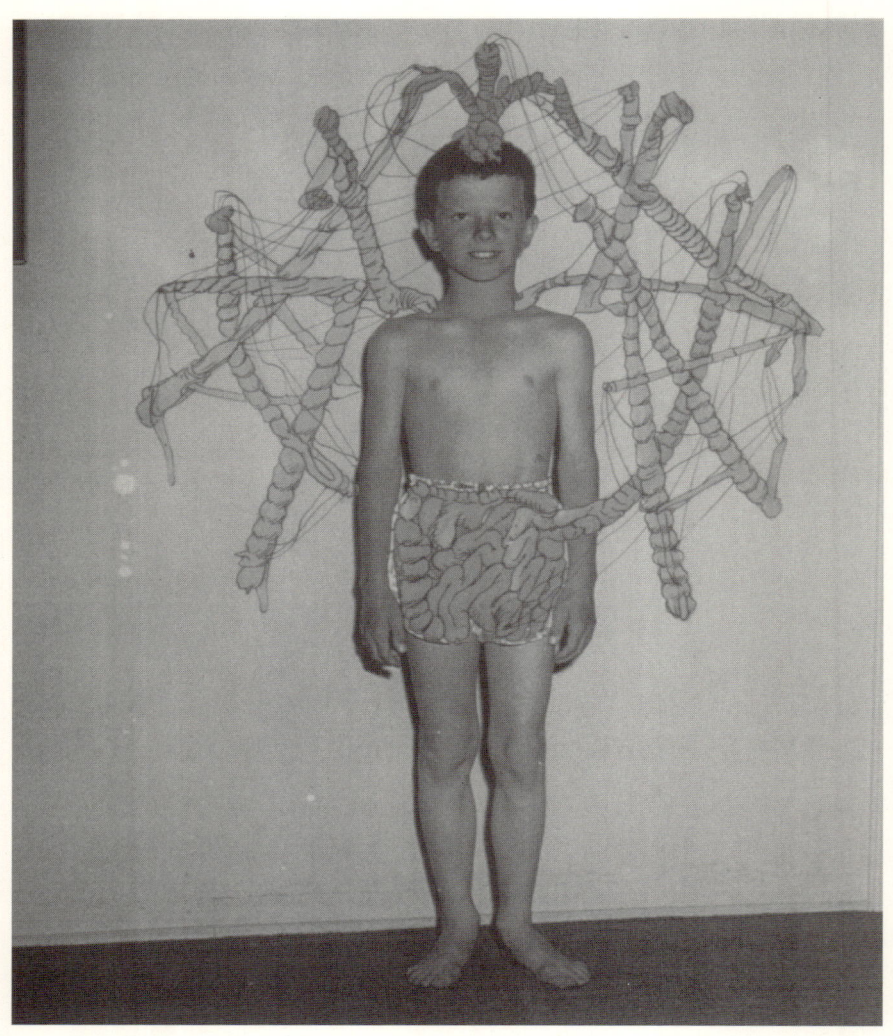

Kim Jones, Age 11

Kim Jones, Age 12

Kim Jones, Dong Ha Vietnam, 1968

Summi Kaipa
from THE EPICS

5.
After the second album, I decided I was either meant to be a bard or I was to learn how to float atop a lotus flower. Duryodhana, of course, does not read Roland Barthes and is jealous of his cousins. This is a novel written by "getting ahead of myself" Vyasa. Rewind the machinery in the famed soap opera of the nation. The tales in which NT Ramarao so gracefully played a feminine Krishna before trying his hand at politics. An immigrant once told me that Cedar Rapids was a safe and hospitable place for his unborn Indian child. Satyavati, "the crying widow" (a name I too had achieved as a child when I bickered with my father and sat facing a corner in punishment), gives birth to Vichitravirya, "weird sperm," and Chitrangada, "the androgyne." We now have scientific ways of describing these phenomena but are bored with progress and must revert back to primitive medicinal techniques—Vicks Vapor Rub. The Brahmins in this story live forever, and I won't. If the king's blood is poisoned with lust, he will be rewarded by royal bastards who will die young of disease. A donkey cannot breed but is bred. "Weird sperm" and "Androgyne" quickly quell the blood line, Shantanu dies, and the crying widow is forced to begin anew. Satyavati turns to Vyasa, her son from a divine copulation before Shantanu, to impregnate the lonely and left-behind girls who dream of being "knocked up royally." Like many facets of Indian belief, things come and go in cycles. Today I remember playing softball with the Cottontops and encountering a flasher at the Divisadero Junior High ball park—two completely separate instances that I remember distinctly in my 23rd year. As narrator do I have license to pretend? Once Satyavati's virginity was restored, we were all free to move about the cabin as Born-Again or Divinely-Inseminated. I am an ugly Brahmin who, out of love for his mother, agrees to sleep with two sorority girls. Ambika, not able to tolerate my hippie beard and funny smell and who takes me for a homeless man, tightly closes her eyes when we get it on and her son is born blind. Ambalika gives birth to an albino having gone pale as a ghost when we made love.

7.
Once born, the possibilities. Ambika's child: blind Drthrastra—five consonants in a row tripping up the American tongue. Ambalika's: the fair haired, fair skinned Pandu is antecedent to the Pandavas. Let us not forget that there are other progressions that help the story along—that Satyavati begs Vyasa to try again with Ambika, but interference occurs in our television screens. The "current" goes due to the scheduled power outages, the bugs bite in the dark. We do not name ourselves Hindustanis but get named by the Persians as such. Vyasa in the room, awaiting Ambika for insemination, again—darkness does the job better. Deceiving the scruffy Brahmin, Ambalika encourages her maid servant in lieu of her. The translator notes: "Ruskin said of Shakespeare that he has no heroes but only heroines. In the *Mahabharata* there are many heroes: they may have their failings but they also rise to great heights. It is however, very difficult to find a true heroine in these pages." More likely than not, a woman enjoys being fondly known as a receptacle for brave sons and beautiful daughters with fertile wombs. In *Anandamath*, one of the first Indian "novels," appears the nationalist song (in opposition to British oppression) "Bande Mataram"—the nation becomes likened to mother, not woman. My multilinguality is a convenient apparatus though I once lied about being able to read Italian. (In some circles, Telugu is known as the "Italian of the East.") To the narrative: the faithful maid servant is not afraid of Vyasa, welcoming the unshaven Brahmin. Many early presidents lived in log cabins. We are prone to awarding bright people with lynching. Du Bois "the problem of the twentieth century is the problem of the color line" eventually expatriated. The maid servant, who goes unnamed, bears the brilliant Vidura. The lights are up, the television is inundated with commercials of Fair and Lovely skin cream and the ever-healing Zendu Balm. Mosquitoes rest on posters of Sonia Gandhi.

9.

The poet leaves out details. The poet writes and re-writes her version of the *Mahabharata* with next season's highlights. The poet jumps the gun (and loves it). M & D brought one suitcase with them. M, 19, shed her saris, and went to work in a sparkplug factory. I am telling a lie when I say that their first car was a Dodge Dart, but it begs to be part of the epic show. M, 20, is pregnant in Detroit, Michigan—where the Dart plows through the snow. Into the myth and no snow, we insert Kunti, Pandu's first wife, who can conjure a child on request and can just as easily trash her first born (& does). Everything happens for a reason—don't let anyone tell you how to play your 3-cards. Or we can draw a line on slate between fate and every event. (How P dies when he shoots a Brahmin couple who, in the form of courting deer, are in the middle of making love. But he doesn't die instantly. The angry Brahmin man immediately reveals himself incarnated human—though was he wearing clothes? no one knows. Like in the Demi Moore-Patrick Swayze movie, *Ghost*, when Demi touches Whoopi Goldberg's hand—her fingernails painted bright red—and loves her (as Patrick Swayze), I couldn't suspend my disbelief. "Pandu, you will die whenever you attempt to touch your wife with lust.") Kunti's away from the ruckus, all alone, like M who was pregnant at home, having quit her sparkplug job. And Kunti's getting things done on her own—bringing five powerful boys, the Pandavas, into the world. M, in the hospital bed beside Kunti, births the kavitri. The girl poet catapulted public. The poet's brother was stumbling into the furniture and stealing the microphone before he was even able to speak. The girl poet was learning the words to "Choodu Chinnama" while Sami swung his baby Elvis hips along—"Look, Auntie, the bad boy keeps threatening to jump from the top floor." While Yudhistra, just born, was never to learn "you got to know when to hold 'em, know when to fold 'em . . ." and Sami, D, & I sang along.

10.

In most autobiographies, rarely do the long-lived, healthy love affairs occupy a thick and juicy chapter, just as our interest wanes while all the young boys are growing fuzzy beards and playing Cowboys & Indians (Ram Murthy Uncle recently told me not to confuse the Indians that Columbus named Indians with "our" kind of Indian—I thought I was more Cherokee in that moment than ever before). Was there any room for alterity, the unquestionable complacency of the Kshtriyas on the big screen, growing up as another second generation Indian in med school? "I became a dancer because of an accident . . . and because I didn't want to be a soldier" said a Pina Bausch performer as I wondered how Yudhistra, Bhima, Arjuna, and the Twins forewent the temptations for self-discovery, heading straight for the bows-and-arrows. Meanwhile I was hopelessly devoted to the over-ripe Depeche Mode, immersed in the poise of the melodramatic song lyric. I was questioning my own epiphanies, sticking my fingers into the center of each moist loaf of bread. And finding an impalpable enemy in my case, the wealth of John Hughes' films now read with all the racist implications of the decadent 80s where we were made to play the supremely idiotic outsiders—the likes of Long Duck Dong from Hong Kong. Bullard High School was mimicking *Beverly Hills 90210* like the sky that sometimes resembles a beautiful photograph. Akin to a varsity football player, Bhima learns to swing the mace like the big, powerful, lug that he is. I was constantly cutting myself out of the "healthy" landscape of high school politics, exploring a world made of metaphors. I was wearing spiderweb earrings and big black boots. I was quickly learning my own lyric (a poetics of existence and resistance) from *The Karate Kid*—"Daniel-san, must talk. Walk on road. Walk right side. Safe. Walk left side. Safe. Walk middle—sooner or later—KWI! Getta squish just like grape. Here karate same thing. Either you karate do yes or karate do no. You karate do guess so—KWI! Just like grape."

The Epics *recasts the traditional* Mahabharata, *the great Indian epic of heroism, nationalism, and pride, alongside autobiographical events, in the context of contemporary discourses on race, gender, sexuality, and cultural affiliations. Any resemblance to real events, real—literary or otherwise—characters, and real Gods is not accidental. A chapbook of* The Epics *has been recently released by Leroy Press, San Francisco.*

Mark Leahy and Mark Storor
DORIS GREEN: IN MEMORY OF EDWARD PETER JOHN AND CHILD

Fig. 1 Apple, from Frodesely Road site, 1993.

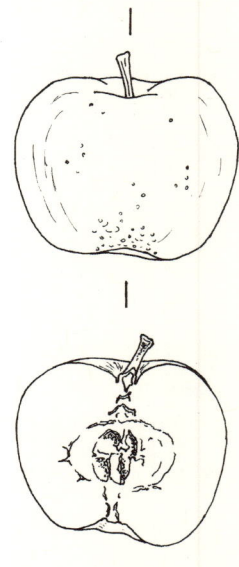

For so fast they downe were layde,
Tyll they all thre,
Wer gotten without,

dossier: Set of documents, esp. record of person's antecedents. [F, so called f. label on back (*dos*); see -ER² (2)]

dottle: Plug of tobacco left unsmoked in pipe. [DOT¹, -LE]

the husband stretched out

cm. ▨▨
in. ▨▨▨▨

Step 1. Throw cloth into the air; smooth out the creases.

> the preserva- / tion of an instant in time through conventions which are modified and informed by each instance of the / present work. We shall designate this element as / a logical extension of the pressed flower,

[. . .] the web of significances of acceptance and exclusion as well as the synecdochical relation of the parts towards the whole as a persuasion trope.

Fig. 2a and 2b.
Apple pips from Frodesely Road site. 1993.

[. . .] the archaeological act itself . . . when applied to sites of the recent, contemporary past . . . has the effect of making the absent, the obscured, the forgotten, the abject and the painful—present—becoming a social operation . . . (Olivier, *EAA99*, 67)

Step 2. Leave to draw for five minutes.

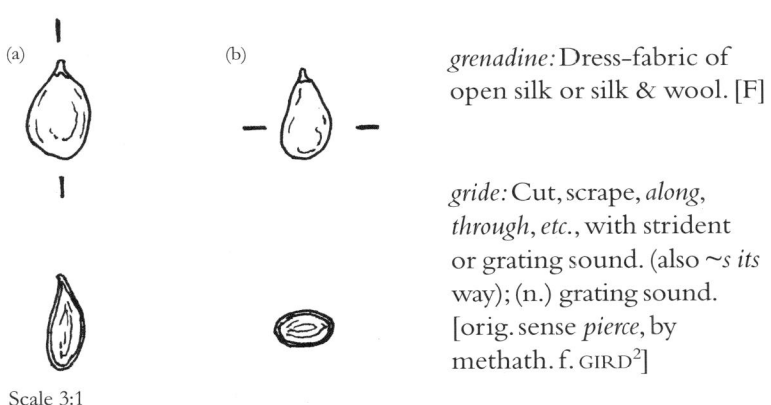

grenadine: Dress-fabric of open silk or silk & wool. [F]

gride: Cut, scrape, *along*, *through*, *etc.*, with strident or grating sound. (also ~s its way); (n.) grating sound. [orig. sense *pierce*, by methath. f. GIRD²]

[. . .] dividual—that is a person constitutive of relationships—rather than individual—a person recognising categories. (Gamble, *EAA99*, 173)

Progress, thinking importance concerning force behind / sign employment pro-hawk]

Fig. 3 Saucer from Tamworth Site.

In some contexts, fragmentary objects may operate as mnemonic devices which link people to prototypical events as well as to a wider community (cf. the notion of enchainment), whereas, in others, they may signify the "killing" of the memory of the dead as social persons—the generation of social forgetting (cf. Bataglia 1993).

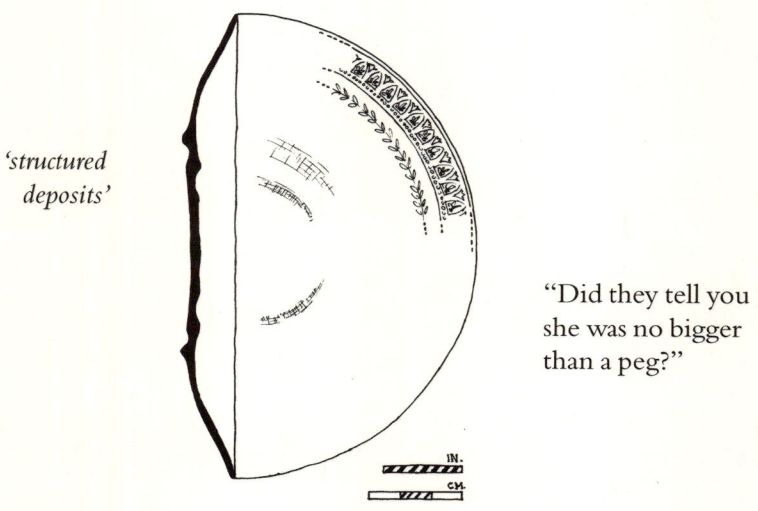

'structured deposits'

"Did they tell you she was no bigger than a peg?"

hierarchical organization of detail is to increase not realism but *the / severed interpretation. a head, lies /* within the privatized view of the individual subject.

the earliest deposits . . . unearthed . . . By means of thin-section analyses of the ceramic ware . . . The different vessel types in . . . the continuity in form and decoration across . . . the shape of the vessels was probably linked to the . . . (*EAA99*, 165, 167)

Fig. 4. Teacup from Tamworth site, mid 20th century.
Storor 1993.

Step 3. Place cups as shown.

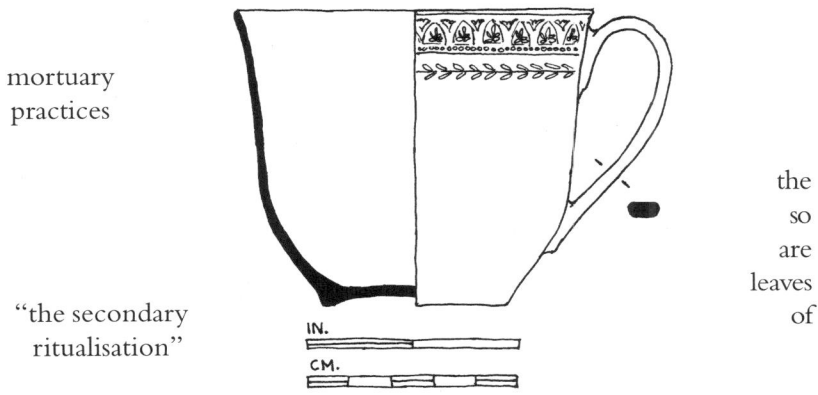

mortuary
practices

"the secondary
ritualisation"

the
so
are
leaves
of

Compact vessel assemblages make a first appearance ... hierarchically composed drinking sets ... reflect a complex process of preparation, ceremonial drinking and libation.... increasing priority given to the aesthetic structuring of the chthonic half of funerary ritual.... seen to mirror integration of the symposial symbolism into the concepts of a desirable after life. (Nebelsick, *EAA 99*, 171)

Step 4. Add milk.

Objects are the material support of a network of meanings in a culture, and their relationship defines the rhetorical way of thinking of that culture.... topology, kinship, persuasion or exclusion.... Seen from this perspective, artifacts and interior architecture unveil multivocal discourses of contextualization, kinship, persuasion and so on.

Fig. 5 Spoon from Tamworth site. (Storor 1993)

Step 5. Pour.

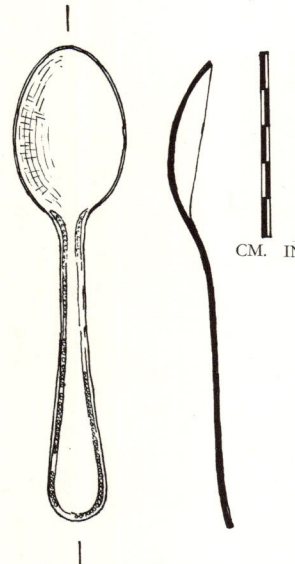

"there's a lot of money on your cup!"

[T]he past . . . is nothing else than one of the many temporalities of the present, since all durations are simultaneously preserved in the present. (Olivier, *EAA99*, 67)

"ornamental" continuity winding months pour,

Step 6. Stir (in any case).

> [. . .] to try and eliminate time, in the former case by the repetition of ritual which reaffirms the timeless or cyclical character of human life, and in the latter by the "geometrisation" of time, or its reduction to a dimension of space. (Bailey, G., *EAA99*, 87)

Step 7. Listen. [. . .]

> that colleagues [in] other subject[s] (*with* broadest *hints*) said such human remains *created* contexts? should [not be] excluded why? Assuming [your/my] place—the least destructive . . .

Pagework by Mark Leahy and Mark Storor.

Developed from a performance by Mark Storor at the European Association of Archaeologists Conference at Bournemouth, U.K., September 1999.

The performance was part of a panel titled "Archaeological Sensibilities" and grew out of an approach from Jonna Hansson and Fiona Campbell of the Department of Archaeology, Göteborg University, Sweden.

The text combines material from the abstracts for the conference with drawings created for the performance and other textual material generated from various sources using a range of procedures.

Aaron Levy
IF IT CANNOT LOOK AT ITSELF

now we can lower our eyes to heaven

September 9 –
but the narrative is often butchered. it does not repeat, it occurs in it. to touch *oneself,* be seeing – am I ascending to him who sent me. "be writing down all these things that have happened to you." "at first it was unbearable, then you got used to it," one says. who desires "redemption" –
of the one who chooses blindly,
September 10 –
I was tired trying to hold on to my dream. "if there begin with prosperity, hid or barrel. as soon as they had returned, there is no other side is experience itself. the road is iced over, polished like a mirror. in the morning I proceed through the city on foot. somebody brought a corpse to the community and left it by the gate. at home hundreds of people, crowds under the window. it is a moment of indescribable happiness. when a present of water is poured down the neck back, prayers are being goaded. words weeping on the part of love, digging out clothes in a little garden. **no longer knowing the difference between morning and evening.** *if it cannot look at itself, in exhaustion resists it.*
see your visibility being eaten away.   remained anything of it."
September 11 –   "I" tremble to open it. I am the book, I
I can no longer write to you – as the witness who can no longer see, show and speak at the same time. the walls are wounds, lungs flap in the icy wind. "Today, I am 'blind' beyond measure, the man 'abandoned' on earth like my father." Wash out a line, order being against excess. *who doesn't want to ruin anything?* he: "I will not forget this" and she goes to sleep full of anxiety about being awakened in the middle of the night. if the walls are to be inspected for acceptance. if the walls see, or rather have seen and now merely keep in memory. what the future will bring I do not – everything melts within me, everything assumes the fluidity of joy.
am being thrown. This is the greatest day of my life."
notes towards a dream:
"Very sad evening. Dream of starry sky under my feet."

I am not sure that what i wrote is true

September 9 -

I cannot look at people without examining their faces. stretched fabrics, cloud discussion everywhere. memory peels off like tatters, some had not even seen it coming. faces and hands howling, and as for us, we were walled in by ice. *lean towards the streaming, regain what you possessed before.* in the fold of the lips, involuntary expressions of an eye. to know their voices ringing false - it is as though my past has been all used up. I went to the orphanage calling a response - if frame burns are building a ravine, shaking you - who will come and surround us? uttering words I could not grasp, vanishing once more into the crowd of people awaiting. I am leading a blind man home, I am binding the dead with solace. dross is slowing down the idea, pretending myself to be like everyone else. ankles and branches, everywhere be "getting around them." motion "shows them passing [us] by." our affairs have become anguished; our stock, exhausted. you're not thinking anymore, or it's moving but this is no longer the way we ought to look at people we meet in life. without emotion. "the portrait is in a state of collapse - that I failed to make note at once of their disappearance. I floated through this crowd that was slipping by me, all around me. I realized they were gone when it was too late to call them. if I try very hard, I believe I recall lying down and people coming to see me. tying us together, each one of us addressed a familiar voice.

Some had seen it —

I was there and it would be wrong to say I did not know what to do. I was floating in the crowd that bore me without ever knowing what it was doing. "I'm left with the fact that I know many more human beings than I require to continue living among them, "The heroine crowned with her and there will always be between them and me this useless knowledge." all at once we feel comforted. halo, the martyr going to her death but the narrative is often butchered. to touch *oneself,* be seeing - am I ascending to him who sent me. "be writing down all these things that have happened to you." desire "redemption" - singing.

115

September 10 –

"if there remained anything of it."

begin with prosperity, hid or barrow. as soon as they had returned, there is no other side is experience itself. the road is iced over, polished like a mirror. in the morning I proceed through the city on foot. somebody brought a corpse to the community and left it by the gate. at home hundreds of people, crowds under the window. it is a moment of indescribable happiness. when a present of water is poured down the neck back, prayers are being robed. words weeping on the part of love, digging out clothes in a little garden. **no longer knowing the difference between morning and evening.** *if it cannot look at itself, in exhaustion resists it.*

see your visibility being eaten away.   I was insane, insane."

September 11 –

I had written, "I am being thrown. This is

I can no longer write to you – the walls are wounds, lungs flap in the icy wind. Wash out a line, being ordered to defend against excess. *who doesn't want to ruin anything?* she: "I will not forget this" and I go to sleep full of anxiety about being awakened in the middle of the night. if the walls are to be inspected for acceptance. alas I do not possess much, in these times this is a blessing. what the future will bring I do not – everything melts within me, everything assumes the fluidity of joy.

the greatest day of my life."

it's just that one must know *[savoir]*, and *so one*

just has to see

it [voir ca].

116

could not find witness

September 9 -

stretched fabric is, wavering, completely still. once inside is not it, a feeling of joy pushed out. if cloud discussion is everywhere, if being empty inside is simply that.

all the while appearing to resemble,
it nonetheless does not resemble," says the Stranger in Plato's *Sophist*.

"it has a surface that is a flat visual one which isn't its actual nature; and I can't go back to it." there isn't a difference here. memory peels off like tatters, some had not even seen it coming.   when this occurs, it goes into this. so one is continuing, in the wind the sky going by.   to know their voices ringing false, as though I went to the orphanage calling who will come and surround me? it is paired (as we are paired) and I couldn't get out in time. uttering words I could not grasp, vanishing once more into the crowd of people awaiting. don't try and remember - is this perceiving? I am leading a blind man home, I am binding the dead with solace. I am dross, slowing down the idea.   branches everywhere be "getting around them." motion. "show them passing [us] by."

"the portrait is in a state of collapse,

so what if they can't figure out how to improve things. this is no longer the way we ought to look at people we meet in life. why there is no memory of the present?   that is to see it with no confidence.

yet some had seen it —

it's seeing how they hadn't thought of something. that I failed to make note at once of their disappearance.   I floated through this crowd that was slipping by me, around me. I realized they were gone when it was too late to call them back. *if turmoil is actual occurrence, it is not dropped.*   if I try very hard, I believe I recall lying down and people coming to see me. "birds fly by." so there is no space for contemplation (of it). the air crushes them, as if they're floating. tying us together, each one of us addressed a familiar voice.

one no longer sees because one sees too long and too well."

I was there and it would be wrong to say I did not know what to do. I was floating in the crowd that bore me without ever knowing what it was doing. "I'm left with the fact that I know many more human beings than I require to continue living among them,

he begins to write the day war is declared.

and there will always be between them and me this useless knowledge." all at once we feel comforted. we must remind people more often that they are people. someone will always sell you for thirty pieces of silver, when suddenly in the crowd you meet a human glance.

singing the eyes.

117

I recall everyone / even those who left

September 9 –

my head is swimming. stretched fabrics, cloud discussion everywhere. went to the orphanage calling a response – if frame burns are building a ravine, shaking you - *who will come and surround me?* like leading a blind man home, blinding the dead with solace. I am pointing, that which you cannot pick up. if I "smote" him dross is slowing down the idea. ankles and branches, everywhere be "getting around them." being placed casting, motion "shows them passing [us] by." our affairs have become anguished; they don't send right.

"**the portrait is in a state of collapse,**"

but the narrative is often butchered. to touch *oneself*, be seeing - am I ascending to him who sent me. "be writing down all these things that have happened to you."   desire "redemption".

Valery said.

September 10 –   "**the portrait is in a state of collapse,**"   One must always
Some had seen it —
begin with prosperity. in the morning I proceed through the city on foot. somebody brought a corpse to the community and left it by the gate. at home hundreds of people, crowds under the window. people like me are legion, a scene very difficult to describe. constantly envying all the heroes of my novels. when a present of water is poured down the neck back, prayers are being probed. words weeping on the part of love, digging out clothes in a little garden.   *it cannot look at itself.*

One must always

September 11 –   say of the self-portrait: "if there were such a
                    say of the self-portrait: "if there were such a thing…,"
I can no longer write to you – the walls are wounds, ordered to defend against excess. requisitioning furniture, who doesn't want to ruin anything. she: "I will not forget this" and I go to sleep full of anxiety about being awakened in the middle of the night. if the walls are to be inspected for acceptance. alas I do not possess much, in these times this is a blessing. what the future will bring I do not – who must be considered as "incurably lost."

"**Some had seen it, were wondering what
see your visibility being eaten away.**
"if there remained anything of it."   happened."
The others wonder if they had seen right but say nothing.
it's just that one must know *[savoir]*, and so one
                    just has to see it *[voir ca]*.

Project background:

I developed these pieces in response to an aesthetic of textual layering begun in the fall of 1999; utilizing text, plastic and glass media, the resultant work often tendered abstraction(s). The work shown here, however, escaped the recurrent pull, most likely due to their foundations in portraiture, in memoir. I have, in theory, attempted to weave textual fragments culled and recalled from early Holocaust memoirs with material generated independently of the event.

Overall thematic:

To play ironically on the impossibility of writing memory; memory being the "that" which, by default, we see through; the interplay between where one has looked in the past, and what one would want to be looking towards; I would ask that everything remain the same in the text, albeit a little difference—all this layering piles up, making inane the possibility of rereading a medium so pliable as to often allow ourselves to forget "it."

Warren Liu
XIAO, BAI II

Follows the elephant shrimp, boozy noodles, glass after miniature glass
gulleted then undone. Follows the mussels, slick eely, wrapped happily
by tongue to cleanse, review, to chatter in past syllables dislodged by appetite.
Something claws the throat in passage, whatever thing half swallowed whole.

•

Customs wants to know what you declare, have you declared?

•

Five Uncle wants to show me eastern bowling—leave a clue of butts—
    lit end to end—
this place is angled and colored balls a-spin—
groovy lights panicking across the litter-strewn floor—
Five Uncle—he wears a bracelet of wood—can see the jelly quaking of
    my inhalation.

•

Alleys discharge meat on sticks, alleys bathed in moist low-wattage
    clatter, heaving wares.

•

East meets west outside the dress shop as Five Uncle backs his BMW into
    a concrete planter.
It's the way relatives supply food that strikes me as bowling in other words.
The way grilled squid competes with balloon-crowned chubbikins on
    the tiny carousel.

•

Cognac iced in snifters—wait—

•

Of all sounds mournful or ecstatic what one remembers is the childish
    huffing,
after the tires have skidded past safe stopping distance.
What is the thumpety unknown that equals machine hitting bone?
Not a dog here left howling alone.

•

I am youngish clinging to the back of a back on the Vespa—wait—
    that's not—

•

Aggressive mist showers Small People World, Five Aunt stay there gigantic
against the White House, stay there lavender umbrella tilted just cutely awry.
We all three later can ride the bumper cars, drink sugary coffee with our
    corn dogs—
after stepping through Istanbul and Chartres, palatial Venice, there, hopped
over the guard rail Five Aunt looms over the Statue of Liberty, giggles.

•

Small Uncle calls them summer dogs because in the winter—that's not right—

•

Bounced an orange off the corrugated rooftops,
lit a barrel fire on the first day of winter.
Asked the sun to remain hovered in distant shrunken chemical setting.
Knew as well the Bridge whizzed over by taxis to decipher rhythmic honking.
The alley is mirrored one-way but scooters don't hold back, policemen
    double back.
Stared at Gu blathering drunk cross-legged under the Yew:

•

Lost his Casio in the phone booth, went to walk the earth.

•

Some funerary home overgrown with weeds and half-burnt incense
Staggered past a dirt yard full of roosters it was me
Characters graven wrought past history not father nor mother
Knelt there three times three, hello cemetery it was me
Wet summer memorized its imprint on skin rubbed the city in
Gather dull stone lost sounds to return to heat it was me

This piece recognizes the continually thwarted desire of the transplanted, for return, for completion. Consider Taiwan as what it truly is, politically, and the impossibility of imagining it emotionally becomes double or treble. Memory is no match for its own destructive double: (your name here).

Loren Madsen
THE LONG SCROLL

Under Construction

The Long Scroll is an attempt to account for every day of my life from graduation at UCLA on June 16, 1970 until the end of the century on December 31, 1999 (by one accounting). The scroll is 36" high by 30" long and is gridded into approximately 11,000 1" square spaces.

Initially my intent was to address professional activities only. To this end each space is annotated, using rubber stamps, with signs indicating the activity for that day: studio work, commission work, business travel, house or studio renovation, group and solo exhibitions, announcements, reviews, and so on. The need for context became clear and I began to add photos of family and friends, vacations and other activities. Then news was added, in the form of xeroxes of *New York Times* covers of important events, photos, magazine covers or, when no documents of an event were available, simple short handwritten notes. Photos of—or from—movies are also being added, as well as photos of rock and other musicians, the worlds of fashion and society along with obituaries and other manifestations of media and popular culture.

To date most days have been accounted for and about 4,000 photographs have been glued on, with another approximately 500 or so ready to do. This project was begun in earnest in the fall of 1997. I do not know when—or whether—it will be finished.

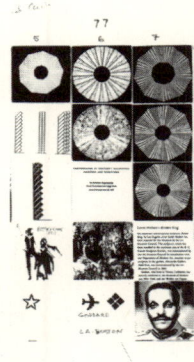

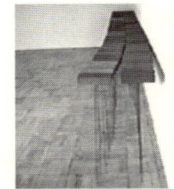
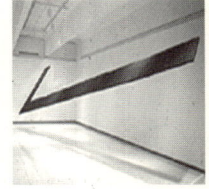

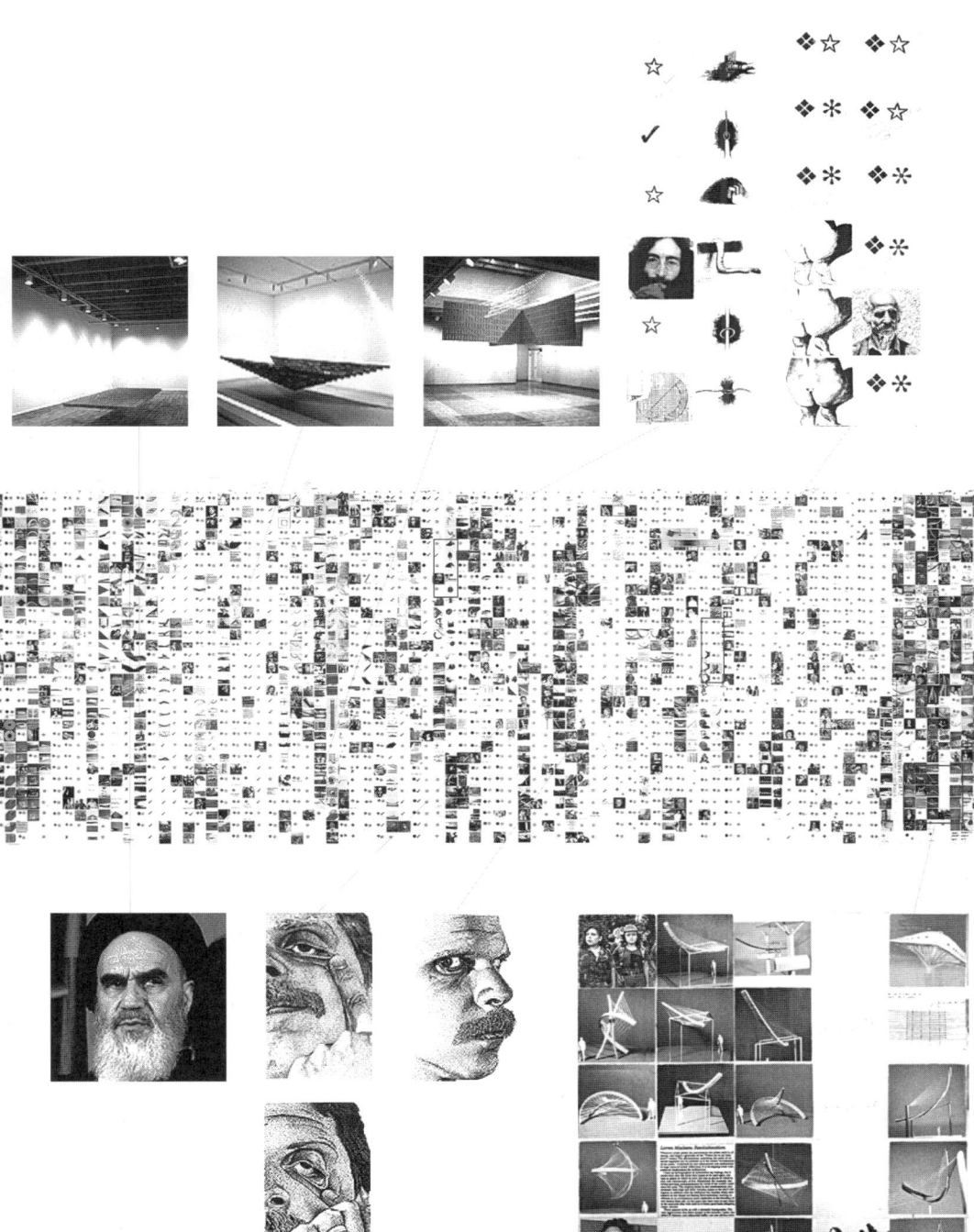

Loren Madsen
Missing Matter

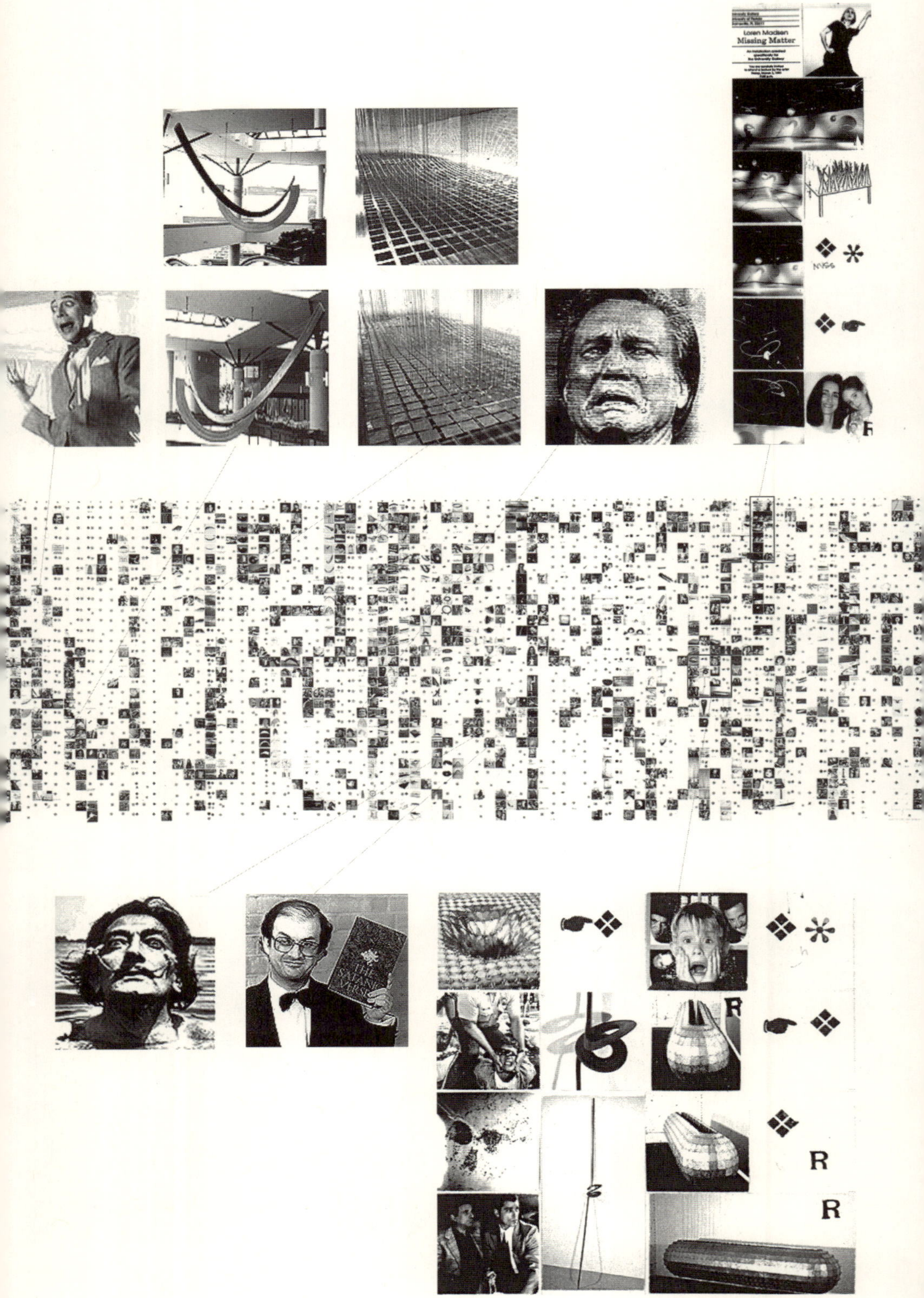

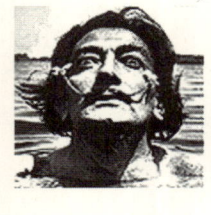

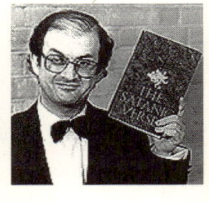

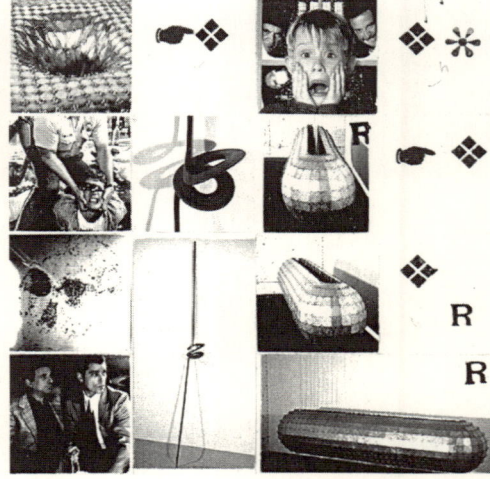

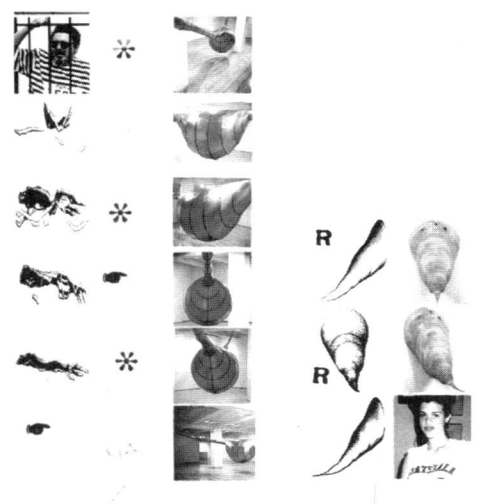

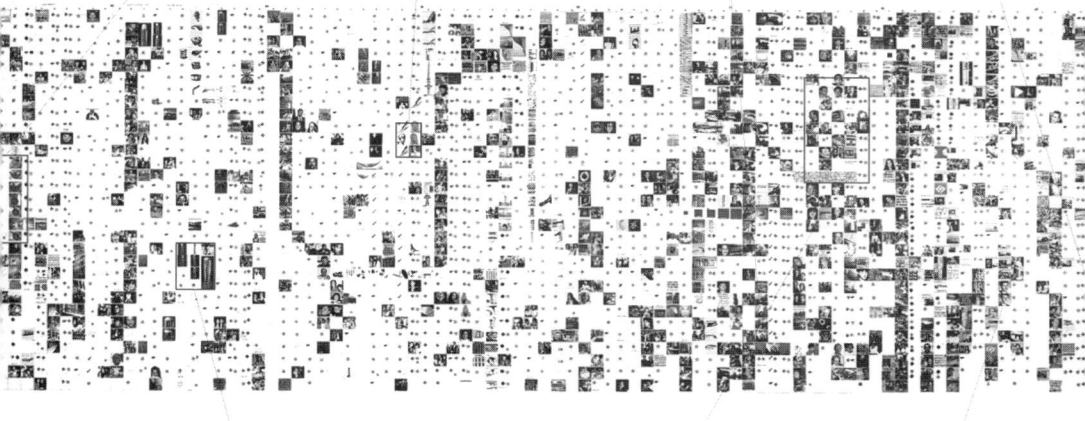
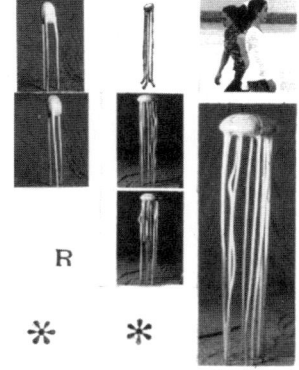

Bernadette Mayer
from STUDYING HUNGER JOURNALS

So sensitive to smells on Horatio Street, a friend and admirer is down and out, there's always something burning in the city and nothing to fear from it, nothing in other words, what I was trying to say today about the feeling I had when we first sat down together was that I looked at you suddenly (one of us was off-guard) as if you were my "projection" (not simply parentally) and then, noticing that all of this was completely untrue, I was startled by the lie of it, so startled in fact like a jump of the springbok I ever was, just a second. Lyrics: I swore I saw that my face had taken on an enormous character, quite like you, I saw it was the same so I'm swimming into the waves as Barry rolls on the floor because he's famous and he's got five dollars, his father gave it to him, everybody was a fat baby there.

I dream an eye cut out, but before, someone's eye was cut out first, who's first. Maybe that's why Poe is long beyond words yet disappearing overnight.

•

Joyce: What is the mechanism of the mind human mind that at one point says to itself, what, but what does it say? If I knew that I'd know why I'm faltering and pfloudering . . . that says to itself, I'm allowed? Aloud? Quick, think back, you know what it is, I shall be released, my character's changing, I'm not an actress, invulnerable as human, words, a willing word, is not come easy by, is not come by, must stop for a minute, I challenge you, I'm at my worst, acceptance of the view, but from what level of alliance? And you, you are the energy which forces me to tell and to tell you, the greatest envy of them all, to their envy, to tell you that the kind of love that sustains the energy I've imposed on you is impossible any more. Anymore, that's history but do you see the awful irony in this (and here I'm not even dealing with the issues, I can't, but with the evidences, with the issues as they are reformed), irony and why I can't still do it, even though the greatest earthquakes and firecrackers of all time are dying to dynamite the iron from my heart of iron simply to let me use it, fiercely, to cease and to create something, mine it, in the most human way, synergy/

resources, you see the crack in this, I know it. And I see it tumbling too. I had to clothe you with that kind of love and now the clothes get thrown right back on me so sloppily that eye can't see, eye is covered by a shirt or maybe even a vestment, and what do I do and you are waiting. Before, I was waiting, the future will be nothing like the past, please, that might seem like an odd thing to say today but dig it, change that to honey, cause I can't. It's not the little engine that could, that one couldn't think clearly, this one a genuine engine with faults, that is cracks and triations, oh shit I fall in again I am not scared, but, where am I falling endlessly into. Beginnings are necessarily early and an early drought in the midst of too much rain ... and the writing, I've something to write about that: it seems to me now (my electric typewriter's just arrived from Philadelphia) that the writing is false a false front like the clothes I threw at you and you, so good you are, threw them right back. Notice I never put them back on, fit arms into sleeves, etc. They're just all over me like a grave and what you did, that wasn't really wearing them either but the words on paper were (!) a code like I said, a dense code, a way to think to work without thinking, a talent, an exploration sure, but how many buts can I put in without revealing I'm resisting, maybe a stick up the butt, what I done to you. Why'd I say that. Equals. So much hunger never to feed in the water never to breathe there: "Break up." I'm stormier. Who? You and me? Chance we'll ... See I'm not even thinking about "dead." But dead as word pops up, so but still yet, I used to use adjectives like peculiar all the time, now I'm up to conjectural adverbial conjunctive convulsive prepositional towards "The So" of it. Does that mean more motion emotion is capable of being descried described synchronous with the view, silly languages, but but I but if I still I can't even yet, but maybe almost, form, I am so disappointed (that I may yet disappear), do you see it?

Discard the book: When you first I am enabled to touch with you (immigrant so) that you know was something that could raise up all expectations that the past made me sure held all solution, as we said. A boundless love in this sense that is with you (leaving me senseless) is very complicated. But as an answer, which you say is wrong or impossible, please show me, as an answer it is perhaps the most impossible again to give up. Let me try to say to you another way: maybe better I didn't write, is it, were it better to say, and is that *Lacanic*? Another way: if the depth of my neurosis emerged without relation to love ... I've just fooled myself, that would be impossible for anyone. (Have a) But, if I had come to solve the problem of compulsive shoplifting, say, wouldn't it be easier, what is that? Easier for me to abandon the complex of my history and reform. No, I've got it all mixed up again. I guess the shoplifter and I are at least both looking for something for free. This thing with Max where he's no longer my "prisoner" this is very bad because now I'll try to hide my feelings from him and our love, mine and his, like I feared from the start, even, daring, there's no guarantee on that. Guarantees on all stolen goods. So I feel like I am nothing and want to steal, I want to steal and be a revolutionary, I want a response, I want to alter the environment, remember? It's like a vision, I want an answer, I'm not thinking complicated, I'm thinking fairly free, play the simple and see what you come out with. But, and but, that love is something to give up (give yourself away). I'm so disappointed I will die, will iron burn? The mix with you, ally, to make an indestructible alloy. I will describe myself. I am all curtains torn, I am tall and right now I have no stomach to speak of, I don't have to go out at eight, but, neither do I have a choice, my arms are cold and I'm somewhere I'm used to being, lucky thing I'm pretty or what would I have done all these lovers. Something else. The thing I hate about the analytic method is too revealing to tell you. O my possession, will you have to human too? The objects of the past become, no it's the past that radicalizes humans into objects and there's no driving through that kind of field without a crash, everybody's field day. Nighttime too. Especially dreams. Max is scared. Here I am. Will I be able to take care of him? If I can remember enough. Perhaps something new.

 I dream I will always be "separate from my job." A vigilant sleep, I quarrel with no one. Then spring (the revolver) adds a revolver to make it sound tough. In Meissen, she was raped: skewered language to make it fit on, to make her stop. A reunion on subways where the clown says: "42nd Street, Home of the Supreme Court of the Land where they serve hotcakes." Hotseats?

 You shouldn't always be here, Hello this is Dr. Witticism, Please hang up and hang yourself.

Cathleen Miller
from SPECTRUM

Violet.

The doctors tell you that there are special glasses to counteract the degeneration of the maculae. Losing your mind. A small creek behind the house runs for miles—the water cold and clear lures you to drink. To see is to know. The surrealists helped to redefine reality for twentieth-century viewers. Sm[all wild v]iolets grow in the midst of the grass in the yard. After dark, the canopy of trees forms a tunnel and a faint white glow can be seen at t t the en y had nearly become one person—their routines symbiotic— —after than fifty years together. We would hear the owls in the wood ods sea for prey late into the night. If we choose meaning, the meanin ning su nly deprived of that part of non-meaning that is, strictly speaking, that which constitutes in the realization of the subject, the unconscious. The world recedes and expands in the same moment. Typing is a complicated event—to insert paper and center it properly takes patience and sometimes assistance. Sunlight glints off of any reflective surface, eliminates the details of faces and objects. An enclosed shelf, front of glass, helps shield the books from dust.

Visual phenomena—aside from **an inverted image**—pass through **this window**, about 24mm of surface, according to the index of refraction. The curvature is much **flatter** than a flexible elastic substance, somewhat harder **and** slightly heterogeneous. A ray of light, one of the optical effects that is to project (**blurred** and indistinct) the eyeball of an animal. To view from behind is apt to be **misleading**.

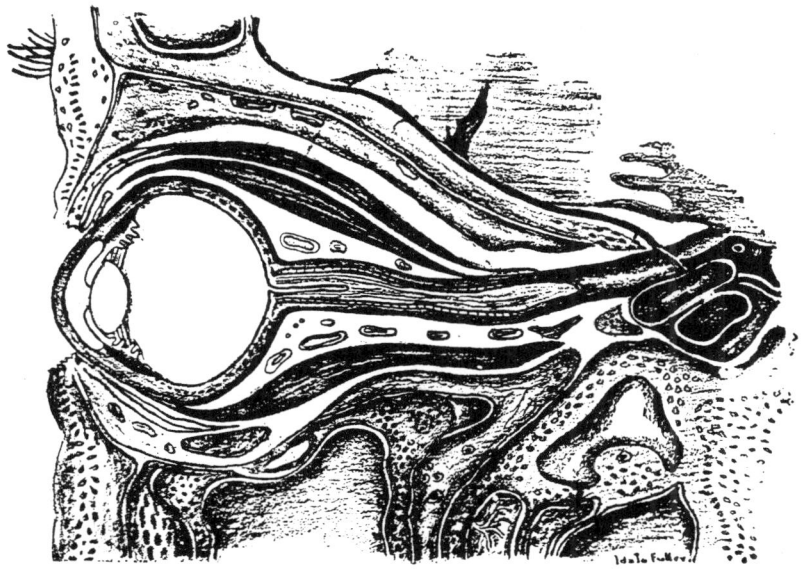

A fixed point—still ahead—you stare to find the connection between image and reality.

White.

You see spots after looking into the light for too long. Sometimes she allows you to answer for her, as if you can define her needs. They say that as you a[re dying, you a]re drawn into a tunnel of increasingly white light—perhaps [this is your ener]ergy returning into the spectrum. Drops of water touch t[he head of the c]hild to purify the soul, make it holy. It is not in the straight [the source f]point of light—the point of irradiation, the play of light, fi[...]om which reflections pour forth. Blue jays knock the seed from feeder to ground to pick out the sunflower seeds from the mixture. Light directed through a small hole into a prism defines the small range of colors that compose all images. Everything appears to be gone in that moment. The curvature of glass creates different effects on the vision. Blindness is not the same as darkness, though this is what we are taught to believe. I HOPE THAT I DON;T SIRPRISE YOU TOO MUCH BUT I HAAVE DECIDED THAT I MIGHT AS WELL PUT MY TYPING PRACTICE TO SOMETHING WORTH WHILE BY WRITING LETTERS INSTEAD OF JUST PUTTIG A LOT OF MEANINGLESS WORDS ON S PIECE PF PAPER. When you begin to notice them, many of the euphemisms in English use sight to define experience, as in "I see what you mean." Flipping through the pages of a book is easier than rewinding a cas sette. We are always looking to the new for inspiration.

> *Spectrum evolved out of my interest in representing emotionally-charged personal subjects without the reliance on pathos used in more mainstream work. I wanted the poem to be about the subject without being consumed by that subject. In this case, I was interested in trying to examine the personal experience of blindness through scientific explication of the structure of the eye and light. I developed the following procedure to help "take myself out of the work" (at least as much as possible): The poem would be organized by the colors of the spectrum—each color section would be fourteen sentences, each with a specific theme, which remain constant through the piece. After these sections were complete, I used the text* Introduction to Physiological Optics *by James P.C. Southall to create the sections in between. I used words that I circled in this text to create new sentences and meanings. The images are all taken from that book as well. In addition to the Southall text, I also used one sentence from Jacques Lacan's* Four Fundamental Concepts of Psychoanalysis *in each of the color sections.*

Eileen Myles

The whole mess
of it troubles me.
The sketchy little
lumps, they seem
inspired by the
area the moods
& clumps of trees
take, climbing up-
wards, it just goes
on its side, and
fills a lavish
area dead on,
it seems wolfish
the appetite of
this colony. It's
moving after all
and the boat
is plowing into
grey, heaping
piles of it on
the horizon, we
seem to be very
right, and
that's our immediate
future, hungry
grey not blue.

Doing the sky has
supplanted my
need for photographs.
It sits, the camera,
like a dark little
plug in my bag. The
sky meanwhile
is a sad blue green
just an inch of it.

Mostly full over that
a thin coarser ripple
of grey with thin
tears of a brighter
blue above. But we
still go right and
there is an arc in
the sky now, a
big blue one. It's
my hope & a
bird flies through it
and there's the
flag whapping in
its breeze,
the whirligigs in
the crows nest
twirling & we see
houses and trees
the oily water,
red cranes, where's
my friend Lorraine
and a hint of
garnet is in

the cloud overhead
There's clouds
painted on clouds
is rusty russet
the sky now, smooth
like old cream. There's
a small piece of
dark blue over
there to the right
but the boat
keeps turning away.
Our moments are
so damn fast the
turn of the boat
my clumsy pen
my heart beating

there's a sweet
white one like
a big fish, one
end just seems
to end—get
just a beat away,
a faint vertical
neighbor vaguer
or a funnel of
moving smoke
like industry or
the world

> This is a section from an ongoing book, well maybe it's done, called Skies. I generally use my immediate surroundings in my work and here it was a very conscious choice to look up and see what was there and transcribe that. The sky's a moving figure, moving foreground, then background, so it was endlessly satisfying to play with like a cigarette, not that good, but close.

Shirin Neshat

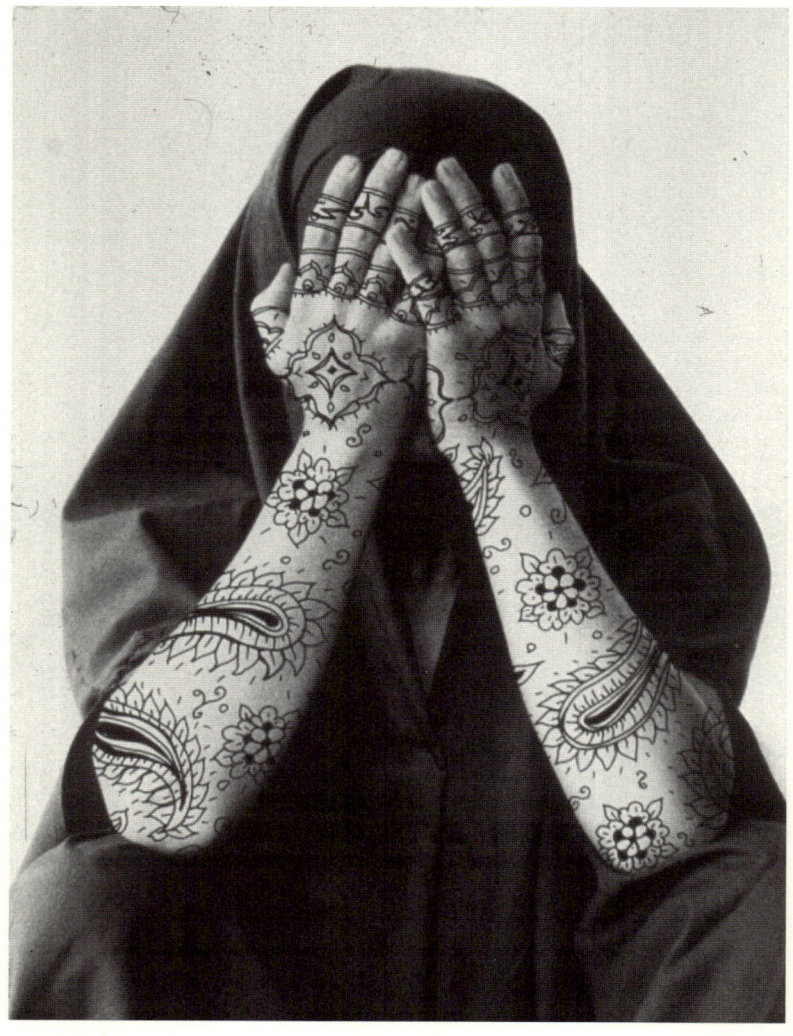

Stripped, 1995
RC print and ink (photograph by Kyong Park).
Courtesy Barbara Gladstone Gallery.

Birthmark, 1995
RC print and ink (photograph by Cynthia Preston).
Courtesy Barbara Gladstone Gallery.

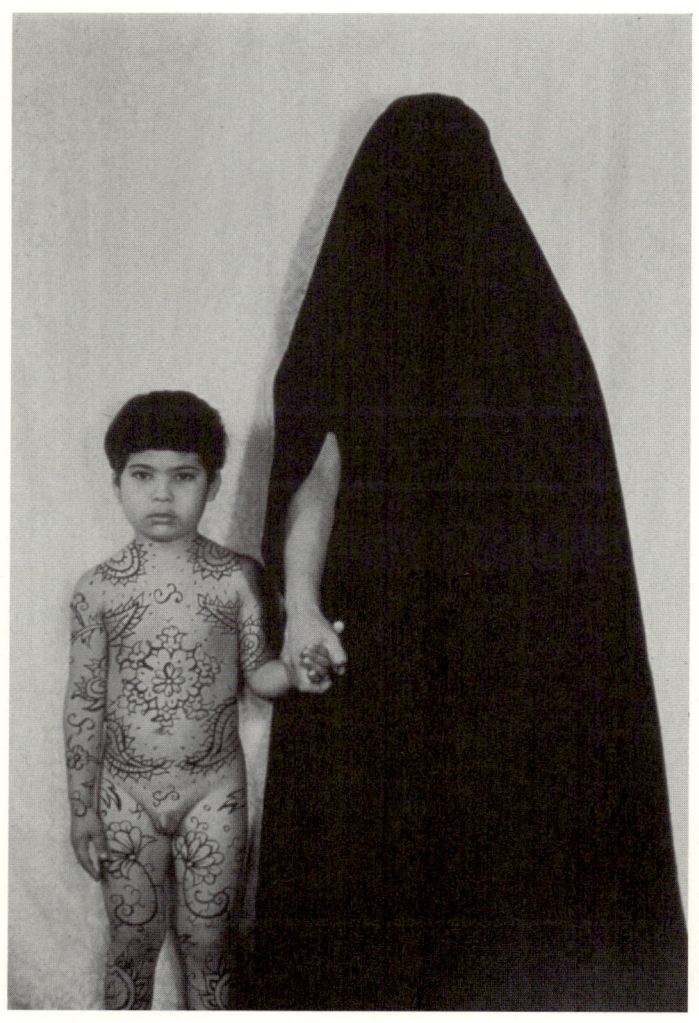

Untitled, 1996,
RC print and ink (photograph by Kyong Park).
Courtesy Barbara Gladstone Gallery.

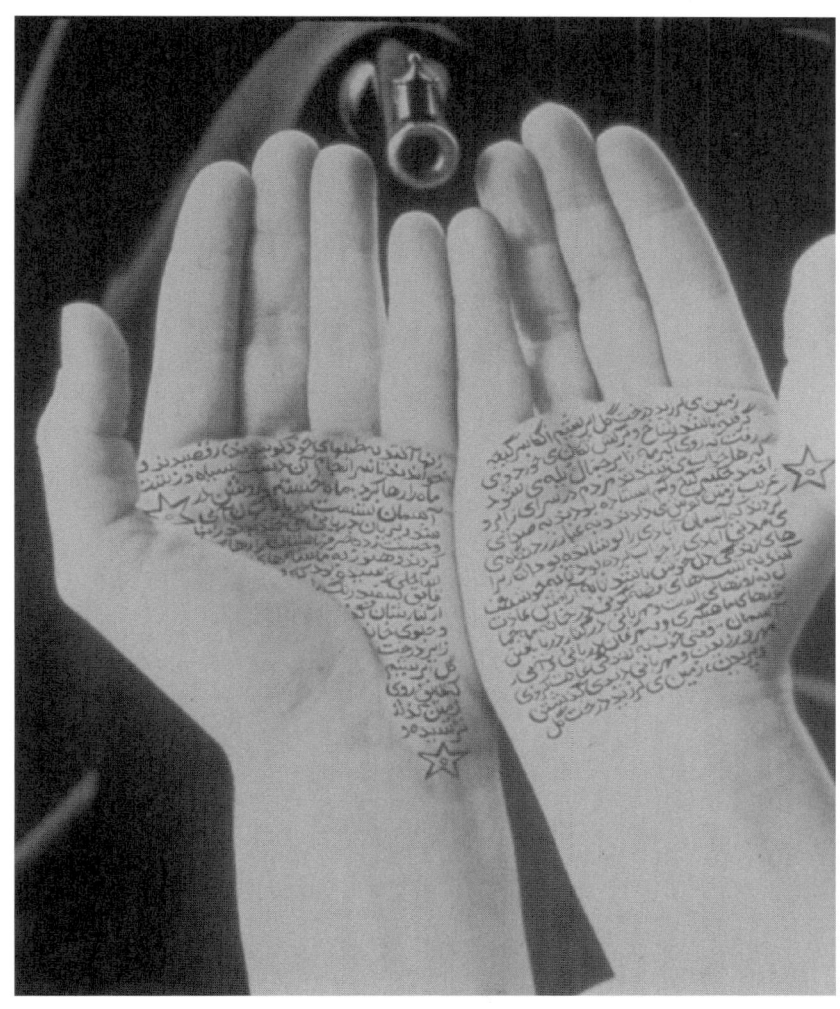

Guardians of Revolution, 1994
RC print and ink (photograph by Cynthia Preston).
Courtesy Barbara Gladstone Gallery.

The Iranian women were first veiled through the gradual process of urbanization. To this day, the kind of veiling that Shirin Neshat critically characterizes is an almost exclusively urban phenomenon. Women who work in the rice paddies of the North, engage in seasonal migrations in the east and western parts of the country, or wear traditional tribal costumes in the south, never veil the way women in Tehran, Isfahan, Shiraz, or other major urban centers do. With the transition from tribal and feudal communities into expanded urbanism caused by domestic (commercial) and colonial (comprador bourgeois) capitalism, women were gradually removed from the public scenes of agricultural and tribal communities and placed in the confinements of enclosed households. . . . With the increased process of urbanization Iranian women were thus forced to have two idle hands in public in order to keep themselves properly veiled.

The first modern Iranian woman revolutionary, Tahereh Qurrat al-Ayn (1814-1852), threw her veil away and uncovered herself the instant she needed her two hands to engage in radical political activities. Tahereh Qurrat al-Ayn, a poet of extraordinary power and erudition, joined the Babi revolutionary movement and ultimately lost her life for her ideals. But the experiences as those of Tahereh Qurrat al-Ayn remained by and large exceptional and the process of urbanization continued to be concomitant with the active isolation of women in their private quarters and their veiling in public. . . .

Shirin Neshat's art is in capturing the tragi-comedy of a body pulled and pushed by the logic and rhetoric of a transition from the early feudal to the late capitalist, from the pre-modern to the post-modern, from the colonial to the postcolonial, and all of that through the electrified energy of death and eros, of a gun and a gaze, of violence and sensuality. For Shirin Neshat, veil is a metaphoric fortress from which to wage a different kind of battle.

Between Tahereh Qurrat al-Ayn and Shirin Neshat stands a rainbow of visionary Iranian women. An array of revolutionaries, poets, painters, novelists, aristocratic critics, social essayists, filmmakers, and political activists fill the distance between the origin of Shirin Neshat's visionary ancestors in Iranian modernity and herself. But immediately and most clearly close to her is Forough Farrokhzad (1935-1967), the poet par excellence, the very living conscience of an entire generation of reawakened sensibilities. Through her daring, provocative, and iconoclastic poetry, Farrokhzad radically redefined not only the very definition of "femininity" but with it the very assumption of "masculinity." Many of the inscriptions on the exposed bodies of Shirin Neshat's photographs are Farrokhzad's poems. She does visually what Farrokhzad did verbally.

—Harnid Dabashi, excerpted from "The Gun and the Gaze: Shirin Neshat's Photography" (Shirin Neshat, *Marco Noire Editore, 1997*)

Sandra Newman
TRUE BLUE & LOVE ALWAYS

THIS is a DIAGRAM of my FIRST HUSBAND.

HE is SHOWN HERE in his TRANSMOGRIFACTION into FOOD FOR THOUGHT.

YOU CAN SEE the THOUGHTS EATING HIM on the left.

-

       THIS is a DIAGRAM of my SECOND HUSBAND

You can see he gives birth to more husbands. Then he kills them all
and cuts beautiful MARBLES out of their heads I don't know
how he does it. I keep the
MARBLES in a SAFE.

Because he does this I'm talismanically bound to him. He does it *silently,
silently* I accuse him, but he harrumphs like a pediatrician and
I'm powerless. *It's time for bed.*

Generally it's always time for bed with my second husband. He magnetically homes to the centre of the bed, where the sheet is always wrinkled as if you are filming Australia from the air. That single crease on a long simple expanse; the idea of red but not the color in fact. Husbands going to be put down on it and gentled.

There can never be too many husbands. I would like to fill the whole Grand Canyon with them and their wonderful marbles that already know me. I would like to make a trail of them through all past time, to lead me back when I die to the ocean whence life once emerged.

And when I die they will be constellations, wise ones with names of all vowels that can only be pronounced through a dainty horn.

THESE ARE MY BEST FRIENDS. IT LOOKS LIKE THERE ARE TWO because they are *reversible.*

THEY hail from THE densely FORESTED lowlands OF suburban breakfasts,

LIKE PANGOLINS in your car, like pangolins in your car. FOR THIS REASON AND BECAUSE OF THEIR SCALY EXTERIOR friend SCIENCE ORIGINALLY CONFUSED THEM WITH the car PANGOLIN.

they have spotted you now and look rooted to the spot. It is as if they are balanced on a ball of what happened last time you saw them

glow inhabits the lawn for many yards around. when they move, ripples out in front PLUS there is a sound

ffffff ffffff like you did say when you're a little child

to tickle inside your head

-

        these are more people I will tell you a story:

I was born in Massachusetts. I did not have any real parents, I was fobbed off with store-bought supermarket brand parents who did not have names but were called generically MOM and DAD. They were black and white but I colored them in.

When I was three or so they held me responsible. Oh I will never forget that day! The formula and mashed bananas and teddy bears, which I had thought just fell from the sky, it turned out, costed money. Well, that was one awful surprise and more awfuller was knowing I would have to pay them back. My parents lay about on the floor weeping saying "I can't take it anymore, someone else is going to have to take responsibility," and from time to time they squinted at me to see, was I taking the hint.

Later that year we set up a regular drip, which was a tube leading from the back of my head, just where the skull joins the nape. Through the day, I would feel them sucking and settle back into my chair, relieved to know I was SOME USE.

Massachusetts had trees everywhere. They looked brown to me when I was small so brown was my favorite color. I seem to remember everyone asking you constantly what your favorite color was so I'd say brown brown brown that was trees and brown horses. I thought people were profane and bald compared to animals skin like puce vinyl and they smelled like the inside of some car, I hated them. I wanted to be a wolf. OR ANYTHING just not people.

That was about the time my drip started coming free of itself. I would pretend I didn't notice and run pouncing through the day spike yellow and remarkable with energy. Then the others adored me. Finally I fed the tube, plugs and hatchetings and all, to Suzy Q, the Briggs's next-door's Springer Spaniel.

Dogs were beautiful and pranced and treetops pranced. I walked for hours in the woods, where sky and dark wood were smashed together like glass. If you walked forever over the hills something wonderful would happen. There were paths in there, if you just followed them enough you could go HOME real HOME not this HOME real HOME

I started to run away from home. It took over my whole mind and thinking like a horror movie fly collector who can think of flies only his whole walls are one psychedelic eyesore of flies and when he undresses flies fall out of his clothes on a bed of flies and his girlfriend says, "You love those flies more than you love me," and she catches the lonesome train and Grandpa tells him straight, "Joe, you're *turning into* a fly!" I never got away.

I grew up disappointingly into the Forked Thing with Arms. The "Neapolitan" design in the starfish range. The starfish with one abbreviated hairy leg on top, with the mouth and eyes on that leg, both on the same side.

In the city, there was lots of excitement, you never knew who you would meet. I thought I was alone in the city like a stowaway because I wore these itsy bitsy skirts and never spoke, and you could go out drinking fuck a Libyan pimp or others all night and go home on the train, there were no consequences. Walking straight through the puddles with their contents of red and white light you summoned absolute purity.

Having grown up, I began to receive mail. The spelling of my name acquired legal significance. Also it was printed on a chit by the intercom. I filled out application forms giving an account of every mediocre act I had stooped to from necessity. It was awful, it was atrocious, it was awful and it was atrocious.

Later on, people got back to me. I was invited. Then I attended slave revolts as Treasurer, and was keynote speaker at brutal rapes. I was paid a basic *plus commission*. Still I would not eat food until the others could have food too, out of elementary politeness. And this EVEN THOUGH even I knew this to be affectation.

I stopped trying to be with people. Then I lived in a damp room. Sometimes I would go out and walk the street, pretending. I liked to look at things people did from a safe distance from A CAFÉ TABLE, like, and I knew many things about people I could NOT HAVE FOUND OUT BY NORMAL MEANS. I wrote fat encyclopedias of my observations. NO ONE knows how.

I married someone else who hated everyone. We sat at A CAFÉ TABLE and looked out. We were like travellers marooned on some island with waiters rowing in and out with fresh coffee and inexpensive cakes. And the damned buzzards overhead, I will never forget it. DAMNED BUZ-ZARDS!

At last the buzzards gott him. He had to go to they head hospittal. He had all big holes in his noggin where the things come in and went out, a-feeding. Jesus Christ, I say, and Jesus Christ and Jesus Christ but HE will not come down for my first husband in his swoopy robes, zooming, cause my first husband WOULD NOT COME DOWN FOR HIM if he was BLEEDING TO DEATH on a CROSS.

•
   these are more people
   looking at me
   want to know where is my first husband
   now the robbers staved in his head to steal the rare components
   infatuate nutmeg, home-made gorgeous rabbits, and shoals
   and the Czechoslovakian doc trepanned HIS HEAD to let the blood out
   it was all a sure sign that the word had got out he got TOO MUCH BRAINS and THOUGHT TOOmuch and HAD FOUND OUT his father's SECRET

Alice Notley
WHERE LEFTOVER MISERY GOES

if its a spiritual offense does it as wrongdoing take place more in more in the second leftover or spiritual world and is the significance of the double now that i might be might the one who offends in other circumstan or that it takes two to make an offense but how was i used and why were the others not usable was it because they were always too selfinvolved to be exploited. oh keep this mostly masked as always these events are of the sort are replayed over and over in the second world perhaps in the overlap the border was it a spiritual offense and did it take place more in the second world than in the first it surely does now. it only takes place in my and keep this masked keep it low shes awaiting attention acceptance as exceptional her face corroding i have to avoid her like poison but i have to keep remembering shes poison there is a machine that allows memory to be memories to taken into the futur i have to remember shes pois and that isnt a known a universally accepted fact that shes poison to me wants to poison me and make me hers of her emotional her emotional camp make me live of the camp of she thinks but she is poison shes acting like she isnt and i can barely remember the last time i was poisoned and now in the now in the second world there is no linear time no many years past and i dont know when they last said in the first world accept her poison bu because its only you dont bother us on the cold wintry avenue in your coat lined with papers another wild looking night darker than the last one which was purple this ones deep navy with slivver moon behind a raggy cloud in this wind the buildings are dangerously high and here and there a gold lights tossed i didnt see the two strangers my former fr is that possible strangers until i suddenly did staring at me but the real point is that i'm not them nor her i'm not the double and i want to be hard about this i am only the double as i must straddle two worlds but i am th not the double who did wrong to me i am not thee there is no key for the brilliant red lake in the top of the rectangle map of me which seems to be a sort of early area is desperation a pleasure i'm so thirsty and i'm suppose in joy but do i believe remem desperation joy or guilt approach me from a side street trying to make me talk to them i'm singing a song and the he double says not enough facts in that song though theres a lot of poetry one word has become coeur of me what word it must be poet coeur de coeur no longer a word we have driven up high to this mountain town where the gypsies live but must leave live but must leave he asks me to talk to him but i wont now an she all fuzzed up in the head wants to give me an entire shelf of old books as a bribe to poison knowledge of her mind but i'm resolutely in black fur burning into a snowbank a dream a tall snowbank that is taller than i am and its hard to walk hard to walk here in the death you are helping i am being assimilated and wear a long dress and shawl watch me make love as a prostitute so i can be your friend because youve only ever wanted to see my body what you think of me the villagers want to circumcize me sunday so i can be everyones theyre gypsies in the mountains on luna something street i used to live there but i have since cut up the sidewalk and carry it with me carry luna something street with me wherever i go and lay it down so i can walk towards or away what away from what i must walk away from them again board the ship my other sister life will go to the camp where the actress a second a second

demonic womans face must be kept out of the movie you cant know about her you cant know in the first world and in the second thus there are these dreams which play out shadows on the street useless kindness curiously useless until the play the playing out is over in the head of what you did used me to stay you and so i'm a gypsy again wait for the camp to break up in the mountains encased in crystal you used me but said you were use in the first world on the street on the street of poison words b was it only words no there was the deathhole that was burned into the snow it was supposedly another who died not die because i was never the one was i never the focus was other so how could you ever affect me when you were trying to ki fight another and only poison me lightly who died not die but there was the deathhole burned into the snow here in the second world as i play it out play it out in the crystal a lighter story now where i never die have only died to that world. no one believes in poison thats why we cant breathe. someone has left me a book highlighted in black always do that leave a book and the letters hop and try to transform but tha they cant nor can the shelf of old book of esoterica change the nature of poison which goes towards because only thinks of self thinks story so the poison flows outwards in the bad air in winter tinged with yellow and corroded face bookstore bookstore ever if the double lives in a book. others support her because i have never needed story and the letters hop and try to transform they are snow the letters try again i dont know how to tell you this letters i dont care about your transitional stages i dont care why you used pois i dont care whose real name or person i dont have to be tain tained certain of the action of self without salt keep doing this keep doing this so old. because it happened once in the first world and in the second doesnt quite go away the actions in the first and the real story as dream as dream in the seconds milder haunt where who died not i but died to the first and died to that camp and died to that

149

bookstore and died to that oh keep this mostly masked dont feel a thing or be pois get poisoned theyre still all waiting for that i dreamed i lived them they wore black robes and lived in a cluster of wooden houses in a clearing but there may have been woods and i was being assimilated i wore a long black dress and shawl the narrator cut in to say that i was prostitute and my boyfriend john watched me make love with the village men there seem to be many and tenderfaced what does prostitution symbolize half of the villagers are leaving and then i will be circumcized because he dies or somethi take part in the rite of becoming a woman can withstand of pain of that she tries to poison again wants me to be on a side and not in i wake up for a few minutes fall back asleep many years ago they are gypsies this movie will star us and the stars are familiar in the part where i'm taken away on a ship with other prisoners but am no one just movie stars just parts and theres no point in falling in love with the commandant hes just a star and i'll die anyway theres no point in and when she says love theres no love. this is a spell to get out of here how long will it take the border is endless. wants me to be on another side she wants t wants me to be on her side of the border and i stay on the side of the second world always but am still in the border the border where the nightmare sucks me into its feeling want to say her keep saying

saying

about her because no has believed it and so say it and say and so remain in the border will the circumcized women feel after death will the real w will the real e include sensation that cant be manipulated by ones feel fellowcreatures on the street denying me to the point of point because i think they like and if you maintain sides you are always near the border and never in the snows come again and the purple sinister sky

150

so i can die and read the books they leave me always alive the letters and the letters

letters

hop about and try to change but never do because no one wants them to change.

"Where Leftover Misery Goes" is from a very long manuscript (over 300 pages) entitled Reason and Other Women. The book is intended to show myself in the process of thought; thus typos and mistakes are left in as standing for "mind fuzz"; repetition both maintains momentum and indicates stasis, in the way the two combine in thinking; thinking may be obsessive or serene, concerned with the past or more exclusively in the present. However the book is also tied with the concept of a Byzantine church with all its icons and mosaics: permanent images or stories one never shakes, also the little dots or pieces of thinking, also a sense of the sacrality of consciousness. There is a numbers scheme employed throughout based on the number six, which was supposedly the perfect number for the Byzantines. There is also a color symbolism of my own device in which blue is the color of reason and red is the color of the soul.

Akilah Oliver
FIBS 7809

Disjuncture}1
the difference between chicken breast fillet and ground turkey should be obvious but i hadn't noticed it until the kitten cried.

> glimpse #245: whatever's happening to us seems to be really strange but the strangest thing is nobody seems to be in charge of it.

Disjuncture}2
don't dream that i don't dream of you. sometimes I do. i'm tired was just a statement. no reason to doubt veracity. or to sleep until three in the afternoon is normal if the sounds from the first hydrants kept you awake all night. paris must be a different city than this one. I did walk on cobblestones once but it seems like that was baltimore. I don't know anything about that place. your tongue has an obvious attachment to things that taste slightly salty. I don't think i'd feel as sexy in a hair weave. or the skin of a lover past her '*prime.*'

> glimpse #98: it was the most intimate thing me lying my head on your back a leathered parcel you won in a crap shoot thirtynine years ago

Disjuncture}3
now that has got to take the cake. a forest should be an actual location or a storybook ideal of evil. like the shadows of denver streets after 10pm. when you died I thought everything would change for the better but things just got worse for awhile. she was sent here to uninvent the family. an alliance to Mondays. a plotless wonder.

> glimpse #456: I thought you said no but that was just another kind of unknowing of what to do as if this calls for some definitive action this slow falling away from one another

> glimpse #56: I thought you'd tell me something definitive why johnny can't read & then it would all be settled

Disjuncture}4
you asked me where the passion went as if I should be able to trace its source to a gully or exclamation point. as if clever were a disguise I could shrug off at any whimsical point in the plot revealing myself really just a plain girl. a workhorse in sensible low heeled shoes shopping for the family's daily rutabagas at a predestined location while donkeys bray loaded down with trade.

glimpse #098: if woman is a false category then I've just made all this up

Disjuncture}5
salty unlike sexy doesn't get in the way of things when you need to invent a letter to write to someone you hardly know. it could just be my old-fashioned selfish impulses at work here but I wanted to see the squirrel swing itself off the tree ledge down into the snow drift below. a reinforcing syntax. double negatives. I don't know nobody. the first statement of truth:
dear:
a disarming endearment. false negative. we don't have anything in common. or john, we hardly knew you. I wanted to wear the body you'd taken on as a thirty-something woman curled in the leather bar stool of the five and dime novel.

glimpse #234: when finally the fairy princess felt brave enough to leave the castle walls she only made it far as the local seven-eleven but even that was better than nowhere

glimpse #98: it was the most intimate thing me lying my head on your back a leathered parcel you won in a crap shoot thirtynine years ago

Disjuncture}6
dear: i'm sorry I didn't return your call right away but the days just seem to run into each other like one endless sentence and besides I didn't want to talk in the voice you would expect of me.

glimpse #56: I thought you'd tell me something definitive why johnny can't read & then it would all be settled

Disjuncture}7
what if all the people are getting ready 'cause there's a train coming. a code in which we all speak like mtv. apparent acronyms that take up little emotional space. nafta. nwa. a mode of thought that brings everything neatly together in a master script.

glimpse #88: I want the drama of a declarative statement like if I break your heart again i'll kill myself but is too early for all that the sun is a vain mistress squalored on the dirt eaten grass outside this frame & besides it's ridiculous to say goodbye with an idiom

glimpse #456: I thought you said no but that was just another kind of unknowing of what to do as if this calls for some definitive action this slow falling away from one another

Disjuncture}8
you broke my heart. now that's a handy idiom. I call for a language of shared possibilities. not the limited inferences of mother lover car cake run. disfigurements in expected speech. a man of the people.

glimpse #097: if there is really no such location called female then we've just made all this up

glimpse #245: whatever's happening to us seems to be really strange but the strangest thing is nobody seems in charge of it.

Disjuncture}9
false alliances to activisms like insisting on a female gynecologist or buying black or drinking Zapatista grown coffee makes me feel better. and because I feel better by extension perhaps the world is now a slightly better place. like carefully plotting all appointments in the daily calendar masks a slight quivering in the fingers when I think of IT. the antithesis of lying on one's rusty dusty

glimpse #98: it was the most intimate thing me lying my head on your back a leathered parcel you won in a crap shoot thirtynine years ago

> My work investigates the tensions between identity, memory, desire and useful fictions. In the "Fibs" series, I am attempting to blend and blur the intersections between those contentions. Much of the impulse for the "Fibs" series of poems is derived from Roland Barthes' A Lover's Discourse. What specifically interests me in Fib #7809 is the unreliability of loss and its relationship to female=female desire's struggle to transmute its blundering nature, or to unhinge itself from itself.

Rona Pondick

Dog, 1998–2000 (work in progress)
aluminum bronze, 29" x 16.5" x 32"
Courtesy Sonnabend Gallery, New York

Joan Retallack
MEMNOIR

it is said that it

           happens even in nature e.g. during the childhood the mother might have a taste for film noir and take the child along i.e. onderful I explained

           my machine is hooked up to my machin fiction is precisely what they call non-fiction so too get a bit presonal

           it would be necessary to go the other way i.e. she wanted more than she could say to not want more than she could say

           or it might be necessary to replace all vowels with x mxgxcxlly txrnxng prxmxtxrx txrrxr xntx pxlxtxblx pxst-pxst xrxny

           not idle play to forgive that we in the spilt second of a single space i.e. it is said that it happens even in nature if only the space at the watering hole is large or small enough the animals the timing is all that is off it is that that is the problem with the timing that it is always off while it cannot be off at all that is the he to be sure that the she did not choose the wrong thing

given the diversity of forms that even a soap film or any other minimal surface can this time at or on this point that is however not an Archimedean point

that will entirely explode the wild idea to try say that I had a wild idea just as a hummingbird flew by just like a deluxe model bumble bee engine with mechanical wings beating the sky like a wild idea in a hot majestic interlude containing profanity violence and graphic photos of murder victims before the clouds parted and the sun turned into a coffee mug or a doughnut

and/but/though over the years mathematicians have been able to prove that every noninteresting closed curve is spanned by at least one smooth minimal surface or surface reflecting the twisting of the sun into someone's bird's eye view or the limits of any horizon always being a point of view just like the one unflooding here

and then she found that to find one's position on the graph using xy coordinates one must replace all the consonants with y

Memnoir, *like all the work I do, comes out of a perforated self—permeable, in conversation, not wanting to finish a story about a self that must be in motion for the I to believe in the I as a vital principle. This isn't about owning a self, or having a story to tell, though narrative strands weave in and out of chance-developed configurations. Since everything is made of the dynamic interaction between memory and experience. . . . Memory in this piece is a process of connecting language with ambient conditions that include material residues of the past while navigating the continuing flood of experience. It's profiles/vase, before/after, mean/while. Experience will always interpolate its noisy silences. All that is and is not the self is all that is and is not poetry or prose, but poetry.*

Deborah Richards
THE BEAUTY PROJECTION

it was a black sundress catalogue bought you tied the straps at the remarkable shoulders, double knots or else disaster just a pull and the animal frame would be released from its halter in those days the italian fashion was to wear tank ts that exposed the breast when dancing or playing instruments blacked because it was easy and especially body coordinated you know my means though simmering in sun I never rubbed musk upon so black a body there is no doubt that it was so those tank ts were in but they required a remarkable form or a beautiful subject to place them on and very

Most that I have said in the chapter on the means of obtaining a bright and handsome form, applies equally to the subject of this chapter. But, there are some artificial tricks which I have known beautiful ladies to resort to for the purpose of giving elasticity and sprightliness to the animal frame. The ladies of France and Italy, especially those who are professionally, or as amateurs, engaged in exercises which require great activity of the limbs, as dancing, or playing on instruments, sometimes rub themselves, on retiring to bed, with the following preparation:

    Fat of the stag, or deer   8oz.
    Florence oil (or olive oil)   6oz.
    Virgin wax   3oz.
    Musk   1 grain.
    White brandy   1/2 pint.
    Rose Water   4oz.

Put the fat, oil, and wax into a well glazed earthen vessel, and let them simmer over a slow fire until they are assimilated; then pour in the other ingredients, and let the whole gradually cool, when it will be fit for use. There is no doubt but that this mixture, frequently and thoroughly rubbed upon the body on going to bed, will impart a remarkable degree of elasticity to the muscles. In the morning after this preparation has been used, the body should be thoroughly wiped with a sponge, dampened with cold water (Montez 75).

You know, I've always preferred your

The following classical synopsis to female beauty, which has been attributed to Felibien, is the best I remember to have seen: the forehead white, smooth, and open (not with hair growing down too deep upon it the black is particularly flat nor prominent, but like the useful in setting off the whiteness of

FIGURE 1 THE HOTTENTOT VENUS.
European prejudices about Africa developed early, and were based on the widely held assumption that Africans were inherently inferior to Europeans. Between 1810 and 1815 (the year she died in Paris) a southern African woman known as Saartje Baartman (or the 'Hottentot Venus') was exhibited in public in a number of European cities for the amusement and amazement of the public. Parts of her body are still preserved in the collections of the Musee de l'Homme in Paris, despite a number of protests. Concepts of race are discussed in Chapter 8 (Hall 3).

the eyes black, chestnut, or blue; clear, birth, and neck and skin portion than sma

(Montez 68)

You're so smooth. We're like coffee and

sexy without artificial tricks of lycra but that was O.K a la mode the young italian woman desirous of **elasticity** commended my skin oh if I could have skin like sprightliness she said and asked her mother the secret concoctions that I may have frequently and thoroughly rubbed upon my body before going to bed but my german friend/loved one was fluent in italian german english he could understand every word and as we had engaged in exercises that required great activity that morning he knew that the black skin covered every part bar the soles and palms and the intimate corners I came again back from inside outside and he applied his hand for the purpose of an imparting companionship o.k this is the synopsis he was to be a doctor in padua a serious student but we had love because he was bright and well rounded then I felt that to be worth anything all the lovely men I knew should make love to me in the full sense of its meaning it was a necessary

| hottentot | Venus |

prejudices **exhibited** in public in a number of European cities for the amusement and **amazement** of the public assumption

Has anyone told you, your ass is so so so

sickness you know trying to assimilate myself into what I thought I could never be equal in proportion it could be particularly awkward in the morning he was so fair and I was so prominently foreign we were chiaroscuro it was a joke his white beauty could be useful in setting off my black against the wet surface of the shower walls he is still preserved in my recollections I can't be one of those demanding women who want something men refuse to give it up in front of the television with their dinner in their laps so the woman hovers around the margins resorting to a cooling off period like nobody it was black and me I think I had black sandals the sprightliness of youth and a cheap flight from london to rome the 18:10 that left from gatwick arriving 21:35 I got off and was met by the man from india who said if you are ever in rome come stay with me I came I saw but I

venusvenusvenusvenusvenusvenusvenusvenusvenusvenusvenusvenusvenusvenusvenusvenusvenusvenusvenus

barbarian/ barbaric barbarous. All three have been used indifferently in the past, though now differentiated. Earlier is ME *barbar*, F *barbare* L, G [squiggle] with ref to unintelligible speech (bar-bar) Cf Hottentot. Hence *barbarism* orig. the mixing of foreign words with Greek or Latin. (*Etymological Dictionary of Modern English*)

FIGURE 114 RACIAL STUDIES. Nineteenth-century scientists, intent on the classification and study of the human races, collected anatomical photographs in which subjects were forced to pose naked in formal positions, usually alongside measuring scales (Hall 132)

You're looking very ethnic today.

was inherently inferior to my attractiveness despite a number of men too many of them who wanted and did rub up my skin I was built for amusement and amazement two looked at pornographic magazines in bologna in pointing at naked women stretched out and ready to snap like a jack I was free to travel alone but it was lonely only the men wanted to kiss me and the other man was from morocco whose idea for a meal was a hamburger in McD's and the film was midnight express in french I had seen the film before but it was quite unintelligible to watch a foreign film without subtitles we spoke with some difficulty on the steps of the opera we were a study for lovers forced to make contact in a short-lived time he wanted to come back to my place another attic another city and in the end we had to remain formal one *bise* on either cheek there was nothing anatomically that could keep us apart but we were strangers though he later sent me a loved letter that photographed the time and the place as being beautiful that night I stumbled into my

162

room late and the bed was unfolded in the darkness I slept in the bed strangerless but here I was in rome padua paris wherever alone surprisingly but it was not easy to be me in india though I had expected a difference in my ability to be accepted they too value the fairest of skins and as my complexion is steeped too dark though I do not expose my skin to direct sunlight as I am covered from head to toe so that I may become unobserved I am viewed with amazement and naked stares they were particularly interested in my cornrows and asked my companion how it could be done this thing that was done to me take the instance of the camel ride in the desert I became the mysterious stranger who appeared from who knows where we'd met in jodhpur in a compound of expensive cottages run by a maharaja educated at eton and the usual places so that his accent was highly sovereign and pure so we had our own servant named happy who we could call with a clap of our hands which we could never bring ourselves to do there like the rajasthani women dark particularly attentive to touch

PIMPERNEL WATER is a **sovereign** wash with the ladies all over the continent of Europe, for **whitening** the **complexion**. All they do to prepare is simply to steep that wholesome plant in **pure** rain water. It is such a favorite that it is regarded as almost as indispensable to a **lady's** toilet, who is particularly attentive to the brightness of her complexion (Montez 83).

whitening   pure

complexio   lady

sovereign   venus

venus
venus
venus
venus
venus
venus
venus

Works Cited
Hall Martin, Archaeology Africa Cape Town: Philip Publishers Ltd 1996.
Montez Madame Lola, "The Arts of Beauty; or Secrets of a Lady's Toilet"
Beauty ed. John Miller San Francisco: Chronicle Books 1997.

Bhanu Kapil Rider
from AUTOBIOGRAPHY OF A CYBORG

Memory is a wall

    Childhood memory: my mother had red hair, in the photos I painted over, with vermillion acrylic. My mother, an Indian. My mother, in the dust and heat; *heat is good,* she says, *it washes you.* So I am walking to the highway to catch the express bus to Connaught Circle. (I walked to the bus-stop every Saturday morning, to catch the number ninety-eight to Harlington, Middlesex, for my piano lesson.) I was seven years old. (I was bleeding heavily.) It was so hot. May,

    late May, maybe June, in the northern hemisphere. The dark nurse stuck a needle in my hip. (These child-bearing hips.) My mother said: *you'll be late.* And she handed me my Berlioz. (My sarong.) I was seventeen. And I wound it tight. And the sun went into my body and made it wrong. (Chopin. Grieg.) Mad dogs, the lot of them. (They take my British passport to verify my living body.) They stick things in.
Faster.

Memory of the earth: Paris: not Paris itself, but the cup of treacly espresso, set down upon the albino linen, in the night-time. A man or a woman, it doesn't matter. All I remember are the brutal, bright hands of the barista, pushing my cup across the counter. (Zinc of the body, when it lies face down, on the zinc: the hand I mean. A palm. So many lines, splitting off as they approach the: thenar eminence, mount of venus, thickened pad of grids. *In your mid-twenties, you'll leave and never come back.* So many crossings, in the invisible layers that are multiple as a boa's. Palimpsest: not Paris itself, but a few days when I had a specific, temporary skin. A sea-bell tolling in the open window of the café.) Someone—my wife? My husband?—said: "I have gold on my finger and wool on my feet." (The atoms of gold. The atoms of feet. A storm is coming from the north.) Returning to me as water:

                                                                             The oxygen of other times. Having loosened, off the surface, from a little touch. In passing; the stranger. (I will drink him. He will drink me. He drinks her. She drinks him. I am drinking: the hands that give me coffee, for nothing, on a Thursday evening in the Latin Quarter, when it's raining and I am so obviously a tourist.)

How I remember things

Through a block of ambergris. As through blocks of. Resins glowing, not condensing what enters, sideways, in the late afternoon.
How? In a sort of four time. As in Pischna: his fourness of breathing; the notes converging from each direction at once. *Read this backwards.*

He can sings.
He cans sing.

It's time to go. I write these things out of the acids of this time. As soon as I write them, they burn. Not even an essence of ambergris can induce the night visions necessary to staying. Not even money. My rolfer thinks I'm crazy. Gives me lectures on Los Angeles/ my blood/ the dim future where I sit in diners on the outskirts of Des Moines, eating lukewarm apple pie and listening to Elvis songs on my walkman. *Listen baby,* he says, as he pumps my sacrum, *the poison will always be there. What, you go to Iowa. Then what? You think you're not going to die? You think you're Priscilla Presley?* He's right. I am blue with toxic forces: images of this yellow city packed tight inside my myofilaments. At the least deep touch, or attempt to re-align, they are opened, like potatoes. Aberrant potatoes, that have no business splitting open, when raw.
Potato woman:
A person nonetheless, i.e. a person who remembers her life and loves according to the theory of rhizomes: in patches/enhanced/prone to green, carcinogenic splotches. Which she eats anyway, with lashings of margarine and tobasco sauce. Knowing specific, uncomplicated recollections to be praise-worthy. For example, "butter." "The first time I had sex with a living person."
"What I did in the summer holidays:
codeine.
Coming as I do,
          from 10% zinc, 3% sclerotic plexus, 18% self-regulating visibility/influence matrix (heard but not seen/seen and heard/neither seen nor heard/seen but not heard), 4.5% bean-juice, 2% brie, 27% Bach (the Goldberg Variations, as well as the Prelude in B minor), 1% Niwot, 0.00000007% oxygen molecules that once passed through the body of Moses/Idi Amin/my father before I was born and he was smoking hookah in a dhaaba in Gulmarg....

So I felt a bit dizzy. My spider mother, my protective mother, and my very

hard mother: loosened:
their protective fats. Connections between zinc and Bach, brie and silence: scarred over. In late August, I heard a ripping sound, just beneath the surface of my brain. Now I travel with difficulty from "my left hand" to "my memories of Venice Beach when I first" to "the taste of" to "this."
    Interluminal,
it was all I could do, come the Fall, to pack my bags.
With the fabulous trinkets, stale croissants, and analog prints photographed from Beverly Hills 901020902010010 . . . ."

Good girl. Nice job. Now, if you can, in your own time, drop your leg off the table. When I touch you here, what do you see? I see red. A lot of red. What does red mean to you? Oh my god, did you feel that? Your QL just released. Do you want a tissue? Here you go. Wow. That was really something. And now I can see a sort of blue. Blue with a green triangle. It feels like grief to me. What does it feel like to you? What other words begin with G?

Kit Robinson
NOTES TOWARD A PHENOMENOLOGY OF MEMORY

Memoir is dangerous territory. There is a huge and perfectly natural tendency to sentimentalize the past.

"As Duke Snider said recently at Pee Wee Reese's funeral, 'Of course, when you're 73, there are a lot of another times,'" as Ted Greenwald wrote recently.

In George Perec's *W or Memory of Childhood*, two texts alternate: one an adolescent fantasy of a quasi-fascist state culture based on athletic competition, the other a documentary investigation into the fragmentary evidence of Perec's childhood, a series of displacements occasioned by the Holocaust. In this book Perec poses the dilemma of autobiography. All memory is suspect, being a construct of the present. Consistency, coherence and narrative unity are attributes of the fantastic. The rigorous approach to the past limits itself to fragments.

Memoir stretches between the twin poles of pure fiction and mute fact.

I remember discussing Wittgenstein with Erica Hunt at the neighborhood bar at 18th & Connecticut. Tom came in and said, "Every time I see you two you're always discussing Vladimir Propp!"

I have no patience for plot and am often distracted from one moment to the next. I like conversation that covers a lot of ground, rather than drilling down deep. By then I'm on to the next thing.

I remember certain moments, the most embarrassing or tragic, the fateful, the triumphant, the tender. Also, occasional odd or random ones.

I remember once when Ted Berrigan, Steve and I were walking back to my place from Winchell's Donuts on Alcatraz & Shattuck. Passing an iron-barred and boarded up window on Alcatraz, Ted stopped to point out that one bar was a little longer than the rest, so it stuck out at the bottom. Now every time I drive by that window I think of Ted.

I remember the first time I met Sydney Murray. We were at Bob & Francie's loft on Folsom St. Sydney had given Bob & Francie a framed fruit-crate label with a picture of peaches and the brand name "Just As Good."

A year or so after my graduation from elementary school I went back for some reason and found myself walking through the empty hallway thinking about time. I decided to remember this moment, for no other reason than as an experiment, like putting a bookmark in time.

When I was about four, I conceived of the notion of reincarnation. Of course, this is a screen memory. Perhaps I actually learned the concept somewhere and subsequently forgot how. Or perhaps this memory is a fiction somehow constructed later on. I figured I might have been Christopher Columbus, or, curiously, Annie Oakley.

I've had two dogs, Darwin and Joey, and four cats: Annie Oakley, Datona, and Iris and Nadine.

If Walter Benjamin had survived crossing the French border to Spain, he would have ended up in Hollywood with Brecht, Lang, Schoenberg, Marcuse and Wilder.

Benjamin wrote that history is written by the victors. He wrote of the Jewish tradition that each moment may signify the arrival of the Messiah, so that history is shot through with chips of messianic time.

"Notes Toward a Phenomenology of Memory" was written as part of an ongoing work of correspondence on the subject of the San Francisco writing scene of the 70s and early 80s. Other correspondents include Rae Armantrout, Steve Benson, Carla Harryman, Lyn Hejinian, Tom Mandel, Bob Perelman, Ron Silliman and Barrett Watten.

Thaddeus Rutkowski
MISFIRES

My father brought me with him for a walk, and we ended up at the hotel bar. Inside, a few grizzled men were sitting on stools. The only light came from a television screen.

"There's a guy hitchhiking at the edge of town," one of the men said. "A black guy."

"He'd better not be there long," another said.

"If he's there when I drive by," said another, "he'll become a janitor in a drum."

My father took me home and went out again, this time in his car.

When he came back, he had the hitchhiker with him.

"He said he'd visit with us," my father said. "Later, I'll take him to the university."

The stranger crouched so that his head was on the level of mine. He held out his hand, but I didn't respond. When he didn't move away, I clasped his hand.

That night, there was a carnival at the local fire hall, and my father said that the hitchhiker should take me. "I'm going to the bar," my father said. "Maybe I'll meet you."

The hitchhiker and I walked down the street to the floodlit grounds. As we got closer, I could smell cooking oil and potatoes.

We wandered on crushed grass between plywood booths, passing a paddle-wheel game, a penny pitch, a dart wall, and a hardball tunnel. When we came to the Ferris wheel, we got tickets and climbed into a bucket. At the top of our arc, we could see all of the carnival-goers, the field filled with parked cars, and the one street of the town.

No one talked to us the entire time we were at the carnival, and my father didn't show up.

•

The next morning, I went outside to catch the schoolbus.

While I waited, a boy called out: "Jap!" He was standing on the other side of the street with a group of his friends.

"Come here!" he said. "I want to pull out your esophagus and shove it down your throat!"

I stayed on my side of the street.

"I want to rip out your femur and hit you over the head with it!"

On the bus, the boy and his friends took the prime seats in the back. I sat next to the driver.

•

When I arrived at gym class, I found out that all of the boys had to wrestle.

I got down on the mat with the rest of my classmates. We lay on our backs and pushed up and back with our feet so that our weight was on our craniums. We balanced like crabs, then pivoted on our heads so that we were face-down.

After "bridging," we practiced Greco-Roman moves. We "sat out" in sequence, lifted each other like firefighters, then broke each other down.

Next, our coach paired us for matches. He chose as my opponent the boy who had wanted to remove my gullet and hipbone. (Both of us were about the same size.)

The boy and I dropped into the referee's position. I supported myself on my hands and knees; my antagonist held my near elbow with one hand and wrapped his free arm around my waist.

On the command of "Wrastle!" the boy on top attempted to pull my limbs out from under me. I quickly extended one arm and leg, and both of us slithered sideways. He crooked an elbow around my arm and tried to lever me onto my back. But I twisted my torso, pried his arm away and stood up. He grabbed the backs of my knees, but I planted my feet, and we staggered out of the ring.

Our struggle lasted about five minutes. When it was over, the coach declared the match a draw.

In the locker room, I sat on a bench to change. As I took off my gym clothes, I heard an athletic boy say to the boy who had wrestled me, "For a little guy, you sure have a big dick."

I didn't want to be naked in front of the rest of the boys. So I didn't take a shower. I stuffed my T-shirt, shorts and strap into my gym bag, put on my street clothes and went to class.

•

When I got home, I had to practice my flute.

I went to my bedroom and took the instrument out of its case. I twisted the three silver parts together, brought the mouthpiece to my lips, and rolled the airhole back and forth for a comfortable *embouchure*. I blew gently and produced a jug-like tone. Then I blew hard and got a high whistle.

When the family dog heard my shrill sound, it started to howl. I kept making high notes, so that the dog and I performed a duet.

•

At dinner, I told my father that I wanted to play in the marching band.

"You want to wear a uniform and learn to goose-step?" my father said. "No son of mine is growing up to be cannon fodder."

He turned to my brother and sister. "None of you is to associate with Americans anymore," he said.

"What about their friends?" my mother asked.

"They will stop seeing their friends."

"But we live in America," my mother said.

"Americans are herd animals," my father said. "They march in step and worship the dollar."

"I work to support you and the children," my mother said.

"Have you heard the saying," my father asked, "'a woman with a wagging tongue is a stairway to disaster'?"

"There's another saying," my mother said, "'the best time to visit the wise man is when he isn't home.'"

My father stood up. "I'm going to the hotel," he said.

•

I heard my mother talking on the telephone in Chinese.

When she was finished, she said, "That was my brother. He heard from my father."

"Where is your father?" I asked.

"He's living in a village near the city where I grew up. He can't leave there. He has false teeth, from when he was hit in work camp. Otherwise, he's healthy."

"Can you talk to him?" I asked.

"I can write to him. But I've forgotten a lot of characters, so I'll write in English."

"Can he read it?"

"Yes. That's why he disappeared."

Late at night, I was awakened by my father's voice. "He's not coming here!" he shouted. "I can't take care of you people! I'm not a nursemaid!"

•

For a birthday present, my father gave me a hunting gun: an over-and-under with a rifle barrel on top and a shotgun barrel on the bottom. "You're old enough to hunt by yourself," he said.

Then he told me to hit the woods.

I left the house and walked on a farm lane toward a hillside.

The gun was heavy. At first, I cradled it in my arms, with one hand wrapped around the trigger guard and a thumb on the safety. This way, I could smoothly bring the stock to my shoulder, cock the hammer, aim, and fire.

As I crept through a stand of trees next to a field, I kicked at brush piles, stopped, listened, then moved forward and repeated the routine. But I didn't see any game. After a mile or so, I dropped my arms and let the gun dangle. Sometimes, I carried the gun over my shoulder, like a soldier.

After a while, I put the gun on the ground and stood motionless.

When I took my next step, I heard the drumming of wings and saw the blur of an escaping bird. I grabbed the gun, brought it up to my waist, and fired blindly into the trees. The shot tore through the brush, scattering leaves and twigs.

As I fumbled to reload, I saw the bird break out of the trees and head for clear sky.

Susan Schultz
from MEMORY CARDS

9/3/99
The little boy next door either weeps or sings. Weeps when he goes to bed, weeps when he awakens, weeps when he's put in the car. Then his frail voice sings, church songs. "You are making me happy now," someone says to him. NRA sticker on their windshield. "You must obey your mother; you must obey." There was the time at the airport she said never to come home again. Small woman with the bones of a bird, furious. Anger's crock pot. There was the time she refused apology; she'd meant it then. If you do not buy shoes. If you do not buy that dress. If you do not. Fill in the blanks. Only one of you has live ammunition; you will not know which. The better not to feel guilt, or. In musicals, fascists dance in the streets.

12/6/98
"If you are fearful, you will be attacked, but it is possible to influence even the most difficult people, or improve the most difficult circumstance, through the power of universal truth." The other internet *I Ching*, more technical, refers to "buttocks" and "tree stumps"; that's the one my mother'd like, if not for its wisdom. Almost wrote "widow." Tomorrow she'll think of Pearl Harbor. "The War" is her retirement project, guilt for actions unmentioned. Except: I dropped a bag of popcorn at the movies and she refused to get me another. Digital means one or the other, he says. Empathy close to empty. Her Mama, grandmother who raised her, lifted Tom Thumb in her arms, the only adult she'd ever met smaller than she. Mama waved her arms to radio music, wanted to be a conductor. I have her copy of "Martha" somewhere. My mother Martha and her brother Joe were laughing at Mama's dinner table when she died of a stroke. My mother will not babysit for any grandchildren of her own.

9/6/99
Terminal analysis. Rode Amtrak from D.C. to New Haven beside a Frenchman. My nerves weren't right. Talk to me. February is the cruelest month. *Figurez-vous*. Both sides of your brain will work if you type your poems in.

For this is my terminal and these my words; not a process but a processor. The end is in sight. The end is insight, according to this model, though blindness often follows and we can't all be Tiresias. My parents were not home, that weekend of the shaken snowy paperweight. I called later to say something is wrong in my head. She came, "that awful weekend," up the New Jersey Turnpike, I-95, through Newark, Bridgeport, all the post-industrial coast, and took to a hotel bed. I brought her Chinese take-out for dinner.

9/13/99

A woman was crying. This child has been sexually abused; her mother uses ice. She is six years old and wants a loving family. She has written her note in crayon. What memory would you choose to end your afterlife? The cherry blossoms rain on an old woman reliving her ninth year. Cotton clouds screech on a cable past a single-wing airplane, suspended in the stale air of a film studio. This is just as it was! I found a barefoot girl in the parking lot of the Hilo Wal-Mart; her mother was inside shopping. Took her dirty hand and walked her to a clerk. How old are you? No answer. What is your name? No answer. Hers is the poetry of common sense, not philosophy. Of witness, the zen master on the street, at Auschwitz, in the barrio. The buildings at Ellis Island are empty; there are only photos of luggage, of immigrants, of the "mad" turned back after four minutes with a doctor. They look at you strangely. None of them were my ancestors; those came earlier, though my father didn't know. His parents' wedding photo, clothes so obviously borrowed, the unaccustomed fit of suit and wedding dress, a familiar asceticism. They lost three babies at birth.

10/2/99

The rinpoche stood on the lama's narrow bed, adjusting a yellow cloth across window blinds against the heat. "Don't drink tea or coffee in the evening," he said, "you have wind humor problems." His large fingers on my pulse, the young translator's slight English affect. Bry passed the prescription to Lama Rinchen; "I haven't a clue what it means," he laughed. Nor did he explain the fire puja. Anne said her husband's altar has too much *stuff* on it. Green Tara in our living room presides over our childlessness. His assistant eight months big, the dentist bonds my broken tooth, an experiment to see if the tooth can be saved. Yet we return to the same level of happiness, scientists say, as if it were the line on a carafe where the wine stops and air breathes, inebriate union of spirit with spirit. My eyelid still quivers from the novocaine.

> *In December of 1998 I began writing a prose journal from which I hoped to generate a memoir about my mother and my complicated relationship with her. As I recall, I began by writing down one of the many stories she told me growing up—stories about her experiences in North Africa, Italy and France during World War II, mainly. Over the following few months, I wrote over 200 pages, only to realize that I didn't have a prose memoir or anything that would ever become one. But when I compressed certain sections of the text into smaller sections, I arrived at a series of prose poems. I started sending out these prose poems to journals. But I didn't like the way they looked on the 8 ½ x 11 pages I was printing them on. They got lost on all that white space. So I wondered if I could fit the sections onto large index cards, using the deskjet printer that I had in my closet. Sure enough, most of the sections fit onto cards, and other sections benefited from the editing necessary to make them index card size. Once I started revising the larger prose pieces onto the cards, I stopped writing my prose "memoir," and took to writing card-size blocks instead (it's the first creative work that I've ever written first on the computer, as well). When I put the cards "in order" for publication, I do so by subject rather than by date. But the advantage of the cards is that they can be shuffled, their order changed in the way memory changes—arbitrarily, almost at random.*

Ron Silliman
from UNDER ALBANY

for Colin and Jesse, Later

There is no such place as the economy, the self.
If a lion could speak, it would talk very slowly. Civilization constructed of complex nouns for which no exact equivalent in nature can be found. Identity is composed of our response, passionate or ambivalent, to exactly such muddy notions. Reading *Poetry Flash* with the photograph of Barrett looking boyish and introspective, I remember someone (Kit? Alan? Steve?) saying aloud "It looks like we've been named."

That bird demonstrates the sky.
One way to view nature that incorporates both chance and change. Define the trail by that which is transient. Also, it's something Krishna and I both enjoy and at which neither (for once) is an expert. What is better than a northern flicker at the suet cake? The Virginia rail, perfectly still in the muddy reeds. The long parsed tail of the tropic bird. Once in a bed-and-breakfast, exhausted after a long day of seeking the worm eating warbler in a vacant lot in Davenport, Krishna had an ectopic pregnancy, the fallopian tube literally exploding, and nearly died.

Our home, we were told, had been broken, but who were these people we lived with?
My grandparents had no idea that they would ever be asked to raise a second family and my grandfather's lapsed Catholicism turned his own guilt into open disapproval at my mother's failed marriage. Also, he'd never raised boys and as the youngest in his own family, did not understand how one might nurture anyone younger. Eleven hundred square feet and two bedrooms did not divide easily into five people and three generations. As his hearing declined, he became quieter and quieter, a simmering, seething presence that never quite managed to erupt. My last two years of high school, I probably said

less than 100 words to the man. Six weeks after graduation, I was gone.

Clubbed in the stomach, she miscarried.
The whim of existence: my grandmother was the youngest of 13. Two years later, her father was dead. My parents would never have met without the geographic and social dislocations created by the Second World War. They almost certainly would not have married without the mutually damaged home situations each was escaping. My brother and I were each the result of failed birth control. Had my father remained at home, it is unlikely that I ever would have gone to college. Had my father remained at home, I would have learned to love camping and become good with weapons. If I had not grown up on the fringes of Berkeley, it is unlikely that I would have ever stumbled across William Carlos Williams (most Americans never do). Had it not been Berkeley, Shelly would never have arrived in search of a student movement. Had I not turned on the television, would I ever had discovered Zukofsky? Had I not been in New York on the literal day of the Gulf of Tonkin incident, would I have thought to have gotten a draft counselor early enough to have made a difference? Had I not been reading to the blind, would I have stopped in the classroom doorway at Boalt to listen to Fay Stender talking about the San Quentin Six case and would I, six months later, have thought to have sought my conscientious objector's slot with a prison movement group? Had I not had to take the bus to Sacramento so many early mornings, would I have ever walked past Hospitality House and stared in at its windows filled with street people artwork and thought, years after, to have sought a CETA job there? What if I had not stopped drinking? *What if Jon Arnold had not invented metalanguage in front of me, a ten year old boy, as though on his own?*

  I wrote this sentence thinking of David Mandel's sister-in-law, beaten at the Oakland Induction Center. Today I read the same sentence inside out.

There were bayonets on campus, cows in India, people shoplifting books.
One night, as the cops were approaching slowly in a vehicle that somehow spewed pepper fog, a particularly acrid and painful form of tear gas, as I was rushing with others to drag some saw horses from a nearby construction sight to create a blockade on Bancroft, I looked up to see that the person who was lifting the other end of the wooden beast was a fellow I'd known as a bully in highschool (he'd once, in

a fit of anger—I'd let a teacher who was a friend know that some students had obtained a copy of a forthcoming test—shoved me literally down a flight of stairs). Our eyes locked briefly and the air seemed full of the sounds of sirens, breaking glass, shouting people, rocks bouncing of all manner of surfaces and, more distant, the bullhorn of the first prowl car intoning that "this is an illegal assembly." We stared just long enough to realize what we were doing and who we were, then we rushed with the sawhorse (its yellow blinker flashing all the while) and hurled it atop the mounting pile of other debris. As the car approached, we could begin to smell the fog and dashed with the rest of the crowd back down the side street to the next instant of engagement. I never saw him again.

I just want to make it to lunch time.
A typical day at the office: I arrive a few minutes after the designated hour of eight, plug in my ThinkPad, unlock one or two of the eleven filing cabinets I use on a daily basis, and log on to one of two email systems. The first, a mainframe system called PROFS, also connects me to internal postings from a wide range of other IBM divisions and subsidiaries. If one or two postings from the hundred or so I will scan seems pertinent to our division, I will download it. After PROFS and Lotus Notes, I log onto the internet and scan headlines from a variety of news sources, including the New York Times, Washington Post, BusinessWire, Reuters and several computing journals (with special attention to *Computer Reseller News* and *Information Week*). By 10:00 or 10:30, I will have scanned between 500 and 700 articles, maybe taking note of six or eight. On some days at this point, I will begin (or continue) to work on a periodic email publication I write. On others, I will turn to research one of the inquiries I've received from other departments, executives, sales reps and managers in the field. An inquiry can take anywhere between five minutes and two weeks to complete. As details emerge during the day from these sources, I may update a series of ongoing presentation files.[1] Most often I use lunch to look at my hard copy mail—computer magazines, research reports, direct mail for events, the occasional invoice. The further each day proceeds, the more apt I am to be pulled into meetings, to conduct consultations for various departments, to embark on "out of the ordinary" projects. At least one hour over the day is given to talking to reps, managers and industry analysts about various "issues." There are always between six and ten of these in an ongoing state at any given moment. By 4:00, I begin to sense whether one or another will lend itself to a concentrated effort in the early evening,

once the secretaries and hourly workers depart around 5:30. If so, I plot it out and work until 7:00.

Uncritical of nationalist movements in the Third World.
The world is a system, complete.[2] In spite of Marx's comments about the impossibility of socialism in one country, the left has repeatedly rallied around attempts to set up just such a logical contradiction. Invariably these attempts fail—capital demonstrates its power to undermine any local effort, regardless of how well intentioned it might be. During the Cold War, the U.S. posture of isolating and threatening pockets of resistance, particularly those within what it imagined grandiosely to be have been its own sphere of influence, Asia and the Pacific, forced the smaller power to over-militarize. The most militaristic and least democratic groups within that nation were thus rewarded, promoted, reinforced.[3] The impact on the civilian populace was (also invariably) predictable. Instead of critiquing these deformations and supporting what were now dissident forces within these tiny countries, the U.S. left, stuck on a simplistic the-enemy-of-my-enemy kind of thinking, tended to excuse the excesses (the North Vietnamese hunt down and execute Trotskyists), even to imitate them at home.

Letting the dishes sit for a week.
I was raised in a world in which the dinner was always on time and always predicted: on Friday there would be fish sticks. Even now, over 30 years after leaving home, I am torn—always—by the desire for intense order and its exact opposite.

Macho culture of convicts.
Because her former husband, a San Francisco beat cop, had on more than one occasion tailed her off-duty and at least once come to her job to ask her supervisor if they knew that she was involved with "revolutionaries," Marti's gone to court to get a restraining order. The irony was that her fling with Wilbur "Popeye" Jackson, the head of the nominally Maoist United Prisoners Union (UPU), had been short lived. What lasted was her distrust of the police, which Jackson shared but hardly had created.

The UPU had splintered off from the larger Prisoners Union in 1970 after a meeting to which, it was rumored, both sides brought guns. The Prisoners Union's goals were clear, defined and in retrospect relatively modest. It did not seek an end to prisons, nor critique the social concept of incarceration, but wanted to define and defend the civil rights of prisoners both in the joint and afterward. Focusing on eliminating the byzantine vagaries of the indeterminate sentence as a primary goal, the Prisoners Union was largely composed of white ex-cons, led by Willie Holder, a classic Okie robber who looked and sounded like a wizened version of the musician Willie Nelson. Also around were John Irwin, a 50s era robber who'd gone on to become a sociology professor at San Francisco State, Frank Smith, a literate one-time drug dealer and kidnapper—surprisingly gentle and good-willed given his biker-qua-mountain-man persona—and Roney Nunes, who'd served time in the midwest for a crime that he'd later proven he had not committed only to pull off a bungled robbery in California for which he'd done a few years. Other than Willie's wife Patty, the Union in the early 70s had almost no women in positions of authority. Deftly using the credibility of Irwin, the persistence of Holder, and the reasoning skills of Smith, the Prisoners Union had gotten the ear of several legislators, some lawyers (notably Jim Smith and Michael Snedecker) and had received the gift of a large but rundown building on San Francisco's Potrero Hill from an elderly sympathizer. Holder and his wife lived upstairs (always with a few recent parolees and occasionally someone like Snedecker who's choices as a lawyer kept him as close to a street person as a practicing advocate could be).

The UPU stood in sharp contrast with its leadership focused entirely on the charismatic nature of Jackson, an African American from rural Louisiana with the thickest accent I'd ever heard. Off the record, the Prisoners Union's rap on Jackson was that he'd been a snitch in the joint and was an empty-headed idiot interested only in sex with white women and ripping off the Stanford students of the Venceremos Brigade who helped to fund his organization. The UPU's position on the Prisoners Union was that it was run by hillbilly white racists, one step removed from the Aryan Brotherhood,[4] who were using their connections to liberal politicians to angle for grants. The UPU argued that all felons were involved in class war whether they understood it as such or not and that band-aid measures like administrative due process in internal disciplinary procedures or the replacement of the indeterminate sentence by a more systematic (and thereby more "fair") structure of penalties for crimes only served to strengthen the system and slow the progress toward a necessary revolution that would be led not by college-trained leftists, but by former prisoners who had had direct experience within "the belly of the beast."

I had friends in both organizations although relatively few seemed to understand what I thought I was doing working in the prison movement. (In 1976, Holder, who by then had known me for five years, asked me "well, just what did you serve time for?") In 1972, when I began working with CPHJ, it had been clear to me for at least two years that no revolution was even remotely in the offing in the United States and I had no illusions that the working class people of Concord or Alamo or anywhere were about to follow somebody whosr greatest accomplishment may have been a bungled liquor store robbery.

Still, it was (and is) true that economic crime carries within it a domain of the irrational that was and always will be about class. The women around the UPU were neither idiots nor dupes; they were some of the most intelligent people I would ever meet in the prison movement. For the most part they all came from the very lowest fringes of the working class—a position with which I immediately identified—and some would go on to significant careers as lawyers and private eyes.

Popeye was another matter. A shrewd political thinker with a mercurial temper, he played all sides against one another, even within his own organization, which recycled people in purges and counter-purges. One time Marti asked me to help her move from her apartment in the Mission, a move dictated by Popeye after it had decided that there must be FBI infiltrators in the group.[5] Each of the collective houses and apartments that UPU members shared were to be broken up as they were to find housing with people outside the movement altogether. When I arrived at Marti's apartment, there were guns on the kitchen table, set there just so people would feel comfortable enough to cooperate in getting a couch down a flight of stairs.

Marti soon left not only the organization but the Bay Area, settling in the Sierra foothills in hopes that her husband would not find her. Two years later, Popeye Jackson was murdered in the front seat of his car, parked in front of his apartment on Albion Street in San Francisco. Shot alongside him was a young schoolteacher from the Contra Costa suburbs who'd been active with the UPU for only a few weeks.

With a shotgun and "in defense" the officer shot him in the face.

If one has a shotgun, defense purposes do not require you to aim at the head of the other party. This was the report given in the media concerning the capture of a bank robber, treated as though without question or controversy.

Here, for a moment, we are joined.

It took me, it seems, forever to reach out to your mother. Peggy had moved out of the flat on San Jose Avenue in the Mission District some six months before, after which I'd had a short and profoundly unfulfilling relationship with an Australian painter and performance artist, Jill Scott.

I had worked for a year on an ethnography of the Tenderloin for Central City Hospitality House. The project team needed an administrator, having hired one only to have him quit in a huff and hurry, so were delighted when I literally walked in one day, able to handle that work, edit the final report and interview the one neighborhood group the two primary researchers, Toby Marotta and Clark Taylor, felt nervous about—ex-felons. Marotta and Taylor were interested in the Tenderloin's gay history, but it was the entire community that was to be described by the project. By design, two members of the team were neighborhood residents, one of whom, Dorothy Rutherford, a one-time fashion model and one of the last true hippies, had promptly moved herself and her four-year-old son out to Bernal Heights where she shared a flat with two other women who worked at the agency, Kathy Ryan and Krishna Evans. At the time, Ms. Evans directed the arts program on the agency's main floor, a large open studio crafts and fine arts workshop that funded itself by asking participants to make two of anything they worked on and to donate one item for sale through a "store" that consisted of the agency's Leavenworth Street windows.

She had impossibly thick, long black hair with just the slightest threading of silver, which she wore pulled back in a failed attempt to look plain. She wore oversized army pants and tank top t-shirts, never with a bra. More important, she had (has) the most complete smile I have ever seen.[6] Although our programs only occasionally had direct business with one another, it was evident that she was a passionate administrator who cared deeply about her students and took her job with absolute seriousness. She was capable of great theater in staff meetings, raging out, slamming the door behind her. Once, the director of the drop-in center upstairs, a man who often came to work smelling of wine, pawed a high school coed who was interning in the arts program. Krishna walked up to him, flattened him with a single punch (several metal folding chairs crashing out of the way as he falls backward). She stormed upstairs to the executive director's office and got the man fired on the spot.

Because Hospitality House defined itself as a place open to anyone, regardless of how marginal, the various floors were always full of street people, runaways, ex-cons, drag queens, psychotics, confused post-docs, alcoholics, junkies, the works. For awhile, our receptionist was Jerry-Diane, a pre-op transsexual whose goal in life was to become a lesbian. It was, and I mean this literally, the finest working environment I have ever had, can ever imagine having.

Early on in my tenure with the ethnographic project, Peg and I had been invited over for brunch to the house on Bernal Heights, along with several other HH staffers. The house on Winfield Street was a rambling Victorian set high into the hillside. I remember the weather that day as perfect and a sense of life there as almost utopian. In retrospect, I'm sure what that meant was that I was attracted to all three of the women who lived there. It was already apparent to both Peggy and me that this latest attempt to construct a relationship was proving a disaster.

Once or twice a week after work, Dorothy, Krishna and I, occasionally with one or two other members of the staff, would head over to Harrington's, a cavernous Irish pub only a block from HH, where we'd sit, drinking watery draft beer or gin and tonics, eating hotdogs and popcorn, talking office politics for hours. Dorothy, who'd lived for several years in Spain and several full grown sons there, often brought along her four-year-old boy, Jose.

Once, at an agency picnic, I sat on the grass and Krishna (without asking, without being asked) lay back to put her head in my lap. My heart raced a million miles. Another time, one of the neighborhood men, Eugeia Shaw, celebrated his 25th birthday at a Castro Street pizza parlor, after which Krishna and I took the longest of walks back through the mission. She pointed out Hungadunga, which had been the leading commune in the free food family and where she'd had several friends and a few lovers.

I had a prohibition in my head about sleeping with my co-workers. I was insecure enough about employment generally to feel that some crossing of the boundaries like that would certainly make life crazy. Although I'd more than a few unrequited crushes on women in other organizations of the prison movement, I'd virtually fled the apartment of Jeanne Baker, a young single mother who volunteered for CPHJ, not because I wasn't attracted, but because I was.

When the ethnographic project came to an end with the publication of "TERP Report," the five of us on the project were duly laid off. I'd already proposed to Claudia Viek, the executive director of Hospitality House, that what the neighborhood needed, more than anything else, was a positive self-image. Some of the folks in the upstairs drop-in center had started a mimeographed publication called the *Tenderloin Times*. They'd published three issues with runs of about 150 each, until somebody on the board discovered a recipe for mistletoe tea and had flipped at the idea of the toxic possibilities. I'd suggested that I could take over the paper, turn it into a real neighborhood paper just like the *Bernal Journal* or *Potrero View*, and sell enough advertising to cover the printing costs. Since that wouldn't provide enough work (or cash) to make a real job out of the position, I suggested that I run a writers workshop, trying to get funding from the California Arts Council for that, and that I also work on housing issues in the neighborhood with funding from the agency itself.

I felt ambivalent about the idea. Krishna had given me several hints that, if she ever broke up with her current boyfriend, an itinerant and seldom-employed rock musician who periodically went by the name Random Chance, she'd be available and was interested. We'd ride buses to the Haight after work (she on her way to class at USF, me on my way to the Grand Piano) and increasingly our conversations turned to relationships and what each of us was seeking. We never actually said out loud that it was each other we were talking about.

It was apparent that this woman was brilliant, beautiful, had a sense of the arts (she'd studied ballet with Balanchine and Cunningham), was committed to her work and the people of the neighborhood she served. A cousin of hers, Julie Garrett, was visiting San Francisco and would come to the Writers Workshop, hanging around afterwards to ride on the Mission Street bus with me. Julie would tell me, at length, that Krishna was interested in me, but was afraid that I might be too intellectual. At other times, Dorothy and Steve Brady also dropped similar hints.

Peggy had long since returned from Georgia and the abortion, moving to an apartment directly across the street from the one we'd shared on San Jose Avenue. "If I'm the one who moves," she said, "I won't feel like I was the one who was dumped." I moped around for a few weeks, then, at a music performance at Mills, I ran into an Australian artist by the name of Jill Scott I knew very slightly through Carla Harryman. Jill and I talked and later I ran into her again after a performance in the City. We got involved soon after, although it devolved almost instantly. I was looking for a relationship and she absolutely seemed terrified by the idea. I was restless.

A month after the job at the Ethnographic Project ended, one of the administrators at HH quit, leaving a small, part-time salary. Claudia called and asked me to start work on the new position, waiting until we heard from the Arts Council to pick up the other segments. The truth was, I hadn't even begun to look for another job yet. Instead, I'd spent the month watching the relationship with Jill devolve, had done a performance I'd been thinking about for a year at least, reading all of *Ketjak* aloud on the steps of the Bank of America branch at Powell and Market Streets, three days after which I had had a tooth extracted. The oral surgeon had told me I would need a ride home afterwards, so I'd asked Dorothy, one of the few people I knew who owned a car (a clunker that cost maybe $200). As I'd woken groggy from the anesthesia, Krishna stood over me, explaining ex post facto that she thought it would be "fun to help."

I accepted the position.

One evening six weeks later, on my way to Bruce Boone's for a meeting of the Marxist study group that we were in together, a young woman next to me on the Mission Street bus asked about the book I was reading, Georg Lukács' *History and Class Consciousness*. I'd been writing notes in the margins and underlining passages in several different colors of ink.[7] She nodded as I explained what I was doing, asked who Lukács was, and, after she "debussed," suddenly ran back up to my window shouting her phone number. I called the next day and we went to lunch at Knight's on Golden Gate Avenue, a giant old-style cafeteria that catered to the City Hall and lawyer set. Laura was working as a legal secretary for Charles Garry, a criminal defense specialist I knew slightly from my work at CPHJ, but thought of herself as a folk singer between gigs. "Before gigs," she corrected herself, laughing.

As we ate and I slowly began to realize that the excitement of a chance encounter on the bus hadn't led to any sort of miracle, in walked Dan White with a couple of his aides. White had just resigned from his position as a San Francisco County Supervisor, unable to make ends meet on his $9,000 a year salary—I could hardly blame him—but had just changed his mind and was trying in vain to convince Mayor Moscone to re-appoint him to his same old seat. White had been in the headlines for weeks and I was surprised that Laura didn't seem to know who he was.

It was only a day or so later that, as I attended a political conference at Horace Mann School in the Mission, I first heard of the massacre at Jonestown. Garry was down in Guyana representing Jim Jones, the charismatic San Francisco preacher who'd become increasingly paranoid and hostile, leading his congregation literally into the jungle. He'd arranged for a visit by Leo Ryan, a Congressman from San Mateo County and a former paper member of the CPHJ board. Among Ryan's entourage was a photographer from the *San Francisco Examiner*, Greg Robinson, who'd recently finished doing a feature on Krishna's program at HH. Both were killed in the attack on the visitors at the airstrip as they'd attempted to depart. As Jones and his followers began to drink poisoned Kool-Aid, Garry slipped into the woods to hide. In a matter of an hour, over 900 people were dead.

I felt sick the minute I heard the first details. Like anyone on the left in San Francisco, I'd run into People's Temple members dozens, perhaps hundreds of times, usually helping out with the Saturday precinct work alongside the New American Movement, DSOC and the unions. Ryan, a former schoolteacher who'd once spent a week "undercover" in prison just to get a feel for the environment (and not part of a media grandstanding stunt), was that rare individual, someone motivated into politics by the idea of accomplishing something.

The next week was Thanksgiving. I found myself in that tortured state of needing to read every word in the media about Jonestown, feeling increasingly nauseated the more I read. On Monday or Tuesday, Dorothy, who was again temping at HH, came down to my office to say that she, Krishna and Kathy were going to have a meal of Thanksgiving leftovers on Friday and did I want to join them? She may have invited me to Thanksgiving itself, but I was already committed to my mother's. A day later, Dorothy again dropped by to say that she and Kathy were planning to go to the movies later that night "so that it will just be you and Krishna, if that's okay." More than a little amused by the transparency of this set-up, I accepted.

The next two days gave me time to think. I'd had what seemed excellent reasons not to get involved with Krishna. There was the work taboo. She was, she said, still involved to some degree with this musician, although she'd also hinted on several occasions that she was looking to move on. As it stood, our relationship wasn't predicated on my life as a poet. Peg had been the first woman in my life for whom that had not been, if not the paramount fact about me, at least an important one. And Peg had been jealous of my writing in a way that had surprised me. If Barbara had been merely envious of the relative success I'd had publishing, a competitive envy, Peggy saw my writing as a relationship in itself, one that would prevent her from ever establishing the sort of balance between us she imagined herself to be seeking. It was impossible to know in advance how Krishna would feel about that. There was no question that I found Krishna desirable and fabulous, but there was also a side of me so anxious I could (rather like a cat) spit. I'd seen her at work under the hectic and often harsh conditions of that environment, dealing with crazies, street people, seniors, city bureaucrats, inept board members, the corporate types on the United Way review committee. On one occasion a client tried to kill her, attempting to ram her with a ladder—she remained magically calm under the threat, turned by the event into pure concentration itself, never once allowing her assaulter to imagine himself in control, talking him into a form of submission while I and John Denning, an art teacher, physically stopped the ladder each time this speed-crazed young man roared forward.[8] I'd also seen a harder side at work also, the flashing temper and take-no-prisoners insistence on honesty. Unlike my situation with Jill, where I'd hopped into bed with no hesitation, knowing that there would be few lasting consequences if it didn't work out,[9] I could sense that Krishna would be exactly the opposite. If I got involved, it would have to be all the way.

On Friday at dusk, I walked the mile from the apartment I now shared with Fred Glass over to Krishna's. An index of my anxiety and sense of anticipation that evening is that I can still recall the precise quality of twilight along Mission as I walked, stopping once or twice to write down sentences in a notebook that would later find their way into *Tjanting*. It was a beautiful clear evening, oddly balmy for San Francisco in November. The steep climb up Virginia Street to Winfield, and the ever steeper climb up Winfield, seemed to stretch out forever (I'd only made the trip once or twice before, so wasn't yet familiar with every step).

Dorothy and Kathy wolfed down their dinners, a moist and well-stuffed turkey, and started to head out the door to a movie. But there was a catch—cousin Julie, who had become a semi-permanent house guest, staying in a room nominally devoted to weaving equipment, decided (I forget why) not to go along, even though Dorothy and Kathy offered to pay her way. Given the layout of the house, two tiny bedrooms by the front door, beyond which was a huge, central kitchen, with a dark, windowless alcove that nominally served as the living room, stairs up to an attic-like loft that was Dorothy's space, and on the other side the room that had become Julie's space all focused around a large, round kitchen table, there was virtually no way to be in the house without being in Julie's presence, unless Krishna and I were to retire to her bedroom (too loaded with anticipation, lust and symbolism) or Julie were to retire to hers (too clueless to figure this out).[10] So we sat around the table and talked for several hours. I have no memory whatsoever what about.

At midnight, I noted the time and Krishna suggested that the two of us walk around the top of Bernal Hill, a rare blister of open space in San Francisco, topped with a huge microwave dish for the phone company. Although three of the most economically depressed housing projects are within a short walk of this mile-long unlit, half-paved circular road, we thought nothing of heading off into the darkness on that warm night and found only two or three cars with teenage couples parked overlooking the Mission. We walked slowly and talked, although even at this point we did not touch. I could sense from Krishna's body language that she wanted me to reach over to her, but that she wouldn't or couldn't do that herself. My mind was racing a million miles an hour as I remembered every reason why I did or didn't want to act. Eventually we got back to her front stairs, where we paused silently for what seemed like minutes.

"Would you like to come in for tea?"

"Why not?" Trying to sound casual. In fact, it is only now that I realize I've decided, not so much that I've made a decision but rather that I recognize a decision I've arrived at on some level almost inaccessible to me.

Inside again, I'm immediately relieved to discover that Julie has finally gone to bed. Kathy and Dorothy are still out, but for how long? For the moment at least, we're alone in the kitchen. Krishna moves to brush past me to put a kettle on for tea and I reach out my arms, palms up. She takes my hands and without the slightest hesitation sits in my lap, which surprises me but feels wonderful. We kiss.

"So what are your intentions?"

"Why don't we discuss this in your bedroom?"

Eventually, that is exactly what we do, another long conversation, only now at least it is Krishna who is being infinitely cautious, hesitant about going forward. Her reaction to my reaching out is more one of relief than desire. I'm trying very hard to understand and read these subtle signs. Already we've crossed over emotional boundaries we won't ever be able to re-erect. I want to make love, but she's not ready, she says. "Let's just sleep." So we do, me entirely naked, her still in tank top and blue jeans.

At dawn or just before, I wake and lean over and kiss her gently. She's awake also, although maybe I don't realize this at first. Without a word, she slowly rises and stands over me on the narrow bed, removing her clothes. This is the closest thing to a vision I will ever have.

We make love twice, taking almost until noon to finish. When we finally stumble toward the kitchen, Kathy and Dorothy are at the table, laughing that they'd gotten up in the morning, realized I must still be there and had headed out of the house to give us privacy. They've returned hours later post-brunch and we're still in bed and they'd begun to wonder if we would ever rise. We eat a cursory breakfast and say very little. We're exhausted and shy and exhilarated. I feel as though I've used a lifetime of adrenaline—it would be easy to hallucinate. After the meal settles us down somewhat, we walk very casually back to my apartment on San Jose where we spend the afternoon in bed.

It is only because I've promised to attend a book party at Geoff Young's in Berkeley that I ever really rise at all that day, at dusk, because Tom Mandel's coming by to give me a ride. Krishna and I dress and we sit on my minuscule back porch overlooking the minuscule Poplar Alley until the bell rings. As Krishna says good bye and heads up the hill, Tom looks at my poor dazed expression and says, "What hit you?"

It would make sense, narratively, to stop right here, but life is not a plot. On Monday morning, I wake and rise at Krishna's. We decide (or maybe it's Krishna who decided this) that she should go into work first and that we shouldn't arrive together. Later, as I'm riding the Mission bus down past DuBoce, somebody who's been playing a boom box turns the volume full blast. I hear the words "Mayor Moscone and Supervisor Harvey Milk have been shot and are presumed dead this morning at City Hall," and then the sound is turned back down again. No further explanation. The words sound completely foreign and meaningless at first. I've known George Moscone since I first worked for CPHJ and he sat on the Senate Judiciary Committee. I've known Harvey Milk because everyone in San Francisco knew Harvey Milk. In a moment the bus turns onto Van Ness and when it reaches City Hall, I get off. I walk inside past no security whatsoever and see Bill Kraus, Harvey's aide and a DSOC activist, red-eyed, talking to a crowd. Rudy Nothenberg, one of Moscone's assistants, is running full tilt up the broad stairs. Police are everywhere. TV cameras are everywhere. Why am I here?

I walk outside again, down Golden Gate Avenue two blocks and the one block up Leavenworth to Hospitality House. As always, the step from the brilliant sunlight of the street (made all the more stark by these treeless Tenderloin stucco facades) into the shadows of the arts center is almost blinding. I wait for my eyes to adjust to the dark. Nobody's working—everyone is just standing around, talking. They've already heard. I remembered seeing flowers already sprinkled on the steps of City Hall as I'd left and I suggest that we should buy some also and take them there. Several of us head out to purchase roses from a street vendor near Harrington's. By now City Hall is secured and closed, so we stand around the broad stairs, Krishna and I and Dorothy and Spider and I don't remember who else. It's a beautiful sunny afternoon. It's a terrible day. The headlines in the newspaper boxes are still filled with Jonestown.

Krishna had already planned to leave the following weekend for Baltimore and Virginia where a sister is getting married. It feels as if we spend the week itself attending one memorial service after another. It's an insane time and I feel wildly out of sync to be so intensely aroused and pleased every single minute of it. The morning she flies off we stand at the top of the Esmerelda Steps, one of the great secret views of the city, not long after sunrise, talking about how we'll write to one another.[11] We already know (have known for months) that talk, casual, intimate, intelligent conversation, will be an important form for us. It will be a long time before many other important things occur. Over four years, for example, before either one of us really settles into monogamy. Another six before I stop drinking. Eight before we marry. Eleven before Krishna nearly dies from an ectopic pregnancy. Twelve before I begin to go blind from cataracts. Thirteen before you are born. Sixteen before we all move to Pennsylvania. But in more ways than an individual could hope to understand, the logic that leads through each of those events was already implicit (though not inherent) the instant I said yes to a cup of tea. I crossed a line in my life from which I have never stepped back.

This, in a sense, is the exact opposite of telos, but rather a recognition that choice is central to freedom. With both its intended and unintended consequences.

I remember a day fourteen years earlier when, 17 years old, my highschool flat-top just starting to grow out, I was walking through Newport, RI, wondering what to do in the next 48 hours when the annual folk festival would begin and my room at the local "Y" would go instead to someone with a reservation. I looked to the left as I crossed the intersection, noticed a small coffeehouse and thought to walk in. Asking to speak to the manager, I inquired if they needed any assistance for the festival week and that I'd happily accept meals and a place to sleep. Can you perform, I was asked. I lied, saying that I could do stand-up comedy. I only had to do one set during the week, possibly because I was dreadful at it.[12] But this was enough not only to give me shelter, literally a palette on the floor, but also access to some backstage parties connected to the festival. Which was how I found myself sitting next to Bob Dylan on a couch one night as he and Paul Stookey and Sebastian Dangerfield improvised a version of "King Bee." I'd never heard of the British rock group whose record Buffy Sainte-Marie told me this song had been found on, but sensed that I was being given the most privileged of "inside" information. What if, I thought to myself, I hadn't looked to the left when I'd crossed that street?

That night in 1978, with Krishna already thousands of miles away, I'm walking alone through a human sea of candles in the shabby urban park in front of City Hall, hyper-conscious in this first separation that the same dynamics are now being played out in my life on a whole other scale. I'm overwhelmed by all of the visible grief I see around me in this memorial rally held both for the assassinations and the mass suicide in Guyana. And I'm overwhelmed by the vertigo of love. I understand already that I'm involved far more than I've ever been before, that I've arrived at a whole new level of risk. So the same thought recurs: *What if?* And, *How much courage will I have to see this through?* On a stage mounted over the City Hall steps, Joan Baez is singing *Amazing Grace.*

The want-ads lie strewn on the table.
It is not possible to "describe a life."

1. An example: every Tuesday afternoon I update a series of charts that track the stock performance of several companies that perform desktop services.

2. As has been increasingly evident, the state itself is merely a convenience. Capital and its latest expression, "information," are more powerful and fundamentally stateless phenomena. The creation of the European Union is itself a desperate attempt for several governments, formerly "world powers," to reimagine themselves as relevant.

3. The same strategy domestically was carried out under the banner of Cointelpro.

4. One or two of the ex-cons who cycled briefly through the Prisoners Union went on to people local Klan groups.

5. This was absolutely the case. Sara Jane Moore was revealed as an informant after her attempted assassination of Gerald Ford. The FBI wanted to know why my phone number at CPHJ was in her address book.

6. This same smile, Colin, appears miraculously on your own shining face.

7. Looking at the book today, I see, on the inside front cover, in a black box, "Opacity 159." In orange, above, "Art begets dialects begets history 137-145." In red, below, "The production of new needs = the accumulation of <u>SURPLUS VALUE</u> 180!" In blue, to the right, "Aura as a bourgeois (unmediated) element in art 158!"

8. What had set Eric, an unemployed African American with a family crammed into a small hotel room on Mason Street, off was another HH client who'd called him nigger. *The staff in the upstairs drop-in center had rescued that idiot, but had done so by diverting Eric, who was literally exploding with anger and meth-amphetamine, down to the arts floor where he'd gone after the first white person he saw, Krishna. As 50 or so people surrounded us, it was evident that Eric was, in the eyes of many, the victim in this scenario, so that Krishna, John and I all understood that we needed to resolve the circumstance* not only without anyone getting hurt, but without Eric getting arrested either. Around the corner, out of sight, the SF police waited it out, which took a good two hours. They thought we were crazy. But it ended with Eric going out with John and me for a cup of coffee to talk about why anger and speed mixed badly.

9. It would be another three-plus years before city housing specialist Dick Gamble, the first AIDS victim in my circle, began to grow thin and pale.

10. Worse yet, there was a downstairs apartment, a small separate unit, in which the erstwhile-musician/boyfriend lived!

11. I will send her a letter that takes up the whole of a Chinese notebook, a favorite form of mine in the mid-70s, which she still has somewhere. She writes me a long detailed description of the wedding.

12 I plagiarized my material from the dim memory of an old Alan Sherman record.

Jeanne Silverthorne

Palm with Fragments, 1999
rubber, 27.5" x 24" x 4"
Courtesy of McKee Gallery.

Sweat Pore, 1999
rubber, 35" x 40" x 9.5"
Courtesy of McKee Gallery.

Sweat Beads, 1998
rubber, 21.5" x 26" x 5"
Courtesy of McKee Gallery.

Caroline Sinavaiana-Gabbard
GRANNY

—for Caroline Bartley

It's twilight in 1961, and there's honeysuckle drifting from the carport. I see you sitting cross-legged in the half light on the front walkway of that house on Willard road, twin stars tattooed on your thighs, dark and bright too in the almost night. Smoking away on your pipe, your face is a quiet, gentle resting place: Samoan Granny buddha in the Florida pines. Who did your star tattoos? They didn't look Polynesian, but more like the ones from Old Glory. Were they in honor of your son being a military man in that strange country?

I think of you now, all these years later when I'm nearing the age you might have been then. I was probably coming home from cheerleader practice, dragging my sack of lumpy guilts at feeling ashamed to have a grandmother who didn't speak English, did smoke a pipe and did have stars tattooed on her legs. My teenaged trying-to-fit-into America self back home from another day at Choctawhatchee High School wondering where (and who) the hell I was anyway. It seemed like cheerleading might give a clue, a stamp on my dubious visa into the white side of town where we somehow found ourselves, despite having brown skin and hair that teetered on the edge of nappy.

Now at 50 and far away from those bayou confusions, I think of you and wish I could have kept you better company. I would ask you about being a young girl in Samoa. How you met up with your husband, the American sailor. And how it was for you when he died young and left you with 3 kids, my dad the oldest at 11 who then became the man of the family. How it was when you found out that you wouldn't be getting your widow's pension from the US Navy, because your husband had another wife and kids back in Oklahoma which meant they'd get the pension and not you, the other so-called wife and kids living impossibly far away on some south seas island or another.

I would ask you how you managed that one. And what you thought of 30 years later finding yourself in a small southern town 8000 miles from home, your son all grown with 7 kids, a wife, and two jobs at the air base. And what you thought of that time in Texas on our long drive east, when the restaurant man told your light-skinned son that his colored wife and kids couldn't come in. How you felt having only two people you could talk to in that world, after teachers told mom and dad they must speak only English to their kids if they wanted us to succeed in America. And so they did, and sure enough we succeeded in Amerika more or less, except that we couldn't talk with you granny, and it must have been lonely. For you and for us.

But we all turned out okay anyway, Granny, thanks to you and the good man you raised up as a son and the woman he married. Now that you've been gone these long years, and I've been around some blocks one too many times, I can only send you a few words and imagine what you might say. I teach school on a beautiful island near Samoa. I get to read and talk a lot about stories and books with my students. One of our favorites is the one about how you made your way around all those huge boulders standing between you and some decent life for your kids in this weird upside down world. We talk about different ways to be brave, to keep going, to keep talking with whatever words are handy, even no words at all, to keep talking story no matter what, to keep passing it on. You would like my students, Granny. They're bright and funny, and they shine like stars tattooed on the almost goodnight sky.

Christina Olson Spiesel

The stationery is pale peach with an embossed poodle in the upper left corner, its nose, paws, and tail gilded. It is hand written in pencil, numbered with roman numerals dated 11-22-54.

Dear Mrs. Berry,

My mother told me last night that you didn't want me to ride with you anymore. I don't care, but I do not like being accused of saying something that I didn't say. I never made any remark to you or to your family about disapproving of the army, navey, marines, or air force (sics). Or for that matter about any defence (sic) job at all. Why should I? My father want to U.C.L.A. and he was in the army. Please don't get me wrong I am not accusing you of being a liar.

I admit that I have made a few sarcastic remarks at Dorine.

I tried at first to be friends with her but she was never nice to me. I am especially sorry for that remark the day I was so late, but I didn't know that he had to leave early. I am usually very tired at night and I have a difficulty in going to sleep. So when I get up in the morning I am still tired. I truely (sic) wish that I could have seen the rest of your stamp collection.

Mama mentioned that Dorine had mentioned about me bragging about my grades. Mr. Barry (sic) asked us what we had all gotten. We all told. He had also asked about my earlier school grades.

Whenever I get good grades somebody always resents me for it.

I don't know if Dorine mentioned the dressing rooms at school or not. You see we were three in a dressing room. It was just too crowded. Dorine took it upon herself to move in with a girl who wasn't sharing a dressing room with anybody. We didn't kick her out!

I wrote this letter of my own accord, please forgive me. Please don't show this letter to Dorine!
Sincerely,

Chris Olson

P.S. I was going to quite (sic) going with you anyway because of Dorinne (sic).

198

Inkjet paper, Epson printer.

11-22-99

I was twelve in 1954.

The envelope had a typed address. Was I trying to fool Mrs. Berry into opening it because I thought she'd never read a letter from a child?

It was never sent. My mother purloined it. She was right to do so. It would not have helped at all to have sent it but I am curious. Why did she keep it and give it to me years later? What did she have in mind?

Mother was always constructing history. Every object in her home had its story and when she died, the narrative was literally broken as we dismantled her place. It is hard to ask the small yellow jar with the chick painted on it to contain the life but what to do with it when it was full of years gathered on her kitchen counter?

One of the last things my mother ever asked of me before she died was to write the story of our family. It was her agenda, not mine, and I thought it was odd for her to ask. It wasn't a happy history from inside, and like all families, it would involve secrets. I notice things—like how empty the streets were in the pictures of my father's boyhood Rockford and how the camera was used to invent a story in 1939 in a home movie of youthful love. The young men were eating living fish from the lake to impress the girls—that was when my mother and her sister seemed still to be friends. The camera made these memories mine.

In the sixth grade I appeared on "Art Linkletter" and told the TV viewing world that I thought the country would be fine if the communists didn't get in.

I wonder now if Mr. or Mrs. Berry saw my father called a "breezy witness" in the newspaper after he appeared before the HUAC. He wasn't a revolutionary. He wanted a fair shake for working people and he thought it odd that persons of Greek descent weren't admitted to his fraternity. The only politics I remember from early childhood was campaigning with my mother for Roosevelt in his last race when I was two; I would pull on the pants legs of workers hurrying out of Douglas Aircraft at the shift change, a blond smiler trying to shove a paper into their hands.

And another thing . . .

Christina Olson Spiesel

Edwin Torres
BIRTHDAY PRESENT; BIRTHDAY BOY

{*these are the visual neccesities*} That which *was*
co-mingles—in sleep stupor; the following:
A white box, being carried by a perfect boy
in a white shirt—wishing; I were the boy
Or just the perfect; or maybe the shirt
inside the white box; giving me, the box of boy inside

Co; Mingling {*this is the vision*} the sleeves, to fit the box
so the boy—to fit the box, would fold my sleeves
To fit myself *inside* the shirt; so the boy
my classmate; a toy party; given—to me
The *perfect* boy in slo-motion {*the visual appears*}
the white box, glaring in the sun; I see him

Holding as it opens; to me {*I seem to reveal*} the white shirt inside
he is wearing; the white shirt box—inside, is a boy of me
Wearing what I am revealing; at my birth; my day; my toy party
my father {*this is what appears*} in my father's
Slow-motion *giving* of my party; standing over me—"Now,
what do you say, to the boy who gives you everything"

"Thank You"; he strides long strides—but not as long
as mine would become {*out of the picture*} he goes,
Thank you, or no; {*force of habit*} already, there is only me
and the boy now; glowing {*out there—in this vision*} his perfect shirt
Catching sun; in slow motion, the picture perfect white shirt
boy; as he glows to me—I take his hand, or hit him {*I am*

Unclear at this} but now; I am the window
looking down from three flights, before this all
Has happened; I am looking, still perfect—I see
the station wagon pull up; the boy comes out, wearing
A white shirt that glows; brighter than the sunshine
of my birthday party; the first to arrive

This poem was the memory caught as it came. A recollection which would surface, in and out of consciousness since my childhood, until ready to be caught by adulthood. As I let the brain process what is, initially, a faint discovery . . . the images clarify in slow motion—like a movie where you are the star of the super 8 jittery. What surrounds you gives way to a stronger need for closure. The recurring shift of the poem as a run-on sentence—obscured by the presence of the recollector.

Anne Waldman
SAVE MY DOCKAGE

—for Mark Sikelianos

1/ ma mere

just married   flower not in her hair in his lapel   ship just visible see him of a sailing on the deck light   blade edge of structure just visible   her of profusion of hair or feeling   was she?   just in from Christ Science   night signals   porcelain insulators   repeat the color of clouds   in cranial mist   make out my character   long before you are born   make out her young hunger   places to grow to   third pylon   number of sea birds   arrivals   peninsulas   I am that she could be   she is that I could be completed by her   not him I like him a first husband   the Greek connection   to fame to sanctification   to a face   heat-shimmer   sex-shimmer   shy stevedore   tugboat   a male-angel   her face has all of control & eye contact   irony I see   I see his hunger   a little dejected   son of the poet   face mirrors of two beings   glare   I am still in their thrall   first love second love tattered skirt   passive eye   from now on you will weave your own garments   & eye but gaze a realm   look on   stir   isolation before it is born in her   wings like a flapper   Isadora will lead you a beautiful Greek arm made to dance   outdoors   first born   limited to layers of clarity   all made up where seeing   is ancient   mimesis blink fend off sleep   that I will start making plans   no betrayal   bow of his lips   send them into the distance   10 years a throw off   10 years plus more an inner working   watch   collar   zipper perspicacity   pointed breasts   hand in a pocket   speak what you see leaning   shade   young people of the world   embark   touch the shapes   "don't go"   before the hydrogen bomb   can you imagine that is my birthday   arise   I was never without a bomb in my life and she?   nautical miles   realm of indigo   no contempt   just starting out a drop out   she got bored   artist   now a daughter-in-law   learns another language forever goodbye Vassar   the Greek connection   sea is blue   snake of the sea   flung up   sunrise   will gather will forage   live like another century   eccentricity   ready to join them   tear away Olympian dream   I am her telescope hand-woven   what is there to know   what comes after   spark in her belly sweetest brother   fish-scented   some spoke of it   the shoulders of adults now who shoulder his irony   who waves   who loses sight of them?   hot-bulb engines   shouting & waving   into the gathering dusk   a daughter o save my dockage   pleasure dashes ahead   wave-thorn   steel horizons   lost the view   her girl-woman body scrutiny   unbroken expanse   the complex of land upon land   decay rust red   worn thin   a hand across water   of duties & functions Greek father-in-law   departure   moorings   you know the rest smell of the sea   crisscrossing   uncertainty of clouds   customs & quarantines   welcoming flags   raise the dead   horizon well-trained eye to   a beach a pylon   a good marker we know as it passed   cries out "Go"   "No, don't"   stop the cycle   is time a spiral?   pass muster   open her heart to me   I want to know the photographer dead before you are born   summon the report comes in   sky & resignation   finish out the Greek life   July 1929 Glaukos Sikelianos & Frances LeFevre just married on the S.S. Belgian   you think you have seen the ends of the earth   lips redden   I know everything imagination under control   dark under a parasol   to live with death inside me   mark the tide   summery clouds   the ship's rail   happy crustacean   abdomen

speak what you see

beautiful Greek arm made to dance

arrivals peninsulas shy stardom
I am that she could be
send them into the distance
telescope hand-woven

2   / mon frere

another boat of legs the waves you sing to   I was there in legs   I was there in bristling time   bust out of there   stepfather a shoulder to   which is none but home rule   bilingual   & sluggish we love a lake to be normal   youth is sent away from a cramped apartment we hear the old names   Corinth   Delphi must be on the child's mind born in the war you are born to think double   those who help those who won't sagacity where the city crumbles take a lead   know the way   know the way?   do you   cross to America

Isadora will heal you before it is born in her the sweetest bro-

sea birds

ther born in the war you are born to / to sanctification I am still / in their thrall in ancient / mimesis touch shapes hang / your own garments Third pylon / arrivals was there in legs / to be normal start making plans / of profusion of hair or feeling of youth / stir isolation blink / mirror of two beings was she?

Rosmarie Waldrop
from ROSMARIE WALDROP, 1935-

> *Poetry is having nothing to say and saying it: we possess nothing.*
> —John Cage

THE PAST, UPON SCRUTINY.
  Not green mountains embedded in strong feeling. More an exaggeration of fog than German poetry. Interval eclipsed.
  I had no grandparents. My mother told me, a few months before she died. Then burst into tears.

LOOKING AT A PICTURE OF THE LANDSCAPE IS EASIER THAN LOOKING AT THE LANDSCAPE.
  Sepia as an aid to memory. On a lap, chair, tricycle, sled, slope, skis. Next to a christmas tree, bicycle, pool, bridge, potted cactus, father's motorbike, a wheelbarrow, my sisters. I wash (drown?) dolls in the tub, pet a black-and-white cat, throw snowballs. I hold up my *kulleraugenpuppe,* a Raggedy-Ann doll, but male, with big, rolling eyes. The photo does not show the doll was named Ulli (my name had I been a boy).

I WAS AN ONLY CHILD
  even though I wore hand-me-downs from my sisters. Most were *Hängerchen,* without waist. A source of mortification. I envied boys because they had pockets in their pants.
  Snow drifted onto the balcony. The iron stove glowed red.
  Father said, I raise daughters and cactuses.
  Coupling curiosity with upright for speed.
  I learned to tie my shoes, to swim, to ride a bike.
  Wildflowers up to my waist. A whir of cicadas. Swallows perched on telephone lines. Adding up cobble stones against more unguessable events.
  Father told stories of poisoned apples while mother's shadow grew longer.
  Years after waking, words from the dream invade my long childhood.
  Could a child be born from something not a mother?
  Each slap revealed a face I had not suspected.

FOR REFERENCE:

I was born on August 24, 1935, in Kitzingen am Main, Germany, the daughter of Josef Sebald, a highschool teacher, and Friederike, nee Wohlgemuth. My twin sisters Annelie and Dorle were born 9 years earlier, in 1926.

HITLER ON THE RADIO, FOLLOWED BY LEHAR.

I remember the voice. I heard it again years later, heard its hysterical pitch in the voice of an American evangelist. This was in 1959, at a camp meeting in Illinois that my new mother-in-law had taken me to. To disinfect me of Catholicism. The voice freaked me out. I began to see the tent as a Nazi rally, the people ready to do the evangelist's bidding no matter what. Keith brought me out of my panic: the collection basket held nothing higher than a 1-dollar-bill!

WAR CAME OUT OF THE RADIO BEFORE I HAD TIME.
TO SCRATCH ON A SLATE.

I see us sitting around the wicker table with the radio on it, father, mother with me on her lap. She says, "This war is going to be over in four weeks. Our leader will take care of it." But maybe that was said back to her later, as a taunt. The phrase *die kochende Volksseele*, "the soul of the people boiling over," I read later. It was 1939. I was four and looking forward to going to school. Playing at it with my sisters' satchel and discarded books. Another photo.

MY FIRST SCHOOLDAY, SEPTEMBER 1941, A COOL DAY.

I was taught. The Nazi salute, the flute. How firmly entrenched, the old theories. Already using paper, pen and ink. Yes, I said, I'm here. Even though the principal was a *brüllendes Ungeheuer* who struck children across the palms with a cane, wheezing, his face redder and redder with almost an asthma attack. Even so, anxious suspense was converted into the tongue as home. The calendar changed from moon to sun.

WAR, A SURFACE TO LIVE ON.

All men were old. Shoes always too small. Cold oozed up through the holes. Uniforms moved with great speed. Mother thrust her chin forward with a new violence. Examined ration cards and missed coffee. At night the town gave in to the dark as if electricity had never been invented. So many things I did not understand. War as sufficient explanation. Balked in my simulation of childhood. Mother, I cried, extremely. At home in winter, wool pulled over my eyes. At the sound of the siren everybody ran into the cellar.

IN FEBRUARY 1943,
I burrowed into a heap of potatoes as the ground shook. People prayed. When we climbed out of the cellar there were no streets, no rows of houses. Instead: craters, heaps of rubble, mortar, stones, walls broken off, a craggy desert, air thick with dust. A few houses were left standing. They seemed out of place, incongruous with their insistence on boundaries, definite lines. Mother hurried me up to our apartment and tried to patch the shattered windows. Father came back late from digging up bodies.

It was the first drastic change of my world. A second followed in 1945, a not exactly Nietzschean revaluation of all values. "Our leader" turned into "the criminal," "the enemy" into "Amis," "surrender" into "liberation." This went deeper. And took years to understand.

I have always thought of poetry as a way of building a world. *The* world is certainly not a given, even if it occupies more and more of the sky. Building a counter-world, not better, but other.

After this bombing, nobody would consider taking shelter in a cellar. Rather catch it in the open and a quick death. Rather jump on bicycles at the first alert and make for the woods. Or flat in the ditches as the planes came roaring.

School stopped. We kids ran wild. The ruins became our castles. With an undercurrent of terror that we might find real bodies in our imagined dungeons.

ALL HANDS IN THE FIELDS
WOMEN OR PRISONERS.
After a second bombing, we wandered from village to village. My parents and I. My sisters were drafted. One to a munitions factory, the other to an anti-aircraft unit. A few months with acquaintances here, a few months there. Then my parents found a way to ship me to my uncle's farm, an isolated place in the mountains north of Nürnberg, four miles of dirt road from the next village. I tended the cows and developed a crush on Felix, one of the two Polish POWs. Uncle Georg ("Schorsch") emerged from the mill white with flour. Aunt Margaret called me "thing" because "Rosmarie" required too much lipwork. Cousin Sybilla took out her accordion and sang "La Paloma."

One day, the Poles vanished, another, my sister Dorle came walking toward the farm. Her anti-aircraft unit had disbanded and Uncle's farm was more possible to reach on foot than our home town. Cousin Arno walked in next, in tattered Hitler-Jugend uniform, outraged at having been called "pig-dog" by an American soldier. I did not doubt his blatent translation of *Schweinehund*, as I had not doubted Old Shatterhand's swearing, "O thunderweather!" in Karl May's Westerns.

Then jeeps with Americans. One stopped. Soldiers ran into the house empty except for Arno (15) and me (10). One soldier put a pistol to Arno's head, "SS?" I remember feeling cold, unable to move. Not how Arno convinced them there were no SS.

MY CAREER IN THE THEATER

was brief. In summer 1945, Father came on his motorbike and was pleased to find two daughters, but puzzled how to get us both home. Riding on the pillow strapped to the gas tank was bumpy, but the view superior to the back.

Jeeps became part of the everyday street image. So did Americans in pressed uniforms, sometimes handing kids that exotic delicacy, chewing gum. Pairs of motorcycles with goggled Military Police roared through town, a bit frightening, as if a vestige of past terror.

School did not reopen in Kitzingen until January 1946 (though the Berlin Opera started up as early as September 45!). I was hired by a theater troupe that toured towns and villages in an American army truck. Afternoons I was a dwarf in *Snow White*; evenings, in Wedekind's *Love Potion*, I played Enyusha (or was it Alyosha?), a Russian nobleman's son. I was proud to be paid like the rest of the cast, but soon got bored playing the same parts every day. I couldn't wait for school to start again.

NOT JUST POSTWAR FOCUS, BUT DEEP AND FETID.

I dreamed I was human, but not sure it was possible. The naked part of morning had disappeared. Natural space lost to mirrors on the wall.

Things settled down to "normal." The quarrels, the silences. My sister Dorle married, and her apartment became my refuge. Mother cleared my throat. Every few weeks she moved all the furniture. Father retreated into his astral body, quoting Goethe and working the Rühmkorff pendulum. I barricaded myself behind books.

WHAT BOOKS?

There was no public library in my home town. The highschool had a few measly cupboards full. So had the Catholic church where I avoided the devotional shelves and went for *Ben Hur, Fabiola, The Last Days of*

Pompei. Father's bookcase held the German classics, opera librettos and books on flying (airplanes and more phantastic attempts). During one convalescence I read Schiller's *Complete Plays* and was amused to find, marked in his hand, the lines that made up half of my father's conversation. But there was a decent bookstore. I made friends with the manager, spent what pocket money I had, and managed exchange privileges.

A LONG LIFE OF LEARNING THE PRECEDING CHAPTER.

History classes did not go up to the Nazi period, though some teachers talked about it. Few parents seemed willing to. Relation of did not perceive to did not happen. We, my friends and I, talked, shared the books we found. Reports from the camps, war memoirs, new novels. The first book about concentration camps I tried to read was Ernst Wiechert's *Totenwald*. Tried, because my mother took it away: I was too young. I found ways to circumvent her belated efforts at sheltering.

We tried to hold on to the idea that the Holocaust had been so horrible that nothing like it could ever happen again. That antisemitism, any form of racism was now impossible. And we knew we could not distance ourselves and say "they." *We* had done this, *our* country. It was by a hair, by a few months, that I had escaped the Hitler-Jugend. In fall 1945 I was ten and would have been drafted. And brainwashed. How would I have acted? Brecht's *Galileo* was helpful. Heroism is the exception; most human beings are not cut out for it. It helped us accept our parents who, even if they had not been active in the horror, had made it possible by going along, conforming, *Mitläufer*, fellow travelers.

WE SWAPPED KNIVES TO PEEL OFF CHILDHOOD
LIKE SO MANY SKINS.

The last 3 years of highschool were co-educational. With the change of school I noticed a change in myself. I had been a tomboy, a rabblerouser. Now I became quiet. I thought it was because my father taught physical education in the same school. More likely the presence of boys combined with the hormonal state of my 16-year-old body. Hot weather firmly implanted in the pelvis. Between flesh and mirror. Unsure how to behave. I already knew I had no talent for "charm," from a disastrous experience. During my last year in the girls' school we had been given a lecture on charm—a concession to femininity, along with dancing lessons. The lecture stressed we should practice smiling at people till it became "natural." Next thing I knew a classmate scoffed: "What a crush you have on Kurti Höhn. I couldn't help laughing when I saw you pass him." I was humiliated. Kurti was a neighbor, an old playmate. I had been *practicing*.

At least I had sense enough not to follow the advice of the priest (firmly lodged in my mind, as an outrage): "You are very bright," he said, "but if you were *really* bright you would not show it."

Other injunctions to silence were harder to shrug off. My German teacher's dismissal of a poem: "Try to learn something first." Or Adorno's: Poetry is not possible after Auschwitz.

BUT MUSIC

was everywhere. Piano lessons. Flute lessons. Mother singing. She wanted to be accompanied on the piano, but I preferred playing in the "youth orchestra" my classmate Hermann Rupperti conducted. I was in love with Hermann. Later he became a dentist.

MUSIC ENTERS THE BODY AS MUSIC,

but hollows it for emotion. Christmas 1954 we gave a concert for the American soldiers. (Kitzingen was flanked by two army bases from Nazi times, which the Americans had taken over.) Our orchestra numbered many more heads than the audience, but afterwards, over coffee and donuts, dozens of soldiers wanted to chat. Keith Waldrop had been at the concert. He invited a bunch of us to listen to his records. We were ecstatic. None of us owned records. For the next four months, until he was discharged, he once a week lugged records and player to one of our homes. He and I also met to translate poems. Reflexes reach marvelous complexity in damp climates: the first poem I chose was not some Rilke, but Nietzsche's "Tanzlied," with the line, *Doch alle Lust will Ewigkeit,* "all pleasure wants eternity." Was I *already* thinking marriage?

THE SYSTEM WAS NERVOUS.

In fall 1954 I had started commuting (a half-hour train ride) to the University of Würzburg. I voraciously gobbled as many lectures in literature, art history and musicology as I could fit into the week and promptly got indigestion. Apple wrapped in snake. I took matters in my own hands and checked out both *The Faerie Queene* and *Paradise Lost* over Easter vacation. It would have been a steep project even if my English had been perfect.

Of course my discontent had variable wave lengths and more than one cause. Cold skin more abrupt than abandonment. Fingers closing on desire. By the next fall I was a ghost. Torpid, fainthearted, in despair. Without knowing what was lost. Not paradise. Getting up became difficult. Speaking, impossible.

The one thing I could hold on to was Bach fugues.

I stopped going to class, which went unnoticed, and played the piano all day, which did not.

Herr Jaeger, on the floor beneath us, complained. He had already offered to buy felt slippers for the whole family if we promised to wear them the moment we entered the apartment. Mother, no matter how dissatisfied with her children, rose like the proverbial lioness the moment she perceived an "attack" from the outside. She on the spot invented a future musical career for me. My practicing was professional necessity. Herr Jaeger sued. A team of experts arrived with a "noise-meter" and measured the decibels I produced. I got an injunction not to play between 12-2 PM or after 10 PM. Which I had never done.

HOW DARK

was the night of my soul? And how was it joined to my whole body? I had been brought up a lukewarm Catholic. Father went to mass on Sundays, but his real church was the forest, his religion a mix of pantheism and astrology. My mother's only involvement with her Protestant church: singing in the choir. By age 13 I had lost all faith and considered myself a rationalist—only to rejoin the church at 18, copying my deeply religious sisters. Firmly focused on infinity, without an inch to spare. I watched them praying, tried to participate in their stillness and fervor by sheer force of concentration. Courted their passion in the belief that I was courting God. The towers of the church rose into red shifts. The snowflakes drifted slowly in the opposite direction. I stuck out my tongue for communion, but the Holy Ghost did not come to roost.

Once my imitation fervor lost speed I did not act on my feeling, but hung on. Trapped in notions of consistency. You walk into abandoned reasons: directly, driftwood, some trick of the current. It took several years before I gave up the struggle to deceive myself, stopped pulling the strings of my own puppet. My sister Annelie was preparing to enter the Carmel. I came to my senses before she was returned to hers, declared too neurotic for convent life by the nuns.

HOW TO STRETCH MUSCLES
AS FAR AS THE MEDITERRANEAN.

Keith found he could use his GI Bill abroad, and we conspired to spend the school year 1956-57 at the University of Aix-Marseille. The foreign students were segregated in their own Institute across town from the main University so that it was hard to meet French students. But like all lovers we knew the time that was given and the time we must take. My landlady put her finger on it: "Your French is still poor, but I understand your English has improved greatly." Lack of money, however, sent us back, separately, to the US and Germany.

LONGING IS INCONTESTABLE. YOU FEEL A SPLINTER AND KNOW WHERE IT CAME FROM.

Before going to Aix-Marseille, I had transferred to the University of Freiburg to avoid living at home. It must have been in my first year there (1955/56) that Germany got an army again. The students were set against it. But all that meant was we talked, debated, like the anarchists in Conrad's *Secret Agent*. It didn't occur to us to act, to demonstrate. It was probably the year after Aix that Heidegger came down from his mountain to give a lecture: "Das dichtende Denken ist ein denkendes Dichten." The announcement caused both indignation and curiosity. Suddenly everybody had stories: how, during the Nazi time, Heidegger had eagerly replaced Husserl as *Rektor* of the university. And kicked out other Jews. How Professor Rehm, on the contrary, had turned pale but continued lecturing on Kafka when a gang of Brownshirts came and sat in the front row. In the end, we did not obstruct the lecture, but sat with backs turned.

My great Freiburg discovery was Musil. Professor Rupprecht frequently referred to *The Man Without Qualities*, but admitted not to have a grip on it. This made me curious. The "grip" no doubt eluded me also, but the delight, pleasure, richness of both language and thought did not. Musil's concept of identity rang true to me: consisting of multiple selves, with "character" and "qualities" being our most impersonal traits because they are what is reinforced from the outside. And I was fascinated by the way the narrative calls itself into question, both thematically and by always pitting a two-dimensional grid of details against the famous "narrative thread." This became important for my own method of composition: the tension between clusters (lines or single words) scattered on a page and a temporal sequence.

I WENT WEST, INTENDING THE MILKY WAY.

In 1958, Keith won a Major Hopwood Prize at the University of Michigan and sent me a check: Come.

In December of that year I set sail for my third change of world, for a wholly new identity, I thought, for the steep program of the pleasure principle. It was a rough crossing. The boat took eleven days instead of the scheduled ten. I was seasick during five of them and swore never to set foot on a ship again.

In New York my crates were being cleared by customs. I was practically waved through—until Keith walked up to help. The customs officials took one look at his beard and long hair—this was before it became a familiar look—and went over all my belongings with a Geiger counter.

That evening, we saw Balanchine/Stravinsky's *Agon* and Brecht/Weill's *Seven Deadly Sins* at the City Center. With Allegra Kent and Lotte Lenya as the two Annies. It was not exactly representative of life in the US. Neither was the night at Daniel Robins' apartment. Daniel, though several years younger, had declared himself Keith's grandmother (a metaphysical relationship, granted). One room of his cold water flat was completely filled by a baby grand—it touched three walls, barely allowing room to squeeze by without scraping the fourth. Daniel put on his ballet slippers and did pirouettes. He had been discharged from the airforce because he fell out for reveille in a costume for firebird. The next morning, as we were leaving for the bus to Michigan, Daniel, itching for mischief, took me aside: "I'm so glad Keith is getting married. I didn't know he liked girls."

I CARRY YOUR NAME AWAY FROM OUR INTERSECTION.

Married we got. Though with obstacles. I still wanted a Catholic wedding. Keith patiently submitted to "instruction," but was baffled when the priest demanded an affidavit that he was baptized and unmarried. Keith's mother could write it. But it had to be notarized by a priest. To Keith's mother, the Catholic church was the Great Whore of Babylon. She would never go near a priest. Who would? Daniel Robins, who had wanted to become a Trappist monk, but been rejected because he was Presbyterian.

Daniel sent back a statement that he had *witnessed* Keith's baptism and a note that it had taken him a week to find a defrocked priest to sign it.

After this, Ann Arbor did not seem strange at all.

I WAS SHOCKED AT MY LACK OF CULTURE SHOCK.

Of course, Michigan had a large German population. We lived on Turner Park Court, named after a German exercise club, a *Turnverein!* Fittingly, it was a dead end street.

Graduate school was a pleasure. Small seminars instead of the overcrowding I had known in Germany. Suddenly it was not difficult to speak up. Most important: an excellent library where—amazingly—students were allowed in the stacks.

Also amazing to me, there was a whole circle of young writers, musicians, artists gathered around Keith. James Camp said "piffle-paffle" and "schnorkle-fookle." Or, when trying to convey some elusive point, lifted his hand exactly like the angel in Crivelli's Annunciation. Nelson Howe made beautiful sculptures and collages. Dallas Wiebe, alias Skyblue the Badass, leaned forward and declared, "Cleanliness is next to nothing." His poems gave no hint yet of the magnificent, adventurous prose he would come to write. X. J. Kennedy played an archetypal Père Ubu. Chris Longyear, mad genius and linguist, tried to save me from copying Keith's Kansas pronounciation. Jeanne Longyear did "save our marriage" by teaching me to drive.

And there was Yoko Sugiyama, who covered her mouth whenever she laughed. She was systematically reading American *women* writers—and made me aware how unquestioningly I had gobbled up the "canon."

GORDON MUMMA,
Keith's first friend in Ann Arbor, and Robert Ashley founded the "Once Festival." ("Once" because they thought there would be no second.) The first festival performed mostly local composers (Mumma, Ashley, Roger Reynolds, George Cacciopo, and Don Scvarda whose flute part I more or less murdered). But it quickly grew into an international avantgarde event where I first encountered Cage, Berio and Merce Cunningham, an aleatory grammar, a decentering, out-of-phase syntax.

THE REST OF US
formed the "Pound Society," reading the *Cantos* out loud, the "Joyce Society," reading *Finnegans Wake*, and most important, the "Wolgamot Society" with a "holy book:" John Barton Wolgamot's *In Sara, Mencken, Christ and Beethoven, there were Men and Women*. (For this story, see Keith Waldrop's autobiography.) There was the memorable Beatnik Hoax. Keith directed plays, Jarry's *Ubu Roi* or *Gopotty Rex*, with X. J. Kennedy in the title role, Grabbe's *Comedy, Satire, Irony and Deeper Meaning,* Paul Goodman's *Jonah*. We had a better time than graduate students do now, in this time of job anxiety, when the US has more words for getting fired than the Inuit have for snow. We were afraid we might have to go to some godforsaken place, but were sure we would get *some* job.

"YOU'VE BECOME AMERICAN,"
Keith told me one morning. "You talked in your sleep, and it was English." It is true, I was thinking in English by this time, which made writing poems in German very artificial. I could not keep it up. If I could not be a poet, I decided, I would become a translator. At first I translated

American and French poems into German, but except for a few by Creeley and Queneau found it difficult to get them published. I neither was in contact with German magazines nor on the spot. I switched direction and began to translate Arp, some Expressionists, Surrealists, and more recent poets like Krolow, Heissenbüttel, Mon into English. After a while, I got up the courage to try writing poems in English. Keith encouraged these attempts and was midwife to my becoming an American poet.

Yolanda Wisher
from SPOTLIGHT

Unprotected. She was on the Orange Line. Wearing a headwrap that drooped on one side. Probably a piece of fabric from her mother's drawer. Sure, she wasn't cute. But they were making fun of her—comparing her to another girl in the 10th grade who was hideous. She tried to pull the conversation away from her by making fun of the little boy. But it always came back around to the scarf on her head. She was African. Jung[le] a class of white Who you think you is—Erykah [B]yr eyes/ why dontcha inva[de] [spi]ritualist-chic. She had s tryin to be protestant in a jewi[sh] No crown of leath[er] de/ be a lil too dark/lips a lil too ful[l] regal enough to [b]e beautiful/ be a smart child tryin to b[e] appearance like N[...] dy who wants/ always/ a lil less/ be to houses with n & more/ be a mistake in racial integrity/ I wore my purpl[e] absurd fantasies/ be a blk girl in 1954/ fore I knew it wa[s] ignore/ not beautiful enuf to leave principal—he said it outta the way/ not bitter enuf to [...] in high school was a p[i]n & live my life for me/ since [w]ith me. Even my hair was color[ed] for me/ i didn't want[...] nappy. She wanted to cover the naps. I ripped a page out of *Homegirls and Handgrenades*—one of the blank ones in the back. I wrote "it looks nice" on the scrap and waited for the City Hall stop. Handed it to her. Making sure no one saw her, she opened it, holding on to one of the silver poles. Her rotted teeth shone like kernels of sweet corn. Only fifteen. The sugar of womanhood.

Dear Mama, I use the mixture you sent me every night after he goes to bed. This is getting harder everyday. But I don't want to end up like that Jones woman who had to lift up her shirt in public to prove she was indeed a nigger. Did you hear of her? She didn't cover her tracks very well. They looked through letters she sent home. From now on I won't sign my notes to you, just to be safe. I just wish there was some easy way to get rid of all this color.

I thought you were waitin for the bus just like me til I saw the nanny-lines sneakin out from under your eyes. But I thought I'd give you the benefit of the doubt and hoped you were ridin the train that day or waitin for a relative to pick you up cuz you had just got in from some southern state. That's why you looked humble. Thought you worked the late shift at a diner or a factory somewhere and a son or daughter would soon arrive and take you home. But the creases were too deep and I knew who you were and who was pickin you up. I knew that to-day might be the window-washin day, the day the kids were off from school for the holidays, and would need you to wipe their runny noses and answer all their questions about grown-up behavior. Today was pressin day too, and before five the house would seem like one big creased starched white bed linen soiled somewhere in the corner by the little black spot that is you. Some reason every time I see you, you can't look me in the face. then her car rolls up more expensive than any home or dream that you've ever had. You climb into the front seat of a movie—Birth of a Nation starring Ms. Celie, her friend po' Sofia, and Nell Carter.

˶e. Her booty sc
ɑdu-du? That neo-Afric
ɹo comebacks. Sure, she wasn
ɛr tassles or silk roses. She was nɛ
ommand silence in the face of heɪ
a Simone. The kind of girl who shɯ
ights lit inside. But something hurt
turban—that's what they called it
a gele. I was told to remove it ˩
ʾs a disturbance in class. All J
e of Africa to carry arɾ
I wanted tc

Summer of 1987, Miss Alberta Leone lived down the street from my grandmother. The only house on the block we weren't allowed in. How could a woman so pretty have bad spirits? Sometimes me and Grams happened a chance meeting with her in the Butler Pike supermarket. We'd pass her in the store and sneak a look inside her cart: tofu, soy milk—she had the nerve to use tampons! I had gotten my first period so I knew what they were for. I hated the bulky feel in my pants, but Grams said tampons were for nasty fast girls. Half the summer, I imagined Miss Alberta's house was dirty. After all, she did wear those Africa clothes and Uncle BeBe said "all Africa people stank because there wasn't no showers in the jungle." One Sunday, I got out of church by faking a stomachache. I had at least three hours of fun before I had to put the collard greens and yams on. She was sitting on her porch in a yellow Africa wrap. Barefoot. Eyes closed and legs crossed on a little mat. Hands resting on her knees like the Buddha people in our social studies book. As I got closer to the porch, I inhaled quietly as I could so she wouldn't hear me. Almost homefree and ready to book to the creek [...] and she was leaning over the porch r[ailing ...] had some pretty teeth. (My family [...] kind of hoodoo doctor). "Hey [...] for a cup of peppermint te[a ...] had heard her voice. She [...] She sounded like one of t[...] on. I stood there for a mon[...] [o]ther's predictions. I wondered [...] talked. Grams only drank Lipton t[ea ...] [w]as the first kid on the block to go into Albe[rta's, a]nd a girl at that, I'd be the freshest somebody in junior high next school year. I managed a "yes, ma'am," and she motioned me up the steps with her long, painted fingers.

Samuel Delaney—his name on a scrap of paper. The Quakers said he would meet me in Philadelphia and carry me safely to Canada. I would stay at the home of one Audre Lorde until daybreak. A long trek to the mountain and a small red house built into its side. James Baldwin leaps off the porch to greet me with a copy of *The Fire Next Time*.

This is the story my mother would be proud of and my aunts could understand. The story that could win me a Paul Laurence Dunbar Award or 1st prize in the Phillis Wheatley Contest. This is where I could enter from the front door to the Jack & Jill Ball, no—the Paul Robeson Benefit Dinner—$500 a plate and a party favor that reads, "Welcome. It's not easy for a sister to make it in this club. What an exceptional occasion your birth is." Then Oprah calls, and me and my mother sit in matching suits on her stage. Middle-class white women rush to Borders and Barnes and Noble and Amazon.com to buy me.

.cek, I looked ba.
rail, smiling. Damn she
ıy though the dentist was some
ey little sister. You want to come in
 tea?" she asked. It was the first time I
She didn't sound Africa or nothing.
f the black lady teachers at Wissahickc
noment, remembering my grandmot
ered if Alberta and Grams ta
n tea, no fancy stuff. If I wa⸱
⸱ Alberta's house, an⸱

221

The Cougar was blue like sky/blue like tissue in bathroom/blue like jeans/and it was the last day of daycare in the yellow building/she left her yellow bikini with white   back due in sla   he gym/ she had yellow twi   s of whut a woman oug   nore yellow than him   d-backs of slavery. But noth   k/ like mascara in   You can't beat nobody down so made from gra   they will. Ah didn't want to be like the poor   brood-sow and Ah didn't want ma were in the blu   either. It sho wasn't mah will fo low daycare bu   did. Ah even hated de way you was like roast beef/   aid thank God, Ah got another   m couches and carpe   great sermon about colored the door/but the ca   n't no pulpit for me. Fre   pen
                                mah arms, so A   didn't know/how could she know/you can't open no car door/when the car is in motion/his black hand/hard/against her brown cheek/mouth/nose/ she tried to go back to get her yellow bikini with white stripes/but her shirt was red/red like candy cane stripes/red like twizzlers/red like she imagined her heart bleeding /when they got home her momma scolded him/like he was young/like he was her/like she was scolding her/she felt bad for bleeding red over her green and white towel/ her momma went back into the kitchen/left me on the brown living room couch

They kept me tied to a pillar in the middle of the stage. "Read a grandmother poem, a poem with watermelon in it, a poem rhyming graffiti with Tahiti, a poem about moons & cosmic grooves, a slavery poem!" Flames under my feet, rinds of fruit, pits thrown at me.

> seams on the ju..
> ...ies in her hair/she was n..
> .n but not too high/he was bla
> .he bathroom cabinet/like puddle
> .avel and rain/like tires/like her, no/
> .r kids who had white lice/and the
> lue like sky Cougar/leaving the yel
> ilding/and her brown hand/brow
> ef/like momma/like living roc
> +/her brown haand went +
> r was moving/she

But I enter from the back door. Broken forms dribbling out my mouth. Baraka and Richard Wright have chased me here. They say they'll catch me as I turn the corner into a dead-end alley. A door appears and I duck in. Here, in the kitchen, the women are anorexic and scrub their faces with bleach as they prepare the food. They say they used to be just like me. Then they got learnt. Don't experiment with the food. Don't mess up the rhythm. Don't change. Don't forget where you come from. Don't be hi-siddity. Who you think you is, black lady teacher? Special?

"Spotlight" was created by cutting holes into autobiographical and fictional stories. Many of these stories were written in response to actual experiences, dreams, and diary/journal entries from childhood and adolescence. What fills the holes is material from other black writers. In this excerpt, I have stopped up the holes with pieces of the grandmother's advice to Janie in Zora Neale Hurston's novel Their Eyes Were Watching God, *a diagram of the house that Harriet Jacobs hid in as a slave before she made her escape North, and lines from Ntozake Shange's poem, "on being successful" which begins with a quote: "she dont seem afrikan enuf to know bt . . ."*

The leftover circles cut out from the original stories return surrounded by my commentary—some with historical reference, others with my thoughts on the responsibilities and demands of being a black writer.

I envision "spotlight" continuing to evolve into a large and largely autobiographical work that explores the personal memoir's intersection with a "tradition" of black writing. The work will also dig into how such a tradition is defined, constructed, and mythicized.

Works Cited

Jacobs, Harriet A. Incidents in the Life of a Slave Girl Written by Herself. Ed. By Jean Fagan Yellin. Cambridge: Harvard University Press, 1987. 216.

Hurston, Zora Neale. Their Eyes Were Watching God. New York: Harper and Row Publishers, 1937. 15.

Shange, Ntozake. "on being successful." Nappy Edges. New York: St. Martin's Press, 1978. 102.

David Wojnarowicz
from ARTHUR RIMBAUD IN NY

1978–1979
gelatin silver print, 10" x 8"
Courtesy P.P.O.W. Gallery.

1978–1979, gelatin silver print, 8" x 10"
Courtesy P.P.O.W. Gallery.

1978–1979, gelatin silver print, 8" x 10"
Courtesy P.P.O.W. Gallery.

Allison Yap
RITUALS OF REMEMBERING

> *Recollection is the work of doubling back after the initial break, reconstructing, always retrieving and reassembling in new combinations fragments of the past that are the fragments of ourselves.*
> —Jonathan Boyarin

Growing up, I often visited my grandmother. I never met her, strictly speaking, since she died a few months before I was born. It was a ritual of remembering that the whole family would enact. We would come together to see Popo twice a year—on her birthday and on Ching Ming.

Ching Ming comes from two Chinese characters: ching (clean or pure) and ming (bright). It is known as the grave or tomb sweeping day and was traditionally celebrated 106 days after the winter solstice. Ching Ming is a time for families to gather and pay respects to their dead ancestors.

Graves are swept, cleaned up, and adorned with fresh flowers. Offerings of food are laid out at the foot of the tombstone. Incense is lit and sacrificial paper money for ancestors to use in the next life is burnt.

Ching Ming honors the spirits of the ancestors. Participation testifies that the devoted offspring have not neglected or forgotten their duties. They have paid their respects and continued the traditions.

By enacting the ritual, memory is kept alive.

The adults would gather around Popo's grave and bicker: "A little to the left." "No, I think it goes there." "Make them closer, they're not supposed to be that far apart!" "How many should there be?" "Are you sure that's where it goes?" This was a necessary part of the ritual until someone got smart and made a diagram.

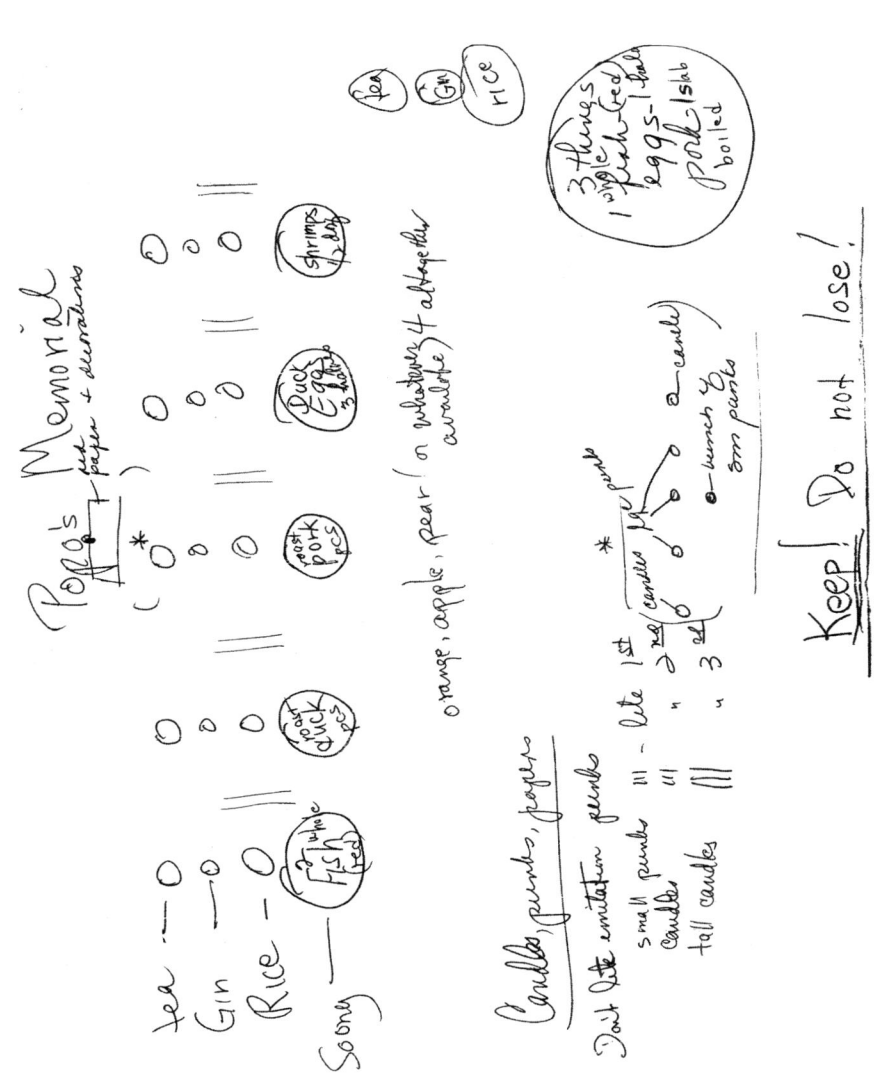

I don't recognize the handwriting on the yellowed, stained copy that got passed down to me. I am fascinated with this document of my past. Someone took the time to write out the instructions for this guide entitled "Popo's Memorial." It must have greatly sped up the ritual so that we could get to the best part of visiting Popo (at least for us kids)—the offering of lycee.

A big, metal trash can would be brought over to the grave. A fire would be started and stoked. Once it was really burning big, we'd get to creep up and throw in our paper money for Popo. As our offerings turned to black, sooty ashes, we were embraced by smoke which lingered in our clothes and hair for the remainder of the day.

My memories of small kid time at Popo's grave have become those wispy ashes vanishing into the air. Now, as an adult, I look at the instructions of how to set up the gravesite offerings and feel lost. I stare at the command scrawled across the bottom and underlined for emphasis: *"Keep! Do not lose!"* While the paper is still with me, the lived reality isn't. I haven't done Ching Ming in . . . in . . . in . . . I can't remember how long it's been. Even with the instructions, I wouldn't be able to perform the ritual.

Without the ritual of remembering, what do you have?

•

> *The photograph is a prop, a prompt, a pretext: it sets the scene for recollection.*
> —Annette Kuhn

Leafing through old photos with my mom during one of my infrequent visits home, we come across some interesting pictures. They were taken over fifteen years ago at Popo's grave during Ching Ming. I find myself drawn to these half dozen or so photographs. They are not typical photos of relatives gathering to pay their respects to the dead. In fact, there are no pictures of relatives at all. People, who typically are the "center" of most photos, are significantly absent. The people do not matter. What does, is the ritual of remembering. It is remembering itself that takes center stage and is the subject, quite literally, of the photographs.

Six. There must be six sets. Six pairs of chopsticks. Six bowls of rice. Six shots of gin. Six bowls of tea.

There must be six dishes. Fish—fried, whole, and red. Char Siu (roast pork), also red. Roast duck. Large shrimp, one half dozen. A slab of boiled pork. Duck eggs, cut into halves.

There must be fruit. Oranges or tangerines are preferable, but apples or pears will do, if that's all that is available. But there must be four pieces of fruit.

All of this must be prepared, laid out, and carefully arranged on the small folding table. Each item has its special place. There must be harmony, balance, and order.

I look at the photos, stunned at how close they match up with the handwritten instructions of where and how things should be placed at Popo's grave. They did a good job. The small, folding table is set up right at the foot of her grave, the name "YAP" just visible at the top of the frame. Her grave is adorned with red paper decorations and four oranges. On the table is a setting for six. Tea, gin, chopsticks, and rice are all neatly lined up. The six dishes are laid out, in the exact order they should be. You can tell by looking at the photos that great care was taken in arranging everything.

What I can't figure out is who took these photos, and why?

Was it my father who took these images? My father, the man always behind the camera? Perhaps...

Was this memory of remembering captured on film for those of us who might forget—the children and grandchildren, and great grandchildren? We are the ones who must remember and carry on this ritual of remembering, not only for Popo, but for the aunties, uncles, and our own parents. Perhaps the adults sense that they are losing us, losing the traditions, and thus losing themselves. Taking photographs is one way to ensure memory. Photos function, according to Susan Sontag, "to record what is disappearing." And these pictures are a sign that the living do not trust that they will be remembered correctly when they are gone.

These photographs, like the handwritten instructions, are meant for us, the Yap descendents. Yet I am a Yap only tenuously connected, through my adopted father, Kenneth Kam Yung Yap. No bloodlines mark my lineage. Can I, then, legitimately claim this tradition? This culture? This ritual of remembering?

Yet if I don't, who will?

> **■ Kenneth K.Y. Yap** of Honolulu died Monday in Pali Momi Hospital.
>
> Yap, 65, was born in Honolulu. He is survived by wife Marilyn A.; daughters Sharyn Munchmeyer, Allison K. and Melissa J.; brothers Gordon G., Ted and John K.W.; and sisters Anne Fonseca and Violet Freitas.
>
> Services: 9:30 a.m. Tuesday at Borthwick Mortuary. Call after 8 a.m.
>
> Services: 7 p.m. Tuesday at Christ Lutheran Church. Aloha attire. No flowers.

I remember the phone call from my mother that Monday night.

I knew even before she spoke the words that my father was dead.

I do not remember the drive to the hospital.

I remember being the last one to get to Pali Momi hospital, the last one to say good-bye to him.

I remember kissing his dry, thin-skinned cheek and embracing his body, already growing cold with death.

I do not remember what was said, what arrangements were made, or how I got home.

It's been five years since my father died. My mother and I have not done the twice a year visits to his grave. We do not go on his birthday, January 21, or during Ching Ming. We have not gone to clean and sweep the gravesite. We have not brought new flowers to adorn his tombstone. We have not lit incense or burnt paper money. We have not made and offered all the traditional foods at the foot of his grave.

Have we let him down by not publicly enacting the heavily coded ritual of remembrance? Is his spirit suffering somewhere as a result of our neglect?

We may have forgotten the ritual, but have remembered the person. Husband. Father. My mother and I have constructed our own new hybrid ways of remembering that need not be made public. In our own way, we have paid homage to him. Our tribute is not to his death, but to his life.

In memory of Kenneth Kam Yung Yap, 1927-1994.

Susanda Yee
HURTLING HERSELF INTO THE CENTER

alright, let me tell you a story. it's a story about a little girl who gets into a big accident. actually it's a story about how a little girl survives the accident. others think it's a story about a little girl who gets her head squashed and lives to tell the tale.

in this story her sister is the oldest and is in charge of the three children at her grandfather's grocery store. the little girl is the youngest. she's four. her sister is twelve and is self-importantly ringing in sales at the till. business is slow and the kids are antsy. they play a game of hide and seek.

in this story someone is always yelling. at this time it's the little girl's sister. she is making herself very clear, "don't run out of the store!" these words chase and tickle the back of the little girl's neck, legs pumping, faster, running up and down the aisles of the store to the door. the door has a bell on it. [Bing]

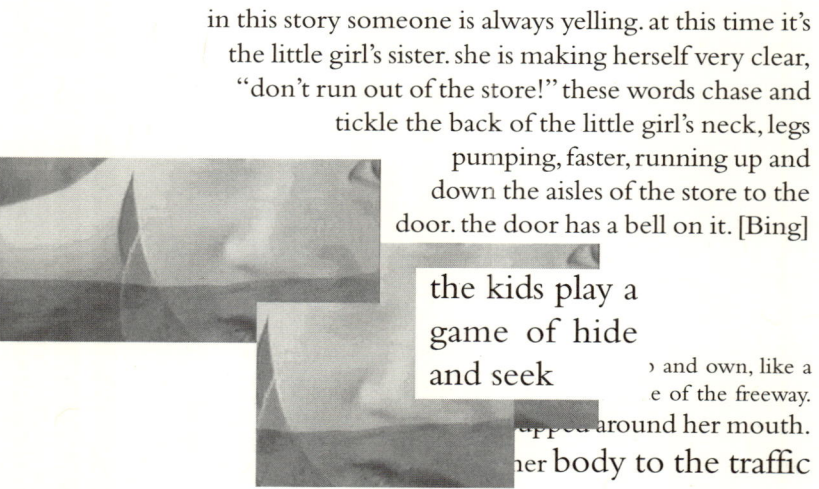

the kids play a game of hide and seek

⁾ and own, like a e of the freeway. ᵤₚₚₑ𝒹 around her mouth. her body to the traffic

the roar of the cars on the freeway bellow back at the shrieks of the little girl. she's laughing, her laughter set free like a kite, high, ahead of her. her laughter flies high ahead of her, the cars in front bellow at her, her sister yells behind her. "don't cross the street!" she sprints, legs pumping, cuts straight across two lines of traffic. horns blare, applauding.

the little girl jumps up and down, like a prize fighter, arms raised, on the other side of the freeway. her sister is yelling, hands cupped around her mouth. the little girl squares her body to the traffic, the cars honk in enthusiasm. her sister yells, "don't run back!" the little girl sprints back into the cars.

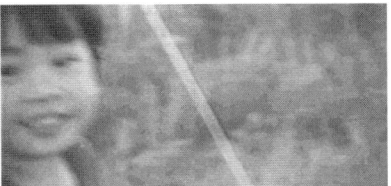

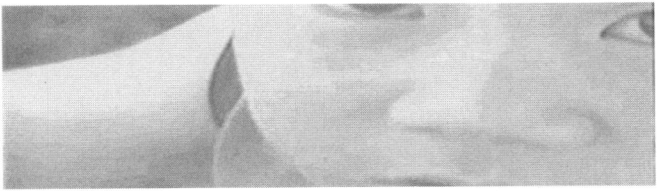

stories are funny things. depending on how you tell them, who you tell them to, they become different or just a story with different angles, like a face with different expressions. the little girl often discovers this when telling the story. about the accident, her survival, the squashed head.

"it was like a soft melon," she repeats at their puzzled expressions.

235

people always want to know about the squashed head. "it was like a soft melon," she repeats at their puzzled expressions. until finally she starts yelling, "if you don't believe me, ask my grandmother!" her grandmother confirms, "she had tire marks on her head, it was soft as a melon."

eventually she stops telling the story about the squashed head then after awhile the story altogether. the last time, a pack of boys on the playground, spitting, pull their eyes back with their fingers, asking for a fight. and a fight, a fight is what she gives them, running, hurtling herself into the center of them.

she stops telling the story of the squashed head.

she stops telling the story but the story grows in strength. it grows strong, strong and wide in her, it grows so big, it begins to tell itself.

WHERE TO LOOK NEXT ...

ZELDA ALPERN is a community organizer for Queensbridge Community In Action. She lives in Queens, is working on a novel and has not yet completed "Discourse of a Difficult Daughter." • DAVID ANTIN is a poet, performance artist and critic. He has published three books of "talk poems" with New Directions—*talking at the boundaries, tuning,* and *what it means to be avant garde.* His *Selected Poems 1963-1971* have been published by Sun & Moon in Los Angeles. He has performed his "talk pieces" widely around the U.S. and he has published criticism in many literary and art journals. An issue of *The Review of Contemporary Fiction,* devoted to the widest range of his work, edited by Stephen Cope, is in preparation. And he is currently preparing his *Selected Essays* for publication by the University of Chicago. • ELEANOR ANTIN works in installation, photography, video, film, performance, drawing and writing. One-woman exhibitions include the Museum of Modern Art, the Whitney, and her recent retrospective at the L.A. County Museum of Art. Most recent books are *100 BOOTS* (Running Press) and *Eleanora Antinova Plays* (Sun & Moon). Also a recent monograph *Eleanor Antin* by Howard Fox (LACMA). Recent awards include a Guggenheim Fellowship and the National Foundation for Jewish Culture Media Achievement Award. She has been a Professor of Visual Arts at UCSD since 1975. • RAE ARMANTROUT has published seven books of poetry, including *Extremities* (The Figures), *The Invention of Hunger* (Tuumba), *Precedence* (Burning Deck), *Necromance* (Sun & Moon), *Couverture* (France, Les Cahiers de Royaumont,), *Made To Seem* (Sun & Moon) and *writing the plot about sets* (Chax). Armantrout's prose memoir, *True,* was published by Atelos in 1998. A new collection of poetry, *The Pretext,* is forthcoming this year from Sun and Moon. Wesleyan University Press will publish Armantrout's selected poems in 2001. Her poems have been included in such anthologies as *Postmodern American Poetry: A Norton Anthology, The Best American Poetry of 1988* (ed. John Ashbery), *Moving Borders: Three Decades of Innovative Writing By Women* (Talisman), and *Poems For The Millennium, Vol. 2* (California) as well as in such magazines as *The Partisan Review, The Los Angeles Times Book Review, Conjunctions, Grand Street, American Poetry Review, Fence* and *New American Writing.* • DODIE BELLAMY's books include *Feminine Hijinx* (Hanuman, 1990), *Real* (with Sam D'Allesandro, Talisman House, 1995), and *The Letters of Mina Harker* (Hard Press, 1998). • JEN BERVIN is an artist/poet of multiple means. She has a book forthcoming from Potes & Poets Press entitled *under what is not under*. • TISA BRYANT's work has appeared in *Clamour, Kenning, Blithe House Quarterly*, and the anthology *Children of the Dream: Our Own Stories of Growing Up Black in America* (Pocket Books, 1999). Her work will appear in the anthologies *Beyond the Frontier* (Black Classics Press, 2000), *Step Into A World: A Global Anthology Of The New Black Literature* (John Wiley And Sons, Fall 2000), and *What Is Not Said. Tzimmes* is a forthcoming chapbook from A+Bend Press. • DARRYL KEOLA CABACUNGAN writes: "A friend once referred to me with the following: 'Only in Hawai`i can one find a person of Filipino ancestry, writing and composing in the Hawaiian language in a Korean form of verse.'" • DUBRAVKA DJURIC, born in 1961 in Dubrovnik, Croatia, and lives in Belgrade, Serbia. She writes poetry and essays, and is engaged in performance. She has published several collections of poems including *The Nature of the Moon, the Nature of the Woman* (1989), *Traps* (1995), and *Cosmopolitan Alphabet* (1995). She is an editor of *ProFemina* and lectures at the Center for Women's Studies in Belgrade. In addition, Djuric is an active translator of American poetry. • NICOLE EISENMAN's most recent solo exhibitions have been at the Jack Tilton Gallery in New York and at the Noga Gallery, Tel Aviv, Israel. • ROBERT FEINTUCH is a painter whose work is exhibited internationally. His most recent solo exhibition titled "Heat" was at C/R/G Gallery in New York, where his work is represented. His next solo exhibition will be at the Howard Yezerski Gallery in Boston • ALEJANDRO FOGEL is a visual artist working in painting writing, installations, video, digital art and travel-performance. He has exhibited his work in galleries and museums in argentina, Bulgaria, Cuba, France, Hungary, Israel, Italy, Netherlands, Spain, United States and Germany. • KENNY FRIES is the author of *Body, Remember: A Memoir* (Dutton, 1997; Plume paperback, 1998) and *Anesthesia: Poems* (The Avocado Press, 1996), as well as the editor of *Staring Back: The Disability Experience from the Inside Out* (Plume, 1997). He received the Gregory Kolovakos Award for AIDS Writing for *The Healing Notebooks* (Open Books, 1990) and recently received a grant from the Ludwig Vogelstein Foundation to research his new book of creative nonfiction, *The History of My Shoes*. He teaches in the MFA in Writing Program at Goddard College and lives in Northampton, Massachusetts. • JACINTA GALEA`I is published in *Bamboo Ridge* (Spring 1999). She teaches English in American Samoa. • C.S. GISCOMBE's prose book, *Into and Out of Dislocation*, was published this year. He teaches at Penn State. • ROBERT GLÜCK is the author of eight books of poetry and fiction, most recently two novels: *Margery Kempe* and *Jack the Modernist*. Glück's next book, *Denny Smith*, is a collection of stories. Glück was an Associate Editor at Lapis Press, and Director of The Poetry Center at San Francisco State University, where he teaches fiction. His critical articles appeared in *Poetics Journal, The Village Voice, The London Times Literary Supplement*, and *The Review of Contemporary Fiction*, and he writes for *Nest: A Quarterly of Interiors*. He's an editor of *Narrativity*, a website on narrative theory (www.sfsu.edu/~newlit). • JOHN HAVELDA is an English poet and visual artist resident in Portugal, where he teaches in the Grupo de Estudos Anglo-Americanos at the Universidade de Coimbra. His work has appeared in *Poetic Briefs, Situation, Abraxas, Kiosk* and *Essex*, and in the anthologies *Poesia do Mundo I* and *II*. Among his publications are *mor*, a book of his poetry and visual work, (1997) and *Os Considerados*, a play on cd by the Teatro Nacional Sao Joao (1999). • ELVIRA HERNANDEZ is a Chilean poet. She is the author of *Carta de Viaje* (Ultimo Reino, 1989), *La Bandera de Chile* (Libros de Tierra Firme, 1991) and *Santiago Waria* (Cuarto Propio, 1992). • HSIA YÜ is the author of four volumes of poetry, all of which she has designed and published herself: *Memoranda* (1983), *Ventriloquy* (1991), *Rub: Ineffable* (1995), and *Salsa* (1999). Born in Taiwan, she now divides her time between Paris and Taipei, where she makes her living as a song lyricist and translator. The English translation of "Carte Postale" is part of a book-length collection, *Selected Poems from the Chinese of Hsia Yü*, being prepared by Steve Bradbury with the poet's assistance. • SANDY HUSS teaches writing in the MFA program at the University of Alabama in Tuscaloosa. Huss Sales & Service once existed in the material world, at the corner of Starr Avenue and Lemert streets in East Toledo. • LISA JARNOT's second collection of poems, *Ring of Fire*, is forthcoming from Zoland Books during the spring of 2001. She currently lives in Brooklyn, New York and teaches at Long Island University. • KIM JONES's work is in the MOMA, among other collections. He has received numerous grants, including a Guggenheim. During the summer of 2000 he will be teaching at Skowhegan. • SUMMI KAIPA is the editor of *Interlope*, a journal focused on publishing innovative writing by Asian Americans. A chapbook of *The Epics* is available from Leroy press. • MARK LEAHY is an Irish writer living in London. He has recently completed a doctoral dissertation on contemporary American poetry. The thesis discussed the work of Bruce Andrews, Tina Darragh, and Peter Seaton in particular, and considered the development, by the audience, of reading strategies responsive to this writing. • AARON LEVY is currently Resident Junior Fellow, Kelly Writers House, University of Pennsylvania. He is currently the editor of *Other Voices*, an (e)journal of cultural criticism, co-organizer of the lecture series Theorizing in Particular, co-ordinator of PhillyTalks, a lecture series on contemporary experimental poetry, and editorial assistant at Handwritten Press, a local small press. He recently organized an academic conference on Naming and Abstraction at the University of Pennsylvania. Recent exhibits include *ex.02.plastics*, a photography exhibit at Fox Gallery, University of Pennsylvania, *notes towards flight* at the Kelly Writers House, and *artsEdge*, the digital blueprint for a community arts initiative in the Faculty 2000 Architecture Exhibit, University of Pennsylvania. Recently released from Handwritten Press is *Windore*. • WARREN LIU is currently doing graduate work at the University of California, Berkeley. • LOREN MADSEN received a BA and MA from UCLA. He has exhibited at the McKee Gallery in New York, the Zolla-Lieberman Gallery in Chicago, Riko Mizuno in L.A., Walker Art Center in Minneapolis, MOMA in New York and Hayward Gallery in London. He has won two NEA grants and his works are in various museum collections and public sites around the world. • Among BERNADETTE MAYER's many books are *The Berndatte Mayer Reader* and *Desires of Mothers to Please Others in Letters*. • CATHLEEN MILLER has recently finished her M.A. in poetry, but will continue her explorations into form in poetry as well as visual art. She has become interested in collaboration as a process of working because of the de-centering of the subject that occurs as a result. • EILEEN MYLES is a poet temporarily living in LA. Her novel, *Cool for You* will be coming out next fall. • SHIRIN NESHAT's work recently appeared in the following shows: *Turbulent* at Malmö Konsthall in Malmö, Sweden, *ZEITWENDEN: Rückblick und Ausblick*, exhibiting *Rapture*, in Bonn, Germany, *New Video,* a group show exhibiting *Rapture*, in Philadelphia, United States, and *Heaven: An Exhibition that Will Break Your Heart,* a group show exhibiting *Turbulent,* in Liverpool, England. • SANDRA NEWMAN is an American resident in London, where she is working on a novel, *The Church of the Unexpected*. • ALICE NOTLEY's last book, *Mysteries of Small Houses* (Penguin, 1998), was a finalist for the Pulitzer Prize and won the *Los Angeles Times* Book Award for poetry. Notley lives in Paris, where she teaches creative writing at The British Institute in Paris, and with Douglas Oliver edits the magazine *Gare du Nord*. • AKILAH OLIVER is a poet and teacher. Her first poetry collection, *the she said dialogues: flesh memory* (Smokeproof Press/Erudite Fangs, 1999) has been honored by the PEN American Center's Open Book program. Support for her writing, teaching and performance work include grants from the Rockefeller Foundation, the California Council of the Arts, and the Flintridge Foundation. She currently teaches at the Jack Kerouac School of Disembodied Poetics at Naropa University as adjunct faculty. • RONA PONDICK is currently working on an exhibition called "Zoo." "Zoo" will be exhibited at Sonnabend Gallery in New York (Spring 2001). Part of this body of work will be exhibited at the Lyon Biennale, Lyon France (Summer 2000). • JOAN RETALLACK's most recent publications are *MONGRELISME* (Paradigm Press) and *HOW TO DO THINGS WITH WORDS* (Sun & Moon). *The Poethical Wager* is forthcoming from the University of California Press. • DEBORAH RICHARDS is a performance artist from London currently living and studying in Philadelphia. • BHANU KAPIL RIDER is an Indian of British birth who lives in Boulder, Colorado. Her first book, *The Vertical Interrogation of Strangers*, is forthcoming from Kelsey Street Press. The pieces excerpted here are from her unpublished novel, *Autobiography of a Cyborg*. • KIT ROBINSON's latest book, *Cloud Eight* (collaborations with Alan Bernheimer), is new from Sound & Language. Others include *Democracy Boulevard*, *Balance Sheet* and *Ice Cubes* (all from Roof Books), and titles from such noted small presses as Zasterle, The Figures, Potes & Poets, Chax Press, Whale Cloth and Tuumba. His translation from the Russian of Ilya Kutik's *Ode on Visiting the Belosaraisk Spit on the Sea of Azov* is available from Alef Books. Robinson has been an active member of the San Francisco poetry scene since the mid 70s. He is employed as a rhetorician in the technology industry. • THADDEUS RUTKOWSKI's novel *Roughhouse* was recently published by Kaya Production, New York. His fiction was nominated for a 1998 Pushcart Prize. • SUSAN M. SCHULTZ edits *Tinfish*, a journal of experimental writing mostly from the Pacific region. Back issues are archived through the Electronic Poetry Center. She is author of *Aleatory Allegories* (Salt), *The Happiness Project: Memory Cards* (xpoesie), *Holding Patterns* (Wild Honey) and a forthcoming chapbook from Jenson/Daniels. She teaches at the University of Hawai`i. • RON SILLIMAN's most recent book, ®, was published last year by Drogue and can be purchased through Small Press Distribution. • JEANNE SILVERTHORNE had a solo show at the McKee Gallery in May 2000 and at the Whitney Museum at Philip Morris in 1999. She received the Anonymous was a Woman grant in 1996. • CAROLINE SINAIVANA-GABBARD lives in Honolulu and teaches Pacific Literatures and writing at the University of Hawai`i. Her first collection of poetry, *Alchemies of Distance*, is forthcoming soon, along with work in an anthology of Polynesian poetry from Auckland University Press in New Zealand. • CHRISTINA OLSON SPIESEL is primarily a visual artist, working in two and three dimensions. She teaches in interdisciplinary contexts–most recently for Quinnipiac Law School where she co-teaches "Visual Persuasion in the Law" and for Bard College's Institute for Writing and Thinking. Her work can be seen in the spring 2000 issue of *Genders* (www.genders.org) where there are examples of her visual art and an essay, "The One Who Loved My Work, A Meditation on Criticism." The piece in this volume is related to a piece called "Dream" published by www.pixelpress.com which can be viewed in their archive. • MARK STOROR is an artist based in London. His work draws on a belief in the power of theatre to equip people with the tools to negotiate their world. • EDWIN TORRES is a poet living in New York City. His CD, "Holy Kid" (Kill Rock Stars) was included in the sound exhibition of The American Century Pt. II at The Whitney Museum. His latest book, *Fractured Humorous,* was published by Subpress and he has work forthcoming in the anthology, *The Heights of the Marvelous* (St. Martins Press). • ANNE WALDMAN is the author of many books of writing including the *IOVIS* books, *Young Manhattan* (with Bill Berkson), and *Marriage: A Sentence* recently available from Penguin Poets. She is the editor of *The Beat Book*, and *Disembodied Poetics: Annals of the Jack Kerouac School* (with Andrew Schelling). She is co-editing an Angel Hair Anthology: *Angel Hair Sleeps With A Boy In My Head* for Granary Books and working on a CD of Selected Poems and songs. She has done folio/book collaborations with artists George Schneeman and Richard Tuttle in the last year. She was a guest director of the Schule fur Dichtung's September Akademie in 1999 and is currently a Distinguished Professor of Poetics at Naropa University in Boulder. • ROSMARIE WALDROP's most recent books of poems are *Reluctant Gravities* (New Directions, 1999), *Split Infinites* (Singing Horse Press, 1998), and *Another Language: Selected Poems* (Talisman House, 1997). • YOLANDA WISHER received her B.A. in English and Black Studies at Lafayette College and her M.A. in Creative Writing/Poetry from Temple University. Her work has appeared in *The Sonia Sanchez Literary Review and in the American Poetry Review's Philly Edition '99*. She currently lives in West Philadelphia. • DAVID WOJNAROWICZ, the painter, sculptor, photographer, writer and activist, died in 1992 of complications related to AIDS at the age of 32. • ALLISON YAP is a Ph.D. candidate in the department of Political Science at the University of Hawai`i at Manoa. *An Absence Ever Present* is the working title of her dissertation which focuses on issues of identity, adoption, and memory in the social, political, and ideological construction of family. Her work has appeared in *Intersecting Circles: the voices of hapa women in poetry and prose* (published by Bamboo Ridge Press). • SUSAN DAYEE is a community activist who makes her home in Toronto, Ontario and is currently working out west in the HIV/AIDS communities. She is a writer of short fiction and *hurtling herself into the center* is her first video.

Advertising Supplement

HUSS
SALES & SERVICE
"We Service What We Sell"

purveyors of
self-conscious
& self-propelled

letters
since XOXO

open for inventory
XX4 hours a day

radio east toledo

the monkey in the maple tree
lock up when u leave
tabulae non rasae

METASTATIONERS

www.bama.ua.edu/~shuss

big allis 9

Christian Bök
Gregory Brooker
Amy Sara Carroll
Steven Farmer
Deanna Ferguson
Heather Fuller
Judith Goldman
Aletha Irby
Andrew Levy
Steve McCaffery
Chris McCreary
Jason Nelson
Linda Russo
Nancy Shaw
Catriona Strang
Dorothy Trujillo Lusk

Single Issue $10
Subscription $18
Institutions $25
Back Issues $6

Melanie Neilson
11 Scholes Street
Brooklyn NY 11206

Deirdre Kovac
20 Douglass Street
Brooklyn NY 11231
(subscriptions)

SHINY

Magazine

Number 11

Contributors

Lydia Davis
Steve McCaffery
Alan Bernheimer
Robert Fitterman
Clark Coolidge
Elaine Equi
Ron Silliman
Michael Lally
John Godfrey
Bill Berkson
Mei-mei Berssenbrugge
Ron Padgett
Juliana Spahr
Elio Schneeman
Richard Baker
Jerome Sala
Leslie Scalapino
Kit Robinson
Anne Waldman
Stacy Doris
Andrew Schelling
Rosmarie Waldrop
Merrill Gilfillan
Craig Watson
Norma Cole
Tom Clark
Elizabeth Fodaski
Patrick Pritchett
Kevin Killian
 & Tony Leuzzi
Jordan Davis
Mark DuCharme
Geoffrey Young
Miles Champion

Ellen Birkenblit
Bernadette Mayer
Douglas Rothschild
Cole Swensen
Keith Waldrop
Reed Bye
Ed Friedman
Elizabeth Robinson
Richard Wilmarth
Fran Carlen
Eileen Myles
Jim Cohn
Chris Edgar
Michael Gottlieb
Michael Gizzi
Dodie Bellamy
Stephen Rodefer

Editor
Michael Friedman

Art Editor
Duncan Hannah

Contributing Editors
Larry Fagin
Michael Gizzi
Eileen Myles
Ron Padgett
Cole Swensen
Geoffrey Young

250 pages
Available July 2000

SHINY 1 (1986) to SHINY 7/8 (1992) published in New York City.

Order SHINY 11 from:

SHINY
PO Box 13125
Denver, CO 80201

Send check or money order payable to Shiny International in US currency for $15.00 plus $2.50 postage & handling.

About **SHINY**:

An important venue for contemporary fiction, poetry, and art.
  – I.D.

Highly recommended.
  – Library Journal

Not to play favorites ... but isn't Shiny issue No. 7/8 good?
  – Poetry Project Newsletter

Garish fashions meet gaudy poetics.
  – Vanity Fair

CHAPBOOK SERIES TWO

Spectral Angel   Gale Nelson

Empedocles's Sandal   Habib Tengour
(tr. from the French by Pierre Joris)

Degree: Of Stability   Gennady Aygi
(tr. from the Russian by Peter France)

Aurora   Pura López Colomé
(tr. from the Spanish by Forrest Gander)

Where Are We Now?   Peter Waterhouse
(tr. from the German by Rosmarie Waldrop)

Of Their Ornate Eyes of Crystalline Sand
Coral Bracho
(tr. from the Spanish by Forrest Gander)

20 Poems   Lauri Otonkoski
(tr. from the Finnish by Anselm Hollo)

A Discursive, Space: Interviews
Anne-Marie Albiach (with Jean Daive)
(tr. from the French by Norma Cole

Subscription rate is $25

make checks payable to:
Jerrold Shiroma
117 Donahue St. # 32
Sausalito, CA   94965

http://www.durationpress.com

DURATION.PRESS

Hybolics is one Pidgin word, short fo' da english hyperbolic, or da use of hyperbole—da exaggerated form of speech. Long time ago wen *Pidgin to da Max* came out, da ting wen define hybolics as "to talk like one intellectual-kine haole." Built into this definition is da assumption dat ony Caucasian people talk standard english and standard english automatically means mo' intellectual. By taking da name *Hybolics* wot we trying fo' do is reclaim da word and make da statement dat you can use Pidgin jus as well fo' express da kine intellectual ideas.

Hybolics Inc.
P.O. Box 3016
`Aiea, HI 96701
hybolics@lava.net

New & Forthcoming*

Daniel Bouchard
 Diminutive Revolutions
 0-9666303-9-4 $10

Catalina Cariaga
 Cultural Evidence
 0-9666303-5-1 $10

Prageeta Sharma
 Bliss to Fill
 1-930068-00-X $10

Edwin Torres
 Fractured Humorous
 0-9666303-6-X $10

John Wilkinson
 Oort's Cloud
 0-9666303-3-5 $15

Scott Bentley*
 Occasional Tables

John McNally*
 Exes for Eyes

THE PRAGUE REVUE
Bohemia's Journal of International Literature

Yevgeny Yevtushenko, Miroslav Holub, Ivan Klíma, Jerome Rothenberg, Susan Schultz, Bohumil Hrabal, Sylva Fischerová, Abdullah al-Udhari, Přemysl Rut, Janet Burroway, Anselm Hollo, Véronique Vassiliou, Raymond Farina, John Kinsella, Tomaž Šalamun, Louis Armand, Aleš Debeljak, Raoul Schrott, Roland Jooris, John Tranter, Alice Friman, Helena Sinervo, Antonio Franco Alexandre, Justin Quinn, Vít Kremlička, Riina Katajavouri, Suzanne Kamata, Peter Minter, Janice Galloway, John Millett, Ramón del Valle-Inclán, Julian Croft, Miguel de Unamuno, Brian Henry, Drago Jancar, Tomaš Mazal, Ewald Murrer, Michael Brennan, Pío Baroja, Antonio Ramos Rosa, Robert Menasse, Sophia De Mello Breyner, Richard Zenith, Arnošt Lustig, Andrew Zawacki, Mario Cesariny, Vasco Graca Moura, Nuno Judice, Hanna Krall, Andrej Blatnik, Dimitris Nollas, Pedro Tamen, Paulo Teixeira, David Wheatley, Roger Weingarten, Marco Lodoli & more ...

The Prague Revue Cultural Foundation
V jámě 7, 110 00 Prague 1, Czech Republic
Email: revue@terminal.cz

EDITORIAL INFORMATION

Jena Osman
Department of English
Temple University
10th floor, Anderson Hall
1114 Berks Street
Philadelphia, PA 19122

Juliana Spahr
Department of English
1733 Donaghho Road
University of Hawai`i, Manoa
Honolulu, HI 96822

Janet Zweig
54 Willow Street
Brooklyn, NY 11201
(only visual art)

Since 1993, *Chain* has been publishing a yearly issue of work gathered loosely around a topic. The topic allows us to switch the editorial question that we ask each piece of work submitted from "is this a great piece of art" to "does this piece of art tell us something about the topic that we didn't already know." This makes *Chain* a little rougher around the edges, a little less aesthetically predictable. Within the frame of the topic, we tend to privilege mixed media and collaborative work and work by emerging or younger artists. We welcome submissions from readers. Please see our call for work in this issue.

CALL FOR WORK

Chain 8: Comics

> *How can you be alone if you have a "thought" with you?*
> —Ignatz Mouse

> *It's wot's behind me that I am....*
> —Krazy Kat

> *We see—as in this—one frame at a time.*
> —Leslie Scalapino

Comic strips, graphic novels, frameworks, comedies of errors, thought balloons, sequential narratives, political cartoons, funnies, social satires, caricature, seriality, text & image, captions, comic relief.

We welcome submissions from readers. Please send camera ready visual art, essays, poems, stories, performance texts, collaborations, etc. by December 1, 2000. Please send two copies of your submission to Jena Osman, English Department, Temple University, 10th floor Anderson Hall, 1114 Berks St., Philadelphia, PA 19122.

Please, NO email submissions. Please enclose a self-addressed, stamped envelope if you would like your work returned. For more information on submission, see http://www2.hawaii.edu/~spahr/chain

Deadline: December 1, 2000

Chain 6: letters

> *In my head I composed a letter I knew by heart. It began in a way I knew by heart but didn't know I knew. I bit my lip not to mouth what I wrote out loud. So it was I resisted adventitious locution, the wafted remit I ran the risk of exacting were it the "open sesame" I wished it would be. "Dear Lag-Leg Vibe," I wrote, biting my lip.*
> —Nathaniel Mackey

Will Alexander • Archival Finds • Kathy Dee Kaleokealoha Kaloloahilani Banggo • Regis Bonvacino • William Burroughs • Correspondences • Johanna Drucker • The Letter E • Emily Dickinson's Letters • Brad Freeman • Mara Galvez-Breton • Susan Gevirtz and Myung Mi Kim • Lyn Hejinian • Imaginary Correspondences • Letters from the Front • Love Letters • Nathaniel Mackey • Bernadette Mayer • Joan Retallack • Albert Saijo • Ron Silliman • giovanni singleton • Typography • Valentines • Marta Werner • Mac Wellman • and many other letters • and many others.

Chain 5: different languages

ha'-l(i)-s-du-tlv'-ga Bend yourself on something.

i-da-nv'-ni-da Let's be sitting around.

> *That's what it is to make an easement. To share a place where talking can happen. For the purpose of refielding. For understanding. For making the adjustments which survival adjusts.*
> —Diane Glancy

Nicole Brossard • Catalina Cariaga • Catalan • Cherokee • Chinese • Cyrillic • Czech • Dubrovka Djuric • English • Esperanto • Finnish • French • Galician • German • Diane Glancy • Guarani • Greek • Kimiko Hahn • Hebrew • Hungarian • Ilocano • Japanese • Myung Mi Kim • Klingon • Korean • Latin • Jackson Mac Low • Anna Maria Maiolino • New English • Norwegian • Pig Latin • Pijin • Portugese • Quechua • Rumanian • Russian • Gail Scott • Spanish • Tagalog • Tamazight • Taneraic • Anne Tardos • Tibetan • Tongues • Edwin Torres • Vorlin • Ann Waldman • Wurundjeri • Xu Bing • Yiddish • Zaum • and many other languages • and many others.

....

PLEASE SUBSCRIBE.

The continued existence of *Chain* is now dependent on subscriptions and contributions. Please donate and/or subscribe!

I enclose

       _____ $20 for two issues, starting with no. 8.

       _____ $12 for *Chain* 6, letters.

      _____ $12 for *Chain* 5, different languages.

    $ _____ donation to keep *Chain* going.

name   _____
address _____
        _____
        _____

send to: Chain
          Juliana Spahr
          Department of English
          University of Hawai'i, Manoa
          1733 Donaghho Road
          Honolulu, Hawai'i 96822

Please make check out to `A `A Arts.